Fair & Balanced
A History of Journalistic Objectivity

Fair & Balanced
A History of Journalistic Objectivity

EDITORS
Steven R. Knowlton
Karen L. Freeman

VISION PRESS

Fair & Balanced

A History of Journalistic Objectivity
Steven R. Knowlton
Karen L. Freeman

ISBN 1-885219-28-8

Copyright © 2005, by Vision Press
All rights reserved. No part of this book may be reproduced
in any form without the prior written permission of the publisher.

Vision Press
4195 Waldort Drive
P.O. Box 1106
Northport, Alabama 35476

```
            Library of Congress Cataloging-in-Publication Data

Fair & balanced : a history of journalistic objectivity / editors:
Steven R. Knowlton, Karen L. Freeman.
    p. cm.
  Includes index.
  ISBN 1-885219-28-8
1.  Journalism--Objectivity--United States--History.  I. Title:
Fair and balanced. II. Knowlton, Steven R. III. Freeman, Karen L.
  PN4888.O25F34 2005
  071'.3--dc22


                                                200406121
```

Printed in the United States of America

CONTENTS

Preface: Fair and Balanced	1
Introduction: A History of Journalistic Objectivity	3
Part I: The 17th and 18th Centuries	**7**
1 Reliable Sources in Early Colonial News	9
2 Puritans and the Foundations of Objectivity	23
3 Neutrality and Colonial Newspapers	36
4 The American Revolution and the Death of Objectivity	51
Part II: The 19th Century	**65**
5 Objectivity During the Early Republic	76
6 The Transition from the Partisan to the Penny Press	90
7 Objectivity and the Mexican War	100
8 The Rise of Journalism's Scientific Mindset, 1832-1866	107
9 Objectivity During a Clash of Titans, 1883-1915	117
Part III: The 20th and 21st Centuries	**131**
10 Progressivism, Muckraking and Objectivity	136
11 Objectivity and the Trappings of Professionalism, 1900-1950	149
12 Readers, Research and Objectivity	167
13 Objectivity and Journalism Education	180
14 Objectivity in Broadcasting Journalism	192
15 The Challenges of Civil Rights and Joseph McCarthy	206
16 Into the 1960s — and Into the Crucible	221
Index	236
Authors	244

Fair & Balanced
A History of Journalistic Objectivity

PREFACE

Fair and Balanced

The genesis of this volume was a panel discussion at an annual conference of the American Journalism Historians Association on the history of objectivity in American journalism. The session was jammed, with literally dozens of people having to listen from out in the hall because the room would not hold all who wanted to attend. The gathering was lively, engaged and – a conference organizer's dream come true – refused to break up when the allotted 75 minutes was over. Conversations continued in the hallways, over dinner and on into the evening. It seemed apparent that the subject had struck a nerve. Was it worth a longer and more thoughtful look than a single conference session could provide?

The idea for this book came out of one of those hallway conversations. While it was widely agreed that the two classic books on journalistic objectivity, Dan Schiller's *Objectivity and the News*, and Michael Schudson's *Discovering the News*, were still largely correct in their assessments, the subject was more complex than any one writer was likely to do full justice to. Further, while cogent arguments could be mounted for objectivity's coming into being during the 1830s on the one hand or the Progressive Era on the other, there were several other tantalizing suggestions as well. Several scholars had found serious bits of proto-objectivity from well before the penny press steamed and hissed its way onto the world stage. Others thought other periods and other technological developments in the 19th century were responsible for objectivity's importance in the pantheon of journalism's guiding principles. And there was the rest of the 20th century: since contemporary believers in objectivity are regarded in many circles as being almost pitiably passé, what happened to the grand idea that reporters could, with care, play it straight and get it right?

In those conversations, the idea emerged that instead of having a single author take on the 350-plus years of Colonial and United States history, scholars who were knowledgeable about particular time periods could pool their expertise and produce a collaborative work that would be stronger than any single author would be likely to produce.

Many of the contributors to this book were at that conference and agreed on the spot to write chapters. Other scholars were solicited for their special expertise in a specific time period or, in a few cases, a broader time period in conjunction with a specific trend or medium. Along the way, others offered to contribute and, where there was no serious overlap or duplication of effort, these efforts were welcomed as well.

Each of the writers deserves a great deal of thanks for signing on to the project and then for tolerating delays not of their making. We hereby thank them all for their work in writing and rewriting, in editing, in helping with the preparation of the index and in reading proof at the end. But mostly, we thank them for their unfailing good humor when editorial delays surely tried their patience.

Thanks are also due to Wm. David Sloan, who agreed to consider the manuscript from his vantage point as consulting editor to Vision Press and who also agreed to lend the volume gravitas by contributing to it from his own vast store of knowledge of the Colonial period of American journalism history.

Special thanks are due to the many journalists and academics, some of them quoted in this book, others not, who took time from their own busy lives for interviews, often at length and over several sessions, to help us understand the tumultuous decades of the 1960s and 1970s. In some quarters of the university, such conversations are called oral history. We still call them reporting. Either way, these conversations reminded us anew of the remarkably high level of both brains and heart that go into the best of American journalism every single day.

Steven R. Knowlton
Karen L. Freeman
New York
March 2005

INTRODUCTION

A History of Journalistic Objectivity

By Steven R. Knowlton

Objectivity is one of the most troubling yet most fascinating concepts in journalism. Most professionals hold to it (by that name or some other) at least as an ideal to strive for, while critics treat a belief in objectivity with the condescension they would have for an adult who swears by the tooth fairy — as generally harmless enough unless taken to extremes, but so far beyond the pale as to make serious discussion a laughable waste of time. When bright and intellectually honest people disagree so profoundly, a wealth of ignorance is often in the way. And so it is here. This book traces the history of journalistic objectivity from the middle of the 17th century — John Milton's *Areopagetica,* with its truth and falsehood grappling, being but the most famous — to the new millennium, with its instant, global factoids for all and yet the continuing nagging sense that the best journalism, in the words of National Public Radio's Scott Simon, "comes from somewhere and stands for something." In this book, 17 scholars, specialists in specific eras of American journalism history, take on a group project to provide the most comprehensive look ever attempted at the development and the changing meanings of this slippery concept.

Historians have looked for the origins of journalistic objectivity for many years, with two major works centering on two periods: the 1830s and the development of the penny press, and the Progressive Era of the 1920s. The case for the penny press as the true origin of objectivity was made by Dan Schiller in *Objectivity and the News.*[1] The most influential proponent of the latter period is Michael Schudson, whose *Discovering the News*[2] argues that it was not until the 1920s that the term objectivity became widely used, and that it was not until then that it became a moral goal of journalism, as opposed to a loose synonym for neutrality or evenhandedness.

In large part because of Schudson's and Schiller's work, the conventional wisdom about objectivity in journalism goes like this: It got its start in the 1830s, when the mass circulation of the penny press first made news into a salable commodity. Like other goods, information was more valuable if it was genuine rather than counterfeit, so there was a premium on reliable information. A generation later, by-the-word telegraph rates helped wring excessive, opinionated verbiage from journalistic prose; and the simultaneous creation of the wire service further mandated a fact-laden, neutral, one-story-fits-all-papers writing style. But it was not until the 1920s and the widespread attempt by soft sciences across the board to adopt the empiricism of bench science that we see the emergence of a moral imperative for objectivity, as opposed to the merely practical. This commitment lasted until the 1950s, when its seeming naïveté seemed inadequate for cutting through "red scare" hoopla, at least in retrospect. Objectivity was finally done in by the postmodernists, who laughed it into well-deserved oblivion. That's the conventional wisdom; but objectivity, in one form or another, has been around longer and has had greater staying power than many suppose.

In *Fair and Balanced*, we acknowledge the debt that journalism historians owe to Schiller and Schudson, even while expanding their fields of inquiry. Although both Schudson and Schiller believed they had determined when objectivity took hold in American journalism, both cannot be right, for their answers are clear, certain and nearly a century apart. This book argues that both are partly right, and yet so are a dozen other answers, depending upon the definition being used. In fact, a proto-objectivity actually predated the birth of American journalism. Then the definition of objectivity in journalism, whether called that or not, evolved. The telegraph and the wire services mandated some changes; Joseph McCarthy prompted others. America's great wars have had their impact, and so have its great social upheavals.

The reader will find that there are different shadings of the term objectivity among the 17 scholars contributing to this book. That is not surprising, given how many different definitions of the term one could come up with in any contemporary group of journalists or journalism scholars, as well as the fact that the concept has gone through many changes over time. It would have been a difficult — and not particularly useful — exercise to try to shoehorn all the writers into one single definition of objectivity, but each author clearly stakes out a position on what the term meant in the context of the chapter. The advantage of having 15 scholars tackle this subject is that each is able to share his or her expertise in various periods or trends, and readers should come away with a clear idea of the issues and background behind a concept that has been called "objectivity" for only a small part of the time it has been an influence on the news media. That is how this volume is unique and how it provides what its authors and editors hope and believe will be a lasting contribution to journalism scholarship.

Hazel Dicken-Garcia reminds us that the first use of the word "objectivity" in journalism may have been when Charles G. Ross wrote in a 1911 textbook that "[n]ews writing is objective to the last degree, in the sense that the writer is not allowed to 'editorialize.'"[3] This century-old use of "objectivity" construes it narrowly as the opposite of "editorializing."

In the middle to late 20th century, objectivity came to be seen as suggesting that journalists must avoid partiality at all costs, even when there were obvious aggressors and victims. Although its meaning remains open to interpretation, "objectivity" is more than a mere separation of fact from "bias" and values. Today, we might define it as unbiased accurate reporting of verifiable facts with detachment and completeness in a manner that is fair, balanced, thorough and clearly separate from the reporter's views and opinions. In contemporary American journalism, scholars, practitioners and readers may agree on little else, but there is a widespread belief that what can be called old-school or simplistic objectivity — that commitment to an uncritical recitation of official facts — is not enough to provide the citizenry with what it needs to know to govern itself. Journalism "that comes from somewhere and stands for something" seems to hold more promise — the idea that journalistic values, grounded in Enlightenment ideology, do support pointing out heroes and villains when the evidence is clear and convincing. The best of such journalism, however, still cleaves to a central tenet of objectivity: to present news and information in a context that is as fair and free of bias as thorough reporting can make it.

NOTES

[1] Dan Schiller, *Objectivity and the News* (Philadelphia: University of Pennsylvania Press, 1981).

[2] Michael Schudson, *Discovering the News* (New York: Basic Books, 1978).

[3] Charles G. Ross, *The Writing of News: A Handbook* (New York: Henry Holt, 1911): 20. Quoted by Harlan S. Stensaas, "The Rise of Objectivity in U.S. Daily Newspapers, 1865-1934." Presented to the American Journalism Historians Association, St. Louis, October 1986.

FAIR AND BALANCED • 6

PART I

The 17th and 18th Centuries: Seeds of Objectivity
By Steven R. Knowlton

While objectivity's shoots appeared in the 19th century, and it came to be known under that name in the 20th, the seeds of objectivity can be found in the America of the 17th and 18th centuries. The first two chapters of this book address two dimensions of the chronic search for truth, which is certainly an element in any concept of journalistic objectivity. These two dimensions have a direct bearing on what would become the American system: a unique combination of the profound religious beliefs of those who came to the New World in the 17th century and the rationalist Enlightenment principles that became dominant in the 18th century, when the American press system was invented. (Most Enlightenment thinkers were religious people as well, but their sense of the order of the universe and the power of the rational mind was very different from that of the Puritans of a century before.)

• • •

The Chapters Ahead

In *Chapter 1*, Sheila McIntyre explores one of those dimensions, the search for reliable truth in a secular sense, which dates at least to the Greeks. It may seem surprising that very early in American history a distinct and demonstrable preference appeared for a scrupulous attention to accuracy and a related bond of trust between the information-gatherer – the proto-journalist – and the reader or audience. From an examination of the letters of some early colonists, the author concludes that eyewitness accounts were more highly regarded than secondhand ones, and that those from trusted friends on the scene were the most highly regarded of all (foreshadowing a time when television network anchors would go to the scene of major news events in an effort to enhance their viewers' perception of their reliability).

In *Chapter 2*, Julie Hedgepeth Williams, also working in the 17th century, finds important religious connections in the search for truth, a powerful American echo of the ringing call by John Milton, a Puritan, in *The Areopagitica* for a wide-ranging search for truth as a religious duty. In this chapter, we hear the Puritan divine Increase Mather thunder: "He that judgeth a cause before he hath heard both parties speaking, although he should judge it rightly, is not a righteous judge." No 20th-century commandment for an objective press ever put it better. The Puritans expected all sides to have a turn at the press in discussions about Puritan doctrine. Only heretics were denied the press. When it came to publications about politics, however, Puritans saw little need for objectivity.

It is a commonplace that newspapers of the Colonial era were partisan in their editorial policy, and so they were. It is certainly true that the sharp division between the news columns and the editorial page that is familiar to modern readers did not exist. Yet at the same time, as Wm. David Sloan points out in *Chapter 3*, Colonial printers had, and knew they had, an obligation to their readers, who expected a level of neutrality and evenhandedness in presentation. Newspaper publishers' concept of neutrality grew out of their experience as job printers for the public. Benjamin Franklin's famous "Apology for Printers" is but the most well-known example of a powerful force in Colonial printing. It was Franklin who likened the newspaper to a stagecoach in which all could ride. Readers expected publishers, even when they were partisan, to allow dissenting views to find a hearing in the columns of their newspapers.

It is one of the ironies – or hypocrisies – of history that the American Revolution was ostensibly fought for, among other things, personal freedom, including freedom of speech, but there was a sharp reduction of neutrality and fair play – indeed, of any commitment to objectivity – at the time of the war. In *Chapter 4*, Professor Williams points out that this deep partisanship in print was especially true on the rebel side. Many Tories tried to maintain neutrality and print both sides of an issue. In the end, that proved to be impossible. The heat of battle made the coolness of detachment impossible to maintain. Journalistic objectivity was a casualty of the Revolution.

CHAPTER 1

Reliable Sources
in Early Colonial News
By Sheila McIntyre

In October 1683, Joshua Moodey, the minister in Portsmouth (later New Hampshire), sent some intriguing and disturbing news to a friend and ministerial colleague in Boston, Increase Mather. Earlier, Mather had asked his large network of correspondents to send reports of remarkable occurrences for him to publish.[1] In response to Mather's request, Moodey diligently surveyed his neighbors and congregation, collecting stories about recent memorable events that highlighted God's workings in the natural world.[2] Moodey shared his full report with Mather in several letters, including one in October that detailed a monstrous birth:

There are sundry reports among us of new things that seem to bee matters of witchcraft, but reports are little to bee heeded, & I have not had time to goe thither to bee more satisfied, & therefore shall not trouble you with any of them at p^{r}sent. Only this I am fully certified of. On the 5th Septr last was this monstrous birth brought forth at Newichuwenoq by the wife of one Wm Plaisted.

From the waste downward it was like anoth^r child & a female.

Above the waste all defective or misplaced.

The Head extraordinary large & no skull or Bone in it.

The face as big as a womans face.

It had no right Arm, but somw^t like a Teat, some say like a finger where the arm should have come out.

The left Arm extraordinary long, the hand reach^g down to the knee.

No Nose, but somewhat like nosethrills, & those in the forehead.

The two eies upon the two cheeks.

No mouth, but a little Hole & (if I mistake not) misplaced also.

The eares, one und^r the chin, the other at the top or near the top of the head.

A very short neck.

Somewhat on the Breast like a Kidney.

The Belly seemed as if it had been ripped open, & the Bowells w^r out, & eithr by one side, or on the back.

It came before its Time. Had life w^n born, but soon died.
The pson had been 4. or 5. years married, & this w^s the first child.

After completing his description, Moodey pledged to travel to interview the witnesses to the birth if Mather thought the story would be useful. He also reassured Mather about the truthfulness of his report, and he shared one observer's analysis of the horrific deformity. Moodey added an important postscript, encouraging Mather to speak to the messenger directly to get more details. Evidently Moodey thought that the messenger's oral verification enhanced the veracity of news.

Joshua Moodey's handwritten report and the messenger's oral additions highlight the role that reliable sources played in early New England news correspondence, well before the arrival of Benjamin Harris's *Publick Occurrences* in 1690 or John Campbell's *Boston News-Letter* in 1704. To the early Colonial reader before and after the newspaper's arrival, the claim of truth was inextricably bound up with the teller or writer of the news. Like printed news, handwritten and oral news, often shared through personal (but not private) correspondence, relied on trustworthy sources as correspondents.

My use of the term correspondence is deliberately multivalent and is designed to tease modern journalists and journalism historians into reconsidering what the term meant to the inhabitants of the 17th century, and even what it means to modern correspondents. Correspondence refers to the handwritten objects exchanged between senders and receivers, in this case the letter sent from Joshua Moodey in Portsmouth to Increase Mather in Boston on Oct. 30, 1683; and it also defines the bridge that this communication built between tellers and hearers, or senders and receivers. The term correspondents refers to the writers and storytellers themselves, and to their role as journalists who gather news and report on it.

Moodey's letter also hints at how 17th-century colonists created their own definition of objectivity. Throughout this essay, "objective" means those stories that Colonial readers and hearers believed to be true, based on their own exacting standards of veracity. Maintaining a divide between facts and values was not an explicit goal, but that does not mean that 17th-century readers could not tell the difference.[3] Like many modern scholars, they also acknowledged, at least implicitly, that all news reflected on the teller, and that such a level of subjectivity was inherent in sharing news. Early New Englanders seemed to believe that subjectivity, either interpretations offered by reliable sources or simply the fact that the story came from a particular person, enhanced news stories. The words "nonpartisan" and "unbiased" do not reflect 17th-century ideas of news and communication.[4] The most useful synonym to get a 17th-century sense of what journalism scholars call "objective" is "trustworthy," because "trustworthy" inherently involves both sides in news-sharing (the reader or hearer and the reliable source) and because it evokes the relationship between them.

Trustworthy news came from a reliable source, whose status, relationship or location privileged the information that flowed from his or her pen and mouth. Trustworthy news gatherers sifted news; they did not indiscriminately share it. In the example above, Moodey opened his letter by describing both his selection process (the recent reports of witchcraft could not be trusted; so he would not share the details) and his preferred methodology (he did not have time to travel to the site of the witchcraft allegation to verify the stories). Early Colonial readers expected their news to come from site-based informants, like Moodey, who performed as correspondents on two levels: as letter-writers and storytellers, and as people specifically dispatched to uncover the truth of the event and report on it. Moodey assured Mather that he could trust the monstrous birth story because Moodey had heard the news from "a sober woman." He was also willing to journey to the scene of the birth to gather more specific details. He offered almost no editorial comment of his own about what the monstrous birth meant, but he shared an assessment that he had heard while gathering the news: his informant had told him that the birth reflected the turbulent times, when everything seemed "out of order."[5] This is not to say that all reliable sources refrained from making editorial comments on the meaning of news, but rather that many sublimated their own analyses to that of their informants. Reliable sources wanted to spread news that was timely and verifiable — two concerns that were often at odds in the 17th century. Moodey shared the news of the birth just as soon as he could be certain of it, but before he had exhausted his verifying options (he had not interviewed the midwife yet). Moodey's reputation, friendship with Mather, location, reporting skills, selective news-telling and limited editorial comment all marked him as a reliable source.

News gatherers recognized that the information in their letters rarely remained private. They usually encouraged their correspondents to communicate the news verbally, by sharing letters directly or by copying portions into their own correspondence. It is that public sense of correspondence that made finding reliable sources particularly crucial — a person's reputation accompanied the news he or she shared. The need to be certain complicated the easy transmission of news, and it suggests that the form news took (printed, handwritten or oral) was less important than the person who shared it. Often, vitally important colony-wide, or even empire-wide, information spread orally first, then later through written correspondence. For example, when Rowland Cotton wrote from Sandwich, Mass., to his brother in 1698 about Native Americans attacking Andover, he based his information on a personal conversation. He also suspected that his brother had already *heard* the news:

Do suppose you have already heard of the *Andover tragedy* because Eben' Lewis carried itt along on Saturday. Now I have nothing certain to Informe But what I hear ... viz Jonathan Fish says to me (who came from Boston thursday night & hither on Saturday night) that 3 posts came into Boston the Last of which sent by Coll Bradstreet wch say as follow, as near as I can Remember.... But ys hardly creditt ... Wee must wait for a fuller acco: Lets hear from you.[6]

How was the information shared? Did Lewis "carry" the information in his hands or in his head? Did the postal riders physically show Fish the letters or simply convey the information orally? Did it matter to the receivers *how* the writer had learned the information he now shared? Were oral sources or written sources more trustworthy? The string of reliable sources in this letter is remarkable; Rowland Cotton admitted that Ebenezer Lewis, Jonathan Fish, three posts and Colonel Bradstreet all contributed to the news he was about to share. Despite the quantity of sources, Cotton remained uncertain, uncertain enough to caution his brother to await a fuller account, presumably before sharing the news any further.

Veracity proved difficult for early New England correspondents. Roger Williams mused to Gov. Simon Bradstreet in 1682 about rumors of political intrigue from England, "We have tidings here of Shaftsbury's and Howard's beheading, and contrarily their release."[7] Rumors and other questionable information spread as quickly as did accurate information in written newsletters, and even more quickly orally. The correspondents recognized the problem and worked within the dual parameters of timeliness and veracity. Writing from England in 1678, Richard Blinman reminded Boston's Increase Mather how untrustworthy shared news could be:

It here pases for currant (which it may be, you know better than we) that by a Hurricane in the West Indies, 8 French men of war, and 6 French merchant men, were driven ashore & lost. ... An eminent blast of God, if true. But our ears are so filled with contradictions & false reports, that we know not how to credit the Reports which come every post.[8]

Although the writers included uncertain rumors in their letters, they worked to verify stories, or at least admitted that their news was unreliable. Correspondents often had to choose between the demands of truth and timeliness; the choice was not always an easy one, and reliable sources qualified their information accordingly. For example, in 1695, Richard Saltonstall wrote to his brother-in-law, Rowland Cotton, with this current news, even though he doubted its truth: "At Salem two men killed 18 wounded by careless overcharging a great Gun as we hear, the truth I dare not assert."[9] While Saltonstall was unwilling to risk his reputation as a trustworthy correspondent by sharing false reports, he also wanted to share important news quickly, so he added the caveat.

Early colonists held exacting standards for the truthfulness of information, but they also realized that waiting for absolute certainty would painfully prolong the exchange of news. The correspondents even joked about the time needed to verify facts. Nathaniel Saltonstall reconfirmed for Rowland Cotton in December 1700 that "Capt. Fosters ship is come lately from England and (*They Say*) brings News that Queen Mary is certainly dead."[10] Since Queen Mary II died in 1695, Saltonstall clearly intended to be humorous. The fear of sharing false information led some reliable sources to exclude doubtful news. When writing European news to his friend Waitstill Winthrop in 1712, Cotton Mather waited until he could confirm some questionable stories about the fate of British troops who may have been taken by the Dutch and the alleged advantage of the British "allies" over the French in Québec during Queen Anne's War:

> I am not willing to impose upon you our Newfound-land stories. ... The Doubtful channel thro' which these things arrive unto us, obliges me to supress them. The first ships will give us better Illuminations.[11]

Mather's concerns about veracity outstripped his desire for timeliness, but he was careful to inform his reader of his specific plans to verify and share the news as soon as he could.

Receivers often requested further confirmation from their reliable sources, especially if more recent stories contradicted the correspondent's earlier version. Thomas Walley asked John Cotton to confirm some information Mather wrote to him in 1677:

> if Mr. Mathers news be true it is very good but we are doubtfull there was some mistake in figures or some other way one of our vessels came home but 2 or 3 days before January that brought other news[12]

Not only did Walley seek reassurance about the validity of information for himself and his community in Barnstable, but he wanted to alert Mather that his own information (based on Mather's letter) might be wrong before Mather shared it any further.

When earlier information was found to be inaccurate, correspondents rushed to correct it. Both accurate and inaccurate information spread quickly, and correcting misinformation was vital to both the reliable source's reputation and to the well-being of his readers and hearers. For example, Samuel Sewall reassured John Cotton that Wells, Maine, did not burn down in 1692:

> These are to inform you that the late Report we had concerning Wells as if that place were destroy'd is altogether a Mistake, and that place is entirely well. It seems they had been clearing some Brush for their security which was laid in a heap & burn'd; and probably that was ye fire mistaken by the nocturnal Post, for garrisons confirmed it.[13]

Sewall realized that Cotton would have widely shared such tragic news, spread both by mouth and by pen, that such inflammatory information would worry the rural residents of Cotton's Plymouth and beyond, and that, uncorrected, the rumor would needlessly upset Cotton's community. Sewall described his verification process to Cotton as a way of both explaining the mistake and reassuring his reader of the correction: the night post had spread the false news, and the garrison later corrected it.

As the examples above illustrate, readers and hearers based their judgments about the truthfulness of information on their knowledge of the teller or writer as a reliable source. Newsletters flowed along the network *because* the receivers trusted the correspondents' information and intentions. The subjective relationship between correspondents may seem problematic to modern readers because at times it appears that early Colonial readers judged the veracity of news based on a correspondent's power, prestige, or personal connection. While a correspondent's status sometimes privileged the news he or she shared, often that status was not the first consideration. The link between news gatherers and their audience always depended on the source's ability to acquire trustworthy news.

Geography was the key factor in someone's ability to act as a news gatherer. Centrally located "news brokers," especially in Boston's busy seaport, enjoyed enhanced access to information, both written and oral, while hinterland correspondents usually depended on them for updates on the latest events and ideas. By the time information reached the last ears and eyes on the frontier, it had passed through many retellings, both oral and written. These early reporters were vital to ensure that information flowed smoothly, even as each hearer, reader and teller altered the final result, filtering and reshaping the information. Some correspondents acted as primary sources of news in each concentric circle that radiated from seaport to backcountry. If they were not centrally located in a seaport, which would almost immediately credit them as informed, then they enjoyed a considerable exchange of letters with correspondents in the information centers.

One Colonial event that predates the first newspaper, King Philip's War (1675-1676) — as reported by two correspondents, Noah Newman and John Cotton — illustrates both the role of reliable sources in 17th-century New England's news and the ways in which news moved in the early Colonial context before the arrival of a locally published newspaper. While rural ministers generally depended on centrally located sources to supply information, news also came from outside Boston. Reporting events on the frontier inverted the usual broker-hinterland relationship. When pursuing the truth of occurrences and replying to inquiries from the intellectual centers, distantly settled correspondents shared the prestige of metropolitan news brokers. Noah Newman's newsletters from Rehoboth about native raids on Medfield and troop movements suggest that the hinterland network could supply news as effectively and as reliably as did its Boston counterpart.

King Philip's War pitted Metacomet (King Philip) and his Narragansett, Wampanoag and Nipmuk allies against English colonists and their native allies (often from the same groups) beginning in the summer of 1675.[14] Metacomet, a Wampanoag Sachem, encouraged natives to abandon their peaceful alliance with Plymouth and rebel against English settlers who were relentlessly encroaching on native land, and whose free-range livestock destroyed native crops. Fearing armed attack, the Plymouth government disarmed the natives, forcibly when needed. The assassination of one Christian Indian, John Sassamon, in January 1675 by three Wampanoag allies of Metacomet provided the immediate cause of the war. A trial in June found Metacomet's men guilty of murder, and they were hanged in Plymouth on June 8, 1675.

Metacomet's devastating raids in 1675 against towns in Plymouth Colony, the Connecticut River Valley, the Merrimac Valley and Rhode Island were extremely successful. By February 1676, attacks on Massachusetts Bay towns such as Lancaster, Medfield and Weymouth continued Philip's encircling of Boston, bringing him within 10 miles of the city. One in 10 colonists perished, and native tribes in New England never recovered from the devastating casualties, making it the deadliest war in American history. As the fighting raged in Plymouth Colony, Plymouth's minister, John Cotton, appealed to his colleagues for news of worsening native attacks. Since his arrival in Plymouth, Cotton had cultivated relationships with neighboring ministers and government officials, just as he maintained regular correspondence with leading colonists in Boston and Cambridge. Cotton's links in both directions — into the backcountry and out to the coast — empowered him to gather and distribute news as few others could. One of Cotton's hinterland ministerial colleagues was Noah Newman, the settled minister in the town of Rehoboth in Plymouth Colony. When war broke out, Cotton naturally turned to Newman for news.

Rehoboth was the central rendezvous for almost 700 Massachusetts Bay and Plymouth Colony soldiers and their native allies, who had gathered to fight against Philip's forces. Newman's location gave him access to news from the officers and the soldiers who filled his town and church, and at first he seemed to relish the chance to serve as Cotton's reliable source. Cotton and Newman had regularly exchanged letters since Cotton's arrival in Plymouth, but Cotton's connections and considerable letter-exchange network usually meant that Cotton was informing Newman. The war's location and the troops' muster in Rehoboth reversed that, making Newman the source for Cotton's news. As Newman wrote to Cotton, "The Northern war which being now come west, by my present situation I consider my selfe to have ye opportunity of a retaliation."[15] Newman's letter on Dec. 16, 1675, reads like a war diary of sorts, listing the movements of the English forces, day by day, with little editorial interference:

> Decemb. 10 All the forces of mass: & plim arrived wth us & Billeted amongst us y[t] night ... some of prov[idence]: coming over that night brought intelligence of some few wigwams neer them w[ch] might be conveniently surprized that night by a pty sent over or otherwise they escaping would give intelligence to the rest of y[e] Armies approach. upon w[ch] the Gen ordered Capt Johnson wth as many of his men as he could muster up that night to passe over & possesse himself of the sayd wigwams accordingly he went but y[e] Indians were escaped a considerable time before he appeared by the snow y[t] was faln since. Decemb: 11 The army past over from us to Prov: at the Narrow passage upon a raft made of Cannows & bands over them[16]

Newman's reporting style included exact information, visual detail and a clear accounting of his sources: "This intelligence M[r] Ames gave to m[r] Browne & m[r] Browne sent to me." Newman was also careful to suggest to Cotton that there was some news he could not provide. He acknowledged Cotton's desire to be as informed as possible but was unwilling to hazard a guess: "I have as yet no thing of certainty concerning o[r] Coneticot forces." He also added a postscript on Dec. 17 with updates on the exact numbers of natives killed in a recent battle, which "is not so plentifull as before related." To save time, he enclosed a copy of the letter he had received that morning: "The Late & true intelligence you have in y[e] enclosed as it came by Letter." Newman's news came from the soldiers themselves, and while he vouched for the truth of their stories, he was careful to inform his correspondents about the origin of news. For example, he included some information that the bearer "doth credibly inform us" regarding "22 psons or thereabouts killd & serveral houses of ... fired." Newman assured Cotton of the soldier's credibility: "he was an eye witness to just before he left the army."[17]

As a site-based correspondent in Rehoboth and Narragansett, Newman actively sought out information by interviewing participants, reading personal letters that receivers shared with him, questioning military postal riders and ministering to the soldiers. Newman's letters to Cotton throughout the war included both news that he had attained firsthand and information gained from his own reliable sources, whom he always identified and validated as "credibel." Newman was meticulous in describing his news-gathering methods. For example, in a Jan. 10, 1676, letter to Cotton, Newman employed many different means to acquire trustworthy news: "When I tooke my Journey to the Island to visit the wounded wch I heard was come thither I was presented with an opportunity of going to Narragansett; wch I tooke hold of ... when I was there this enclosed was presented me by a Plimouth man unto wch I ... refer you for particular intelligence. ... the summe of what I here relate I hrd from one that met them upon the rode." The main body of news contained in the letter recounted some tenuous attempts at English-native diplomacy and listed the numbers of Indians killed during the Great Swamp Fight in Narragansett, R.I., on Dec. 19, 1675: "There hath been an Eng Scout sent out which broght in 2 Indians, who Informe that the Indians lost 300 of their fighting men in the ingagemt. besides women & childr; & old men." Unsure whether some other news was trustworthy, Newman refrained from sharing it, but he promised to be vigilant: "I Looke every day & hour for certaine intelligence of things both at ye Iland & Narrag[ansett] by some gone fro us to visit them. There is of late some losse by fire at Narragan: but I heare it so variously reported I dare say no thing till I have better information."[18]

The fighting moved close to Noah Newman's own community when native forces attacked Medfield on Feb. 21, 1676. Newman's newsletter to Cotton on March 14, 1676, about the attack on Medfield suggests how vicious the fighting was and how adept Newman had become in his role as news correspondent. Describing the early morning attack on Medfield, based on information gained from a visit to the devastated town, Newman relied on the testimony of his ministerial colleague in Medfield, John Wilson, who had survived the attack, and on discussions with other survivors. Although Wilson was still unsure of the exact numbers who had died, he described some of the gruesome deaths, which Newman repeated in his letter to Cotton. Newman's careful attention to place, time, motive and detail distinguish his war correspondence. In the opening lines of his report on "the Hystory of the Medfeild tragedy, as you well call it," he established time: "it was febru[ary] the 21. in the morning." Based on his knowledge of Medfield's location and the rhythm of life in a farming community, he suggested how more than 300 natives were able to surprise the settlers: "It seems probable that the enemy had logd himselfe in most of their barns & waited for the first appearance of day intending to take persons at their first Looking out at their doors in the morning."[19]

After setting the time, place and process, Newman carefully reconstructed the attack, which began when English settlers arose from their beds and stepped into their doorways: "Henry Adams stept but over the threshould & was shot through the windpipe & fell downe dead." Native attackers threw stones at least one house "to provoke [Goodman Dwight] to looke out," and when he did, they "shot him through the shoulder, who is dead since I was there." The wife of one of the visiting militia sergeants was staying at Seth Smith's home, and was attacked as she tried to escape: "She was stricked dead to the enemys apprehansion & a child layd at each hand of her dead as they thought they stript her & tooke her head cloths." While the native attackers thought that she was dead, she survived what must have been a partial scalping. As Newman reported, Goodwife Thurston awoke and ran to the minister's house for safety: "She afterward came to herself went into the house to get a blanket & run into Mr Wilson ... he took me a frightfull spectacle ... not knowing who she was for her hair hanging downe & her face covered wth blood." One of her children also lived — at least the child was still alive when Newman left Medfield — but another Thurston child was "carryed captive" by Philip's forces.[20]

Both the accuracy of his details and the dreadful eloquence of his reporting style illustrate Newman's skill as a news gatherer. For example, he described a desperate attempt by the wife of Samuel Smith to run across a field to the military garrison: "Samuel Smiths wife being big wth child & another child in her arms was crossing over an open feild to a Garison house & was over taken by the enemy & kild, & her child left alive, found standing by its dead mother where they thought it had stood neer an hour." Using vivid imagery, Newman also shared with Cotton the "cry of terrifyed persons, very dreadfull" and the yells of Philip's men, "shouting so as the earth seemed to tremble." Newman's powerful descriptions seemed to want to carry Cotton to the terrible scene itself. At times, Newman was overwhelmed by the tragedy and resorted to a simple list of victims: "Goodman Bowens & his son was kild Thomas Mason & his son kild."[21]

As many New Englanders did, Newman searched for the meaning behind the terrible attack on Medfield and first suggested a providential interpretation: "Oh what a sudden calamity was this & what an emblem of the sudden & dreadfull appearance of the great Judge of the world when he shall come to render vengeance to the wicked." The attack caught the settlers unawares, "few when they lay downe thought of such a dolefull morning," just as sinners slumbered unaware of God's impending judgment. Newman simply wrote what was surely on Cotton's mind anyway: Why was God punishing the settlers through the Indian attacks? He also suggested that the tragedy in Medfield might be a provocation to repent: "It is surely a day of great tryumph wth them; the Lord pray it may be a day of deep humiliation wth us."

Despite his belief that the war was evidence of God's judgment on New England, Newman also transcribed a note posted by Philip's forces as they departed Medfield in which the natives told the settlers exactly why they had attacked: "Thou English man hath provoked us to anger & wrath & we care not though we have war wth thee this 21 years for there are many of us 300 of w[ch] hath fought wth thee at this time we have nothing but our lives to loose but thou hast many faire houses cattell & much Good things."[22] Newman refrained from commenting on the natives' clear statement of purpose and, to modern readers at least, understandable motive for attacking English settlements. While he certainly suggested meaning and causes, Newman devoted most of his newsletters to giving precise and graphic descriptions of the attack and to listing the dead, wounded or captured people and the burned homes and barns. In the March 14 letter, he remained unsure of the total casualties in Medfield, despite his best efforts: "I canot give you an strait number of the persons killd nor their names I askt the Questio 2 or 3 times when I was there & Mr Wilson could not resolve me."

According to Newman, Wilson was still too distraught to give a precise accounting. He then asked Captain Jacob for his assessment, and Jacob "judged there was about 16." Newman was able to provide more specific casualty lists two weeks later. In a letter to Cotton on March 27, he carefully listed the English dead and wounded by town.[23] His clear intention was for Cotton to help him spread the tragic news to people in nearby Scituate, Marshfield, Duxbury, Sandwich, Barnstable, Yarmouth and Eastham whose family members had perished in Rehoboth. On the reverse side of the letter, Cotton listed the people with whom he had shared Newman's newsletter, either directly or by copying portions into his own letters. The list of readers, as listed by Cotton, completes a circle that begins and ends with Newman: Noah Newman (Rehoboth), George Shove (Taunton), Thomas Walley (Barnstable), Captain William Bradford, Captain James Oliver, James Keith (Bridgewater), Increase Mather (Boston), Nathaniel Mather (Dublin, Ireland), Seaborn Cotton (Hampton), Joshua Moodey (Portsmouth) and Noah Newman. Surely, each of these men not only read and shared the news, telling local families about their tragic losses; but they also added updates and elaborations to the story based on their own news-gathering efforts.

Cotton's reliable source (Newman) empowered his newsletters as trustworthy, as did Cotton's extensive letter-exchange network. Some of Boston's leading ministers wrote to Cotton looking for information about the native wars, and they relied on his information, as did his hinterland colleagues. Acting as a sort of central news dispatch, Cotton's correspondence reflects his news-gathering and news-sharing vocations — on many occasions, Cotton acted as a reliable source, once removed. For example, Thomas Walley wrote to him in June 1676 with an update, assuming that Cotton would spread the news only if he could confirm it: "We had news the last day of y[e] week from sea John Hutchins being a fishing and meeting wth a fishing Boat that the week before the United

Forces killed between 2 & 300 Indians, we suspend o^r faith til we hear from yo^u."[24] For Walley, the news would be trustworthy *because* it came from Cotton's pen, with Cotton's reputation behind it. Vital information spread smoothly along a letter-exchange network that recognized the importance of rapid information diffusion, especially during crises, but that also expected the news to be trustworthy.

As the above list of correspondents indicates, Cotton's and Newman's newsletters during King Philip's War traveled far beyond the small agricultural and frontier towns in Plymouth colony. Joshua Moodey wrote to Cotton on April 1, 1676, thanking him for "ye Intelligence" about the Medfield attack, which Moody received from colleagues in Boston as well as directly from Cotton: "I have read it & showed it unto many who have p[er]used it wth great Sympathy. ...If anything remarkeable of like hath occurr among you for ye future...your handing it to us w^d be matter of great Satisfaction y^t wee might know things pticularly & truly. Reports are so many & various y^t one knows n^t what to believe."[25] Moody certainly shared the information as well, broadening Newman's (and Cotton's) audience with each retelling.

News gatherers often referred to untrustworthy news as "burdensome" or "troublesome." To the 17th-century correspondent, sharing news that he or she could not confirm transgressed the understood rules of information exchange, leaving the reader with a difficult dilemma. The temptation to share news could outweigh fears of spreading false rumors. In the example that opened this essay, Moodey alluded to the witchcraft case but decided not to "trouble" Mather with a story that had not been verified. Moodey knew that Mather would be anxious to share news of witchcraft, but Moodey's best judgment did not permit him to leave Mather in such a difficult position. That sense of responsibility to the reader cuts to the heart of early Colonial definitions of "objectivity." The correspondent had a duty to share news freely and quickly, but only after he or she deemed it to be trustworthy. That "objective" news depended on scrupulous self-scrutiny and self-censorship by the news gatherer and on the reader's subjective assessment of the correspondent.

The tradition of the reliable source in the 17th-century sense of the word continues in modern journalism in the guise of the trustworthy anchor. When Peter Jennings, clad in a flak jacket, stands in front of war-torn buildings, he echoes Noah Newman's writings from bloody Medfield. Jennings may not actually need to be there for modern audiences to remain informed, but the symbolism of the pictures of Jennings reporting from the scene seems crucial to maintaining the relationship between the correspondent and the audience that remains part of "objective" news gathering.

NOTES

[1] Samuel Green printed Mather's book under the title, *An Essay for the Recording of Illustrious Providences, Wherein an Account is given of many Remarkable and very Memorable Events, which have happened in this last Age; Especially in New England* (Boston, 1684). Moodey's monstrous birth story did not appear in *Remarkable Providences*. For other letters to Mather containing stories for his consideration, see John Higginson to Increase Mather, 17 August 1683, Massachusetts Historical Society (hereafter, "MHS") *Collections*, 4th Ser., 8 (1868): 285-7; John Bishop to Increase Mather, 11 April 1682, 3 August 1682, 16 September 1682, MHS *Collections*, 4th Ser., 8 (1868): 308-12; John Whiting to Increase Mather, 4 December 1682, 17 October 1683, MHS *Collections*, 4th Ser., 8 (1868): 466-72; James Fitch to Increase Mather, 16 April 1683, MHS *Collections*, 4th Ser., 8 (1868): 474; Simon Bradstreet to Increase Mather, 24 April 1683, MHS *Collections*, 4th Ser., 8 (1868): 480-1; Israel Chauncey to Increase Mather 6 February 1683, MHS *Collections*, 4th Ser., 8 (1868): 627-8; Edward Taylor to Increase Mather, 22 March 1683, MHS *Collections*, 4th Ser., 8 (1868): 629-31.

[2] According to Salem's minister, John Higginson, Moodey, like many ministers in early New England, had recorded wonder stories and providences for many years: "Just as I had finished, Mr Moody came in, & told me that he hath kept 30 years – Almanacks together with fayr paper between every year, setting down remarkable Providences." John Higginson to Increase Mather, 22 August 1682, MHS *Collections*, 4th Ser., 8 (1868): 282.

[3] The connection between facts and objectivity became clear in later journalistic thinking. The historians Bruce Evensen and Doug Ward, for example, make this point in chapters 10 and 12 in this book.

[4] I ground my investigation on the belief that objectivity is not something "out there" but is socially constructed and remade over time.

[5] Moodey's decision to include some basic information about the parents indicates that he did not see the child as the monstrous reflection on the parents' sinfulness. They had been married four or five years, and he suggested no foul play. His description is closer to a natural history catalog than a jeremiad of sinfulness. See Park and Daston, "Unnatural Conceptions," for an interpretation of this shift in monster stories during the 17th century. Katherine Park and Lorraine J. Daston, "Unnatural Conceptions: The Study of Monsters in Sixteenth and Seventeenth-Century England and France," *Past and Present* 92 (August 1981): 30-34.

[6] Rowland Cotton to John Cotton, 1 March 1697/8, Miscellaneous Bound Collection, MHS; quotation by permission of the MHS.

[7] Roger Williams to Simon Bradstreet, 6 May 1682, MHS *Collections*, 2nd Ser., 8 (1819): 196-8.

[8] Richard Blinman to Increase Mather, 9 August 1678, MHS *Collections*, 4th Ser., 8 (1868): 334-6.

[9] Richard Saltonstall to Rowland Cotton, 6-12 May 1695, Miscellaneous Bound Collection, MHS.

[10] Nathaniel Saltonstall, Jr., to Rowland Cotton, 9 December 1700, MHS *Collections*, 80 (1972): 266.

[11] Cotton Mather to Waitstill Winthrop, 15 September 1712, MHS *Collections*, 4th Ser., 8 (1868): 408-10.

[12] Thomas Walley to John Cotton (1640-99), 16 January 1677, Curwen Family Papers, American Antiquarian Society (hereafter, "AAS"); quotation by permission of the AAS.

[13] Samuel Sewall to John Cotton, 11 July 1692, Curwen Family Papers, AAS.

[14] The best account and cultural interpretation of King Philip's War is Jill Lepore, *The Name of War: King Philip's War and the Origins of American Identity* (New York: Alfred A Knopf, 1998). See also Douglas Leach, *Flintlock and Tomahawk: New England in King Philip's War* (New York: MacMillan, 1957; reprint Parnassus Imprints, 1992); Alden Vaughan, *New England Frontier: Puritans and Indians, 1620-1675* (New York: W.W. Norton, 1965); Russell Bourne, *The Red King's Rebellion: Racial Politics in New England, 1675-1678* (New York: Oxford University Press, 1990); Richard Slotkin and James Folsom, eds., *So Dreadfull a Judgment: Puritan Responses to King Philip's War, 1676-1677* (Middletown: Weslyan University Press, 1978).

[15] Noah Newman to John Cotton, 16 December 1675, Curwen Family Papers, AAS.

[16] Ibid.

[17] Ibid.

[18] Noah Newman to John Cotton, 10 January 1675/6, Curwen Family Papers, AAS.

[19] Noah Newman to John Cotton, 14 March 1676, Curwen Family Papers, AAS.

[20] Ibid. See Lepore, *The Name of War*, for a sophisticated cultural analysis of the Medfield attack.

[21] Noah Newman to John Cotton, 14 March 1676, Curwen Family Papers, AAS.

[22] Ibid.

[23] Ibid.

[24] Thomas Walley to John Cotton, 26 June 1676, Curwen Family Papers, AAS.

[25] Joshua Moody to John Cotton, 1 April 1676, Curwen Family Papers, AAS.

CHAPTER 2

Puritans and the Foundations of Objectivity

By Julie Hedgepeth Williams

Samuel Green and Marmaduke Johnson had a delicate matter before them in 1663. The Harvard College printers were accustomed to publishing tracts favorable to the Puritan religion. However, a disagreement had arisen in the church, and it had spilled over into the press.

That year, a synod of church elders had argued about infant baptism. A majority favored loosening restrictions on baptizing infants whose parents were not fully covenanted church members. Child mortality was high, and it seemed tragic to let children die without benefit of baptism. For years the church had resisted pleas for baptizing children of the unchurched, but in 1662 the synod ruled that the children of godly but uncovenanted parents could be baptized. The blessing would last until the children were old enough to choose a commitment to the church for themselves.[1]

A small, vehement group opposed this "half-way covenant," as it was called. John Davenport wrote a pamphlet for the minority in 1663, titled *Another Essay for the Investigation of Truth*. It pleaded for objectivity in its preface, which was written by the Rev. Increase Mather. Mather admitted that few people agreed with his faction, but he asked, "Is *Truth bound up to Number?*" He went on to explain why objective consideration was imperative:

> Variety of Judgements may stand with Unity of Affections. He that judgeth a Cause before he hath heard both parties speaking, although he should judge rightly, is not a righteous Judge. We are willing that the World should see what is here presented.[2]

The argument proved persuasive. Green and Johnson printed the minority's pamphlet.

Another Essay for the Investigation of Truth presented objectivity as a conundrum: Although a man should judge rightly, he was wrongly judging if he had not seen both sides of an argument. Without an objective viewpoint, a right was a wrong.

Although Mather did not intend for the clever word play to represent a puzzle about press objectivity, his conundrum is a fitting way to introduce objectivity in pre-newspaper America. The determination of objectivity in 17th-century America is, today, a word puzzle. It depends on modern definitions of "objectivity," for the word did not exist then as we mean it today. Even though modern concepts are unrighteous judges when applied to the press of centuries ago, this chapter will use modern guidelines to measure statements about objectivity in America's earliest press.

Here in the 21st century, objectivity in the press generally means two things: reporting all relevant sides of a story, and doing so without bias. Beyond those definitions is another piece of the puzzle: What should be objective? Today, we expect objectivity only rarely in published material. Books are seldom thought of as objective — they tell the story of one thing, and if a person wants to read another opinion on the same topic, he reads another book. The same holds true for pamphlets, newsletters and other one-topic media. Journalistic news is supposed to be objective in modern America, but do readers expect every part of the news to exhibit objectivity? Readers do not assume that the editorial page will be objective, nor do they usually expect strict objectivity in feature stories. Even straight news reports often do not report all sides of a story; it is a rare criminal suspect who is able to counteract the police report. However, objectivity is often cited as essential to government reporting. The public relies on the news for its voting decisions, as the theory goes, so the news must report related matters fully and fairly.

The Puritans saw things differently. Puritans had little interest in discussing politics objectively in their press. However, as illustrated by Mather's bold statements in *Another Essay for the Investigation of Truth,* they thought it was vital to be objective in publishing arguments about religious doctrine.

At first that sounds implausible. The Puritans? Objective in religious doctrine? Didn't the Puritans humiliate people if they fell asleep in church? Weren't Puritans the strict, black-clad theocrats whose only joy was to proclaim their own depravity before God?

This popular picture of the Puritans does not square with historical reality. Judge Samuel Sewall's diary, for instance, shows that Puritans wore pink stockings; enjoyed reading poetry and newspapers; partook of delightful things such as cherries, raspberries, fresh air and celebrations; loved fine dinners and fine libraries; went swimming; and delighted in courting the opposite sex and eating cake and gingerbread.[3] The Puritans were not hopelessly dour.

Puritan society and outlook were more fairly summed up in the fact that they championed the printing press. Puritans were an educated, intellectual people. They were raised in the tradition that spawned John Milton's *Areopagitica,* which argued in 1644 for an unrestricted press so

Puritans and the Foundations of Objectivity • 25

that a broad range of religious viewpoints — including his Puritan one — might be heard in England. As Milton complained, "If we think to regulate printing, thereby to rectify manners, we must regulate all recreations and pastimes, all that is delightful to man."[4] Puritans tended to embrace Milton's outlook. They had inherited a tradition of reading and thinking, and they saw the press as one prime way to perpetuate that tradition. That outlook made Puritans more liberal than most of their contemporaries the world over.

Puritans were a sect of the Church of England, but they were horrified by that church's hierarchy and ritual. It seemed to Puritans that the Church of England was Catholicism masquerading under a different name. This was sinister to the Puritans; after all, Catholics of the day denied individuals the right to read and interpret the Bible. Only priests could read the Bible; they, in turn, told the congregation what to think about Biblical issues. To the Puritans, however, it was each individual's duty to read, interpret and understand the Bible. This devotion to the Bible gave rise to Puritans' persistent attempt to educate all people, female as well as male, the poor and the servants as well as the wealthy. Everyone had to read the Bible.[5] It is not surprising, then, that the Puritans were great readers — and as such, they enjoyed reading *beyond* the Bible. They thrived on the spoken word, too, of course; there was no substitute for hearing sermons. But Puritans were true believers in the printed word as part of the quest to understand the nature of true religion.

Puritans at first tried to purify the Anglican church from within, as they felt duty-bound to do. In time, though, they began to flee, first to Holland, then to New England.[6] To assuage the guilt they felt about abandoning England, they embraced a noble idea: they would make their new settlement the new Jerusalem, the "city on a hill" that would illustrate to Anglicans how God's true church was to be lived in daily life.[7]

The big problem that loomed over that project was the Atlantic. The ocean separated England from America by many weeks' voyage. During such a long journey, word-of-mouth communication was not always reliable to explain what was happening in the city on a hill — messages might be forgotten or twisted in retelling. But the printed word could cross the Atlantic while remaining true to the writer. And publications could faithfully carry the story of the city on a hill back to England.

That fact helps explain why the Puritans set up a press just eight years after their arrival in Massachusetts Bay colony, quicker than any other group in British North America. In fact, Puritans owned a printing monopoly in the future United States for the next 47 years.[8] Illustrating the intent of the Puritan press to cast a beacon back to Europe, the funds for the American press came from Europeans: Puritans in Holland and England raised money, bought the press, furnished its type, shipped the press to America and sent Stephen Daye along as printer.[9] Daye printed the first item from the new press, *The Oath of a Free-man*, in 1638 or 1639. Next he printed an almanac, followed by the now-famous *Bay Psalm-Book*. Thus began a rich 52 years of publishing, until 1690, when America's first newspaper, *Publick Occurrences, both Forreign and Domestick*, appeared in Boston. That newspaper lasted just one issue, and the 17th century would turn to the 18th before the *Boston News-Letter*, America's first permanent newspaper, made its debut in 1704 in the Puritan colony.

Since the Puritan press spent six decades laying the basis for the American publishing industry before newspapers appeared on a permanent basis, and since the news media are some of the few places we expect objectivity in publishing today, one wonders if the Puritans helped lay a groundwork for the modern thought that the news media should be objective. Was objectivity a goal in Puritan thought?

At first glance, it seems that Puritans had little interest in telling both sides of the story. The Puritan press, from 1638 to 1690, published 549 items that we know of today.[10] Except for a sprinkling of broadsides, newsbooks and reprinted London newspapers, these publications were pamphlets, which were often long enough to be considered a book in today's terms. True to modern form, a majority of pamphlets put out by Puritan writers dealt with one topic at a time. There was no need to state more than one side or offer a broad look at a subject. Readers of such pamphlets, like readers of books today, did not expect an objective view in individual tracts. Thus it is possible to argue that there was no place for objectivity in the Puritan press before newspapers came along.

Another argument against objectivity in the Puritan press was the intent of the writers. Of the 549 known Puritan publications between 1638 and 1690, approximately 150 were political in nature; some 60 were almanacs; about 40 were educational in purpose; an overwhelming 250 or so were religious in nature. The large number of religious works would, on the surface, indicate a high level of bias. With the exception of a handful of maverick works that found their way to press, those 250 religious publications advocated the Puritan point of view. If other opinions were mentioned, it was to prove their unworthiness. Because Puritans intended to send publications back to England to purify the Anglican church, logically they would send what they considered pure statements of their ideas to England. Puritan religious writers had a mission to spread the word, and they did so by arguing their case, not by covering all sides evenhandedly.

Those statements about Puritan religious writings are true, to an extent. Until the early 1660s, there were only hints in American Puritan writings that the press should practice objectivity by telling both sides of the story. In 1662, however, the synod approved the controversial "half-way covenant." In the debate that followed, compelling statements of objectivity came to the fore. Suddenly both sides needed to have a say to produce a balanced diet of argument and reason.

It was easy for Puritans to let the minority have its say, for they had long embraced minority opinions. *The Oath of a Free-man,* the first item printed in Massachusetts, illustrated a belief in the sanctity of individual consciousness over the will of the majority. In the oath, freemen (male voters) promised to be faithful and obedient to the colonial government, but they also vowed to express differing opinions. The oath stated:

> Moreover, *I* doe solemnly bind my self in the sight of God, that when *I* shal be called to give my voyce touching any such matter of this State, in which Freemen are to deal, *I* will give my vote and suffrage as *I* shall judge in mine own conscience may best conduce and tend to the publike weal of the body, without respect of persons, or favour of any man.[11]

The oath showed that Puritans accepted multiple viewpoints. In another indication of Puritan willingness to consider all sides, by the early 1640s the fledgling Harvard College library was filled with books that examined the entire range of Western thought. Conservative Puritans complained that students were thereby exposed to "heathen authors." However, it was the job of Thomas Shepard to obtain books and to defend the nature of the library's collection. He was able to fend off naysayers so that Harvard students might read ideas from a variety of sources.[12]

Of course, there were limits to freedom of expression, as spelled out in the Massachusetts colonial lawbook of 1648. Laws forbade Jesuits, Indians and Anabaptists from displaying their religions publicly.[13] The Puritan outlook itself was central; no one was to be allowed to try to convert the flock to a "heretical" viewpoint.

But when it came to their own religious doctrine, their own search for truth, the Puritans were eager to examine all opinions. Within the broad circle of Puritan beliefs, all sides of the story *had* to be published. The controversy over the "half-way covenant" in 1662 seemed to crystallize Puritans' thinking on that brand of objectivity.

The "half-way covenant" was no lighthearted matter to Puritans who thought that the synod of 1662 had erred. To them the sanctity of church membership was at stake. A writer for that faction questioned the synod in a tract titled *Propositions Concerning the Subjects of Baptism and Consocation of Churches.* The piece had to be licensed, which it was, despite the fact that it was written to counteract the synod's decision.

The General Court explained why it was licensing the dissenters' piece. The reasoning could have come straight from the *Areopagitica.* As the court put it, the press was open to free discussion, so long as it did not advocate heresy. Furthermore, it was important that every reader understand the various opinions on baptism. The court assured readers *objectivity or diversity of views*

FAIR AND BALANCED • 28

that it would not have allowed heretics to publish their opinion, but

> ... to bear one with another in lesser differences, about matters of a more difficult and controversial nature, and more remote from the Foundation, and wherein the godly-wise are not like-minded, is a Duty necessary to the peace and welfare of Religion.... In such things let not him that practiseth *despise him* that forbeareth, and let not him that forbeareth *judge him* that practiseth, *for God hath received him.*

The court added that it did not doubt the synod's decision. However, as the court said, it was important that all sides of the controversy offer their opinion. Objective publication was a *duty* vital to the well being of the church. God had received *both* sides.[14]

The debates continued in *Another Essay for the Investigation of Truth*, which called for objective reading on the subject of baptism. As mentioned at the start of the chapter, the preface put forth an interesting plea for objectivity: if a reader did not check all sides of an issue, he could not judge correctly. Increase Mather, writer of the preface, also pointed out Biblical justification for discussing all sides. When Christianity was young, he said, the apostles disagreed with one another, as reported in the Bible. In fact, Mather felt that he was under a moral obligation to make the minority's ideas plain. If all opinions were not published, he said, the truth might accidentally be withheld from mankind. Any valid opinion, he said, could be published as long as it did not take away the flock's affection for God.[15]

The elders of the church allowed *Another Essay* to be published, and another tract along similar lines, titled *Antisynodalia*, though published in London, circulated freely in Massachusetts. There was no attempt to squelch the pamphlets. In time, however, the elders tapped John Allin to write a pamphlet in reply. He wrote:

> When the *Antisynodalia* of our Brethren came to our hands, and *Another Essay* of the same nature was here Published, some godly and wise Christians advised the *Elders* to let them pass in silence; conceiving that they would not so take with the People, as to hinder the Practice of *the Doctrine of the Synod:* and that a Reply would occasion farther Disputes and Contests. But, upon serious consideration of the matter by divers *Elders* met to that End, the *Reasons* on the other side did preponderate.

Allin added that the elders finally decided they would be committing a moral disservice if they did not make *both* sides known.[16]

Jonathan Mitchel also came out with a tract in favor of the synod. His disagreement with the minority faction was gently stated. As he put it politely, dissenters deserved a hearing. "How loth we are to enter the Lists of publick Debate with the *Brethren*," Mitchel wrote, "and such Brethren as we love and honour in the Lord, with whom we are Exiles in the same Wilderness for the same Truth...."[17] As Mitchel saw it, discussion on all sides was part of the American "wilderness experience" as men used American isolation as a haven to come to a better understanding of God.

It could be argued that the willingness of the Puritan press to publish all sides in the "half-way covenant" controversy was rooted in the fact that great divines such as Mather comprised the minority. Their presence no doubt lent legitimacy to minority ideas. Yet the discussion of the need for two sides to be told was so gentle, so full of respect, that it is hard to imagine that the idea of objectivity was born in 1662 simply to mollify the minority. The arguments made by both sides were put forth by a people who were comfortable with debate, who had risen above name-calling, who respected opinions. Puritans, after all, had long fought for their opinion to be made plain in England. In *Areopagitica*, Milton had said, "Give me liberty to know, to utter, and to argue freely according to conscience, above all liberties.... Truth is strong, next to the Almighty.... [It is] not impossible that she may have more shapes than one."[18] Indeed, that was the argument Puritans had espoused from the very beginning, as expressed in the *Oath of a Free-man*. Milton's argument was the same that Mather expressed in *Another Essay for the Investigation of Truth*. Clearly, the acceptance of free expression by all sides was already a part of Puritan culture by 1662. Had the concept of objective discussion not been present, objective publication would not have been so graciously accomplished when the big disagreement happened.

There was another clear statement about objectivity during the 17th-century Puritan press, and this time it was in a nonreligious tract. In fact, it was in a news publication. Very few news publications were published in America before 1690 — there were approximately 15 that we know of today, and that included a reprint of the *London Gazette* and the single issue of *Publick Occurrences*. Others were publications about a single event, such as an earthquake or the defeat of a foreign navy. Given how few news publications there were, it is startling that in one of them, licensers took time to explain that objectivity was one important facet of news.

In 1677, licensers made a statement supporting objectivity in news publications. The licensing board approved William Hubbard's *A Narrative of the Trouble with the Indians* and then explained why pieces would be deemed acceptable for publication. In an essay attached to *Trouble with the Indians*, the licensing board commented positively on the fact that Hubbard had interviewed as many people as possible who were a part of recent Indian wars, and that he had faithfully reported what they had to say. Thus, the board indicated that it looked favorably on works that allowed more than one voice to be heard. These stories had to be told accurately — apparently without the author's bias.[19] Hubbard himself vouched for the objectivity of his information, saying that he had taken "great care ... to give all and every one, any way concerned in the subject of the discourse, their just due, and nothing more or less...." After all, Hubbard said, a publication was a record to posterity, and he wanted posterity to have a complete, accurate picture of what went on in the troubles with the Indians.[20]

Seventeenth-century American Puritans had a clear vision for evenhanded publication in matters of religious controversy, and they apparently let that concept shift into the publication of news. Outside those circles, the press was more restricted and was occasionally decried for bias. Most often, indications of bias in the Puritan press were associated with political publications.

While the Puritans' religious controversies could be discussed freely in the press, politics could not. It is difficult today to separate politics from religion in early New England. Pastors did not run the government, but life in Massachusetts centered on God. Thus, politics and religion were not always sharply separated. However, it is clear that people who complained of biased press practices in Massachusetts were usually speaking of bias related to political writings.

Thomas Morton found Massachusetts officials to be biased against his political publication. Jailed on suspicion of murder, the embittered man wrote *New English Canaan* after his release in 1637. It was, the Pilgrim leader William Bradford said, "an infamous and scurrillous booke against many godly and cheefe men of [Massachusetts], full of lyes and slanders...." Authorities jailed him for what they considered falsehoods in the book.[21] It was illegal to publish inflammatory opinions against political figures. The Puritans did not perceive a need for an objective, all-sides discussion of governing men.

Other authors who published in America also experienced a Puritan bias against the publication of certain political opinions. One instance came up when a man named Briscoe had to go underground to publish a political complaint about a requirement that Massachusetts residents pay a tax to support Puritan ministers. This fact rankled Briscoe, who was not a church member. In 1643, Briscoe talked a printer into publishing a tract against the tax. The printer was well aware that the piece would not have the blessing of authority; as the Puritan leader John Winthrop put it, the piece was "published underhand." When the book came out, Briscoe brazenly promoted it and gave speeches against the tax. The General Court called Briscoe to appear. He admitted publishing the piece and then, apparently intimidated, admitted that he had been wrong to write and promote the book. He was fined £10; and the unnamed publisher, 40 shillings.

Puritans and the Foundations of Objectivity • *31*

Given such examples of bias against inflammatory political opinions in Massachusetts, it is no surprise that charges of bias surfaced during the politically divisive Glorious Revolution of 1688, when King James II, a Catholic, was ousted and replaced by his Protestant daughter, Mary, and her husband, Prince William of the Dutch principality of Orange. As rumors filtered to Massachusetts about the overthrow of James,[22] 15 prominent men of the colony issued a broadside addressed to the hated Gov. Edmund Andros, demanding his surrender. Andros had been appointed by James but had governed harshly, and many Bostonians were eager to see him go. The broadside promised that locals would take the governor's palace by force if they had to.[23] Andros responded by trying to rein in the press. It was too biased against him, he said. He issued a decree:

> WHEREAS many papers have beene lately printed and dispersed tending to the disturbance of the peace and subversion of the government of this theire Majesties Colonie....It is therefore ordered that if any person or persons within this Collony be found guilty of any such like Misdemeanour of printing, publishing or concealing any such like papers or discourses, or not timely discover such things to Authority, ... they shall be accounted enemies to their Majesties present Government and be proceeded against as such with uttermost severity.[24]

Andros's attempt to muzzle the press was to no avail. The dissenters imprisoned him for shipment back to England[25] — despite the fact that formal word of King James's ouster would not reach New England for another six weeks.[26]

No one in Massachusetts was really certain of the situation in England, nor could Englishmen be certain of the motivations behind the coup against Andros. Accordingly, Nathanael Byfield rushed a pamphlet into print in London, hoping to convince the new monarchs that the overthrow had been justified.[27] Andros's supporters wanted their say, too. A Massachusetts resident writing under the pseudonym "John Palmer" wrote *An Impartial Account of the State of New England*, addressing the problems that Andros's supporters were having under the new administration. He himself had been jailed for 10 months and then sent to England as an outcast. Commenting on the bias of the Massachusetts press against Andros and his point of view, Palmer said in *Impartial Account* that no one in Massachusetts would print the pamphlet. He complained about the bias against Andros in the press:

> There was so much Industry used in *New England*, by those who had taken upon themselves the Government, that nothing should come abroad which might undeceive the People, already

wrought to such a pitch of Credulity, easily to believe the most monstrous Lyes and Follies, that the ensuing [pamphlet] could not be Printed without excessive Charge and Trouble; the *Press* being forbid to any that were injur'd, to justifie themselves, though open to all that would calumniate, and abuse them....

He finally got his story published in London.[28]

In the turmoil following the Glorious Revolution, America's first newspaper came and went in Puritan Boston. *Publick Occurrences, both Forreign and Domestick,* was censored after its first issue, ostensibly because it wasn't licensed[29] — but probably the more accurate reason was that the publisher, Benjamin Harris, had gone too far out on an editorial limb and had criticized the Maqua Indians, who were allies of Massachusetts.[30] The colony could ill afford such negative political news in the paper. The licensers apparently felt that the newspaper should show a bias in favor of political allies.

The idea that politics should not be negatively reported continued after the Glorious Revolution. When a Salem resident, Thomas Maule, tried to publish *Truth held forth and maintained* in 1695, Massachusetts printers looked it over and refused it. It defended the Quaker religion, but it also spoke ill of governmental leaders. Maule was persistent. He shopped around until he found a press at New York, and he had the offending tract printed there. He then circulated the work in Massachusetts. The General Court summoned Maule, who arrived with his Bible to prove that his opinions on Quakerism expressed in *Truth held forth* were right. However, the court found that there were so many lies about the other topics in the book that the arguments about Quakerism never came up, "which [I] believe was a surprise to him," Samuel Sewall remembered.[31] It was the political criticism that was summarily dispensed as improper; the religious disagreements were ignored.

Five years later, the authors of *Gospel Order revived* wrote an angry attack on Increase Mather. The writers searched in vain to find a Massachusetts printer who would print the piece. This was an unpleasant surprise to the authors, who could only allege bias. "[T]he Press in Boston is so much under the aw of the Reverend Author whome we answer, and his Friends, that we could not obtain of the Printer there to Print the following sheets...." They, too, ran to New York, where William Bradford put the item to press.

The incident, which took place at the turn of the 18th century, illustrates an important fact: the Puritan monopoly on American printing had come to an end. Quakers in Philadelphia had opened a press in 1685, and in 1689 a press had been established in Maryland. New York had gotten a press in 1693. The press had taken root in America, sprouting from the Puritan press, which included Puritan concepts of objectivity.

As the Puritans saw it, objectivity had to be practiced within boundaries. For the modern reader, that sounds restrictive. However, the key to understanding the Puritans' demand for a limited objectivity is realizing that the modern press also has boundaries. That fact can best be shown by propelling 17th-century values into the 21st. Today it is nearly unheard of in mainstream journalism to give religious doctrine any credence. Modern editors tiptoe around the notion of religious truth. When doctrine appears, it is generally covered as a controversy — factions disagree, and the doctrine therefore makes the religion page — but without a statement as to which side of a religious controversy is true or right. That simply *cannot* be discussed. In the future, perhaps, people will look back on "objective" news media of today and label them as biased for their inability or unwillingness to engage in grand discussions of religious truth. The Puritans certainly would think that, if they were suddenly to be living three centuries hence, the foremost purpose of their press was to search for the truth of God.

Instead, today we tend to think of objectivity as applying mainly to political statements in the news media, for we think of journalism as an important factor of political understanding, of self-government. The Puritans did not consider objectivity necessary in political publications. Objective discussion of religious doctrine, on the other hand, was of vital importance, and it was the job of the press to facilitate that discussion.

Perhaps, then, the notion of the proper subjects for media objectivity from the 17th century to the early 21st show a consistent theme. Society in both eras offered the objective right to hear all sides of the story in publications about the most central, guiding light in society. To Puritans, the press had a duty to discuss religious doctrine. Today, when Americans devote so much attention to liberty and law as the defining parameters of civilization, journalists see a duty to discuss matters of government objectively.

Perhaps at the heart of it, journalistic objectivity is applied in any age to what Americans deem most necessary for the proper functioning of society.

NOTES

[1] David D. Hall, *Worlds of Wonder, Days of Judgment: Popular Religious Belief in Early New England* (Cambridge, Mass.: Harvard University Press, 1990), 152-6. There was disagreement among Puritans as to whether baptism indicated saving grace as given by God, or whether it was merely parents' desire to offer their children every possible protection as an act of love.

[2] "Apologetical Preface to the Reader," in John Davenport, *Another Essay for the Investigation of Truth* (Cambridge, Mass.: Printed by Samuel Green and Marmaduke Johnson, 1663). Although the preface was unsigned, scholars are

sure that Increase Mather was the author. See Charles Evans, *American Bibliography* (New York: Peter Smith, 1941), entry #78.

[3] Diary entries of 30 January 1677, 20 June 1685, 28 January and 25 September 1686, 16 August 1688, 27 June 1689, and 8 July 1689 by Samuel Sewall in Harvey Wish, ed., *The Diary of Samuel Sewall* (New York: G.P. Putnam's Sons, 1967), 29, 34, 42, 46, 57, 61-3. See also diary entries of 3, 6, 10, 11, 12, 17, 24, 31 October and 7 November 1718 by Samuel Sewall in M. Halsey Thomas, ed., *The Diary of Samuel Sewall, 1674-1729* (New York: Farrar, Straus and Giroux, 1973), 2: 957-62, 964-5, 967.

[4] John Milton, *Areopagitica* (London: 1644), reprinted in Merritt Y. Hughes, ed., *John Milton: Complete Poems and Major Prose* (Indianapolis, Indiana: Bobbs-Merrill, 1957), 732-3.

[5] See, for instance, Hall, *Worlds of Wonder...*, 21, 32-4.

[6] William Bradford, manuscript, "Of Plymouth Plantation," excerpts reprinted in Giles Gunn, ed., *Early American Writing* (New York: Penguin Books, 1994), 121, 123-5.

[7] "A Modell of Christian Charity," sermon preached by John Winthrop aboard the ship *Arabella*, 1630, excerpts reprinted in ibid., 107-12.

[8] Pennsylvania established a press in 1685. The laws of Virginia were supposedly printed in that colony in 1682, but no further printing was done in that colony for decades. It is possible that the imprint on *The Laws of Virginia* (Williamsburg: 1682) gave an incorrect location for the press.

[9] Isaiah Thomas, *The History of Printing in America*, 2d. ed., Marcus A. McCorison, ed., (1810; reprint, New York: Weathervane Books, 1970), 5, 45-9.

[10] The number is derived from Evans, *American Bibliography*. See Volume 1.

[11] Massachusetts Bay Colony. *The Oath of a Free-man* (Cambridge: Printed by Stephen Daye, 1638 or 1639). Although the *Oath* does not survive in its original form, a copy does survive.

[12] Michael McGiffert, ed., *God's Plot: The Paradoxes of Puritan Piety, Being the Autobiography and Journal of Thomas Shepard* (Amherst: University of Massachusetts Press, 1972), 6n, based on letters from Thomas Shepard to Hugh Peter, 27 December 1645, and Thomas Shepard to John Winthrop, c. 1642.

[13] Massachusetts Bay Colony. *The Book of the General Lauues and Libertyes concerning the Inhabitants of Massachusetts.* (Cambridge: 1648), 1-2, 26, 29.

[14] Synod of Elders and Messengers of Churches in Massachusetts Colony, *Propositions Concerning the Subject of Baptism and Consociation of Churches* (Cambridge: Printed by Samuel Green for Hezekiah Usher, 1662), preface.

[15] "Apologetical Preface to the Reader," in Davenport, *Another Essay for the Investigation of Truth.*

[16] John Allin, *Animadversions Upon the Antisynodalia Americana, A Treatise printed in Old England: in the Name of the Dissenting Brethren* (Cambridge: Printed by Samuel Green and Marmaduke Johnson for Hezekiah Usher, 1664), preface.

[17] Jonathan Mitchel and Church Elders, *A Defence of the Answer and Argument of the Synod Met at Boston in the Year 1662* (Cambridge: Printed by Samuel Green and Marmaduke Johnson for Hezekiah Usher, 1664), preface.

[18] Milton, *Areopagitica*, in Merritt, *John Milton...*, 746-7.

Puritans and the Foundations of Objectivity • 35

[19] William Hubbard, *A Narrative of the Troubles with the Indians* (Boston: Printed by John Foster, 1677), prefatory statement by the licensers.

[20] Ibid., Hubbard's "Epistle Dedicatory."

[21] William Bradford, "Of Plymouth Plantation," manuscript, published as William T. Davis, ed., *Bradford's History of Plymouth Plantation, 1606-1646* (New York: Charles Scribner's Sons, 1908), 251. *New English Canaan* was published in London in 1637.

[22] See Charles M. Andrews, ed., *Narratives of the Insurrections, 1675-1690* (New York: Charles Scribner's Sons, 1915), 267.

[23] *At the Town-House in Boston: April 18th, 1689* (Boston: Printed by Samuel Green, 1689).

[24] *Order against seditious publications* (1689), in *The Andros Tracts* (New York: Burt Franklin, Research and Source Works Series #131, 1868), 3: 107.

[25] Increase Mather, *The Present State of the New English Affairs* (Boston: Printed by Samuel Green, 1689), in *Andros Tracts*, ibid., 2: 16.

[26] Andrews, *Narratives of the Insurrections...*, 167.

[27] Nathanael Byfield, *An Account of The Late Revolution in New-England* (London: Printed by Richard Chitwell, 1689), in Andrews, *Narratives of the Insurrections...*, 170-82.

[28] John Palmer, *An Impartial Account of the State of New England* (London: 1690), preface, in *Andros Tracts*, 1: 21-4.

[29] Massachusetts, *By the Governour & Council* (Boston: 1690).

[30] Diary entry of 25 September 1690 by Samuel Sewall in Thomas, *Diary of Samuel Sewall...*, vol. 1, p. 267.

[31] Journal entry of 19 December 1695 by Samuel Sewall in ibid., 341. Thomas discusses the pamphlet's contents in a note on p. 342.

CHAPTER 3

Neutrality and Colonial Newspapers

By Wm. David Sloan

From the very beginning, partisanship marked American newspapers. Yet concurrently, there also existed the firm belief that newspapers should be impartial and that they should attempt to be accurate in providing news reports. When publishers departed from those principles, displeased readers tried to make them toe the line.

The concept of neutrality had originated earlier than newspapers, as the previous two chapters in this book have shown. In the printing trade, that concept was particularly important. The need to operate a print shop as a business was especially conducive to neutrality. Printers were willing to print for any member of the public who could pay for the job, with little regard for the customer's sentiments. Once they were producing their own newspapers, however, many printer-editor-publishers* wished to use their papers to express their own views — or to provide a forum for writers who concurred — and thus they found their sentiments divided between the business concept of neutrality and their own partisan preferences.

Another force, however, affected the approach that newspaper operators were able to take. Readers expected partisan publishers to allow dissenting views into their papers. It was not that readers themselves had a broadly tolerant view of encouraging opposing arguments, but when editors published views with which readers disagreed, readers did argue that editors had a philosophical obligation to allow the readers' views to be heard. The readers' expectation — like the occupational principle of neutrality with which printers began — had its roots in the assumption that printing, of which newspapers were an outgrowth, was a public business with an obligation to make available the views of anyone who offered them. Thus even when publishers were biased, they always had to be aware of the public expectation of neutrality.

Although the term "objectivity" would not be coined until the 20th century, the principle was generally acknowledged even before the country gave birth to its first newspaper. The original idea was that printers were obligated to print whatever the public presented to them, whether they agreed with the content or not. It was to play an essential part — perhaps the most critical part — in the thinking of early Americans about the proper role of newspapers and in publishers' journalistic philosophy and practices.

The concept that newspapers should be objective — "impartial" and "neutral" were the terms the colonists normally used to express the idea — originated with the concept of the printing press as a mechanical device used simply to produce material for customers.[1] Later, this function would be called "job printing." Today, we may think of it as related to photocopying at Kinko's.

The printer was thought of, and thought of himself, as simply the operator of the machine, rather than as an independent thinker whose function was to originate and present his own views. Groups such as the Puritans and the Quakers hired printers to operate the groups' presses, or groups and individuals contracted with independent printers to reproduce material for them. The printer acted essentially as a craftsman operating a business. His function was to serve others who provided the content of the publications that the printer reproduced. When a town had competing factions but only one printer, he usually printed equally for both sides. That was true even when the printer was biased toward one of the sides, since the printer looked on any publication as a source of income. When two printers served a town, each faction normally gave most of its business to the printer who shared its views. Thus, each printer tended to do the bulk of the printing for one of the factions, although he was willing to print material from anyone.

Such a tradition in the printing business easily carried over to newspaper printing, leading to the general concept that newspapers should print material from a variety of points of view. For example, even James Franklin, publisher of that most biased of early newspapers, the *New-England Courant*, printed an attack on the *Courant*, a one-shot broadside titled *The Little-Compton Scourge: Or, The Anti-Courant*. Its sole purpose was to attack the *Courant's* editor and chief writer, the controversial Anglican John Checkley.

It was obvious, however, that most newspapers took sides. When criticized, editors found it useful to argue that they were not biased but had printed offending material simply because newspapers were expected to print opposing views.

This dynamic of appealing to the concept of neutrality can be seen in the day-to-day operation of most Colonial newspapers. Publishers did not all share the same philosophies about their purposes, but the conflict between partisanship and neutrality was one that most had to deal with one way or another. In Boston, for example, the most energetic site for early American newspaper publishing, ideology seemed to motivate most publishers. Furthermore, several of the newspaper operators came from a background other than the occupation of printing. Thus, they

FAIR AND BALANCED • 38

did not have the printer's professional sense of obligation to be neutral; but they were, nevertheless, aware of the general public principle of neutrality. On the other hand, in Philadelphia, the colonies' second-leading newspaper town, practical business considerations played a stronger part. There, printers founded the earliest newspapers. Publishers in other towns also found that they frequently had to struggle with the notions of impartiality that readers expected.

America's first newspaper was started in 1690 in the chaotic situation following the overthrow of Gov. Edmund Andros in Massachusetts, whom the British king had appointed. Under an interim government comprised of local citizens, and while Massachusetts was waiting for a new charter, internal order began to disintegrate. Political stability was breaking down, factions had arisen, and the chaos fed a variety of rumors, many of them false.

It was in this situation that Benjamin Harris[2] published the first issue of what he intended to be a periodic newspaper, naming it *Publick Occurrences, Both Forreign and Domestick*. He hoped mainly to use it to support the Puritan rebellion against British authorities. Yet he believed the way to do that was to report the news as accurately as possible. He therefore intended to produce a paper that the public could rely on for accurate information. He also intended to use it to speak out on issues.

Harris hoped that the paper could serve as an antidote to the problems confronting Massachusetts. In his statement of purpose, he went to considerable lengths to emphasize his concern that reports be accurate. He would take, he explained, "what pains he can to obtain a *Faithful Relation* of all such things; and will particularly make himself beholden to such Persons in *Boston* whom he knows to have been for their own use the diligent Observers of such matters." Furthermore, he hoped that *Publick Occurrences* might serve as a cure for the "*Spirit of Lying*, which prevails among us." To that end, he promised that "nothing shall be entered, but what we have reason to believe is true, repairing to the best fountains for our Information. And when there appears any *material mistake* in any thing that is collected, it shall be corrected in the next." He would attempt, he promised, to expose anyone guilty of maliciously providing false information to the paper.[3]

The governing council suppressed *Publick Occurrences* after only one issue, but it was clear during its brief life that Harris's approach to newspaper publishing was not founded primarily on the concept of neutrality. Indeed, his venture is best understood as an effort to bolster the Puritan commonwealth's efforts to free itself from British royal and Anglican control. Yet, he also made it clear that he was interested in providing news that was as accurate as he could get. In that effort, the reliability of his news accounts — rather than partisanship or bias — was of prime importance.

America's next newspaper, the *Boston News-Letter*, was also started with the publisher's explanation that he wanted to produce a journal of news rather than opinion. John Campbell began the paper in 1704 without any conception of its being a true newspaper or of its exercising any publishing independence. In his role as postmaster, he believed that producing a quasi-official report in the form of a newspaper was one of his responsibilities. He thus looked on himself not as an autonomous editor but as an official conduit of information and on the newspaper as a formal, chronological record of news items. With the *News-Letter* tied so plainly to the unpopular, crown-appointed administration of Gov. Joseph Dudley, most Boston residents viewed it simply as a mouthpiece of the government and never a real newspaper.

Criticized for the *News-Letter's* timidity, Campbell stated his editorial policy as having "always been to give no offence, not meddling with things out of his Province."[4] It was this spirit that prompted him to shy away from controversial political and social issues. He published the newspaper with permission from the Dudley administration, with each issue prominently displaying the line "Printed by Authority."[5] On only one occasion was he reprimanded for offending authorities, and he quickly apologized.[6]

It was not until Campbell was replaced as postmaster that he began to publicize public controversies and both sides to issues, a change that meant he began to insert his own views along with those of readers. In December 1719, his successor, William Brooker, began the *Boston Gazette*. By then, newspapers had become a part of Campbell's life. Faced with competition, he began to change his approach. He inserted his personality more; and along with the short summary news items he had always carried, he now began including occasional essays and observations.[7] Piqued that Campbell had kept the *News-Letter*, Brooker printed an article stating that Campbell had been fired from the postmaster's job.[8] That charge led to an exchange of personal insults between the two,[9] and it was not long before they were taking sides on public issues. Generally, the *Gazette* under Brooker and his successor, Philip Musgrave, favored the interests of Gov. Samuel Shute, while the *News-Letter* took the side of the Colonial assembly.

Neither newspaper could be accused, however, of being a tool exclusively for one side. Political issues were intricate, and both papers frequently published material from contending sides. Authors paid for some material as "advertisements," whereas some items were published as straight news matter. Readers began to think differently about the *News-Letter*. The attitude of, for example, the Puritan cleric Cotton Mather, who earlier had criticized the paper as "our paltry news-letter,"[10] had moderated, and he wrote a number of pieces for it.[11] In 1722 he began publishing a nine-part series on *"The State of Religion,"* which among other things criticized Anglicanism — despite Campbell's Anglican membership. On the other hand, in the acrimonious public debate over smallpox inoculation in 1721-1722, it was the *Gazette* that served as the primary outlet for Mather and his supporters.

It was the inoculation controversy that provided the immediate background for the founding of the most partial newspaper of the early Colonial period. That paper, the *New-England Courant,* was founded with not even the slightest intent of being impartial — although its editors and publisher frequently resorted to the public defense that they were fair to both sides.

Because of their moderation, neither the *News-Letter* nor the *Gazette* could satisfy a combative High Church faction among Boston's lone Anglican congregation, King's Chapel; and it was the dissatisfaction of that small group that provided the motive for the *Courant.* Through its columns, members of the group brought the differences between Boston Puritanism and High Church Anglicanism to a head. Ever since the founding of King's Chapel, its members had hoped that Anglicanism would be established as the official church in Massachusetts. The Puritan clergy's support for the experimental and unpopular method of inoculating against smallpox provided the High Church faction with the issue they needed to attack the clergy. They thus opened the *Courant* with a harsh frontal assault.

With the fifth issue, however, the editor's duty passed into the hands of the printer James Franklin. He assured readers that the paper would be much more fair. He claimed to be neutral on inoculation and promised to avoid publishing material critical of his opponents. Despite his pledge, the *Courant's* content did not change significantly, and its purpose remained transparently obvious. Like the *Courant's* founders, Franklin may also have been a member of King's Chapel, and he intensely disliked the Puritan clergy. Members of King's Chapel continued to have a dominant hand in writing its content.[12] Although claiming to be neutral on inoculation and "promis[ing] that nothing for the future shall be inserted, anyways reflecting on the Clergy ... and nothing but what is innocently Diverting,"[13] the newspaper continued its one-sided attack on inoculation and Puritanism. For example, of the approximately 50 items related to inoculation that the *Courant* published from its founding in August 1721 to the end of the year, only one, a report from London, was slightly favorable toward the practice. The opposition clergy continued to believe that the *Courant's* "main intention ... [was] to Vilify and abuse the best Men we have, and especially the principal Ministers of Religion in the Country,"[14] with Cotton Mather declaring the purpose was to "lessen and blacken the Ministers of the Town, and render their Ministry ineffectual."[15]

It was not until the government ordered James Franklin in 1723 to cease publishing the newspaper that even a modicum of moderation and fairness began to appear in its pages. James named his younger brother, Benjamin, publisher. Under him, the *Courant* finally started to acknowledge readers' expectation of a degree of impartiality in newspapers. Benjamin's introductory address began: "Long has the press groaned in bringing forth an hateful brood of pamphlets, malicious scribbles and billingsgate-ribaldry." He described the *Courant's* new operator as having morals that were "clearly Christian" and as a "man of good temper, courteous Deportment, sound judgment, a mortal Hater of Nonsense, Foppery, Formality, and Endless Ceremony."[16] Later, as an editor in Philadelphia, it would be Benjamin Franklin who would write the Colonial period's most famous statement of newspaper impartiality. He would offer it as a defense — an "apology," he would call it — for printers who angered readers with articles that the readers thought should not have been published.

While printing with an ideological motive typified early newspaper publishing in Boston, printers in Pennsylvania were taking a pragmatic approach. In the metropolis of Philadelphia, Andrew Bradford and Benjamin Franklin, who had run away from Boston to escape his *Courant* apprenticeship, were concentrating on the practical concerns of building their printing businesses. Whereas Boston publishing strove after ideological victories and lofty ideals, Philadelphia's printers were more interested in pursuing earthly gains.

Bradford had started Pennsylvania's first newspaper, the *American Mercury*, with the main objective of providing news, not offering opinions. It was clear that one of his motivations was to enlarge his business by trying to avoid offending subscribers or advertisers.[17] In the first issue, he declared that the paper would "contain an Impartial account of Transactions, in the Several States of Europe, America, etc." and asked readers to support the paper through subscriptions.[18] Two months later he published his next statement of purpose, and it emphasized promoting business through advertising. It read:

> The Design of this Paper, being to Promote Trade it is hoped, that it will be Incouraged by the Merchants of this City, by Acquainting Us with the true price Current of the Several Good's inserted in it, which we presume may be Serviceable to All concern'd in Commerce.... We likewise Desire those Gentlemen that receive any Authentick Account of News from Europe, or other places, which may be proper for this paper, that they will please to favour Us with a Copy.[19]

Bradford's approach to the *Mercury* reflected his own character: he was a printer and a businessman who for the most part kept his political and religious sentiments in the background. He hoped to operate the newspaper as a financially successful enterprise. In the *Mercury*, therefore, there was little of the burning idealism and ideology of Boston's papers. Although he was a prominent Anglican and a supporter of the proprietary party in government affairs, as a businessman he willingly printed material for Quakers and the popular party. Although partisan, he generally avoided controversy. Responding in 1734 to some irreverent remarks in Benjamin Franklin's competing *Pennsylvania Gazette*, Bradford avowed that his own motive was to publish material that had "a tendency to raise and refine human kind; to remove it as far as possible from the unthinking brute; to moderate and subdue men's unruly appetites; to remind them of the dignity of their nature; to awaken and improve their superior faculties and direct them to their noblest objects."[20] On those rare occasions when he did offend the government, other people had usually written the offensive material, and the government accepted that explanation as mitigating Bradford's culpability.

When Bradford turned to another publishing venture in 1741, America's first magazine, his explanation of its purpose referred to the generally held expectation that newspapers be impartial. The fact that too often they were not provided good enough reason, in Bradford's opinion, for having another forum available. "[S]everal Colonies have no Printing-Press," he explained in the first issue of the *American Magazine*, "and in others where there is but one, and even in those Places where there are more, it is complained (whether with Justice or no we do not undertake to determine) that the printers are often under the Influence of Parties, and cannot, without much Difficulty, be prevailed upon to publish any Thing against the Side of [the] Question they are of themselves." Thus he offered his magazine "as a Remedy against those several Inconveniencies" and promised that "any Person, in whatever Colony residing, will find a ready Admittance to a fair and publick Hearing at all Times" in the magazine. "In the Disputes, that may be thus transmitted to us for Publication," he declared, "we shall *inviolably* observe an exact Neutrality, and *carefully* avoid mingling, with the Arguments on either Side, any Reflections or Remarks of our own."[21]

For both his magazine and his newspaper, Bradford faced continuing competition from a young, imaginative, pragmatic printer. No Colonial publisher was more successful than Benjamin Franklin. In many of his dealings with others, he left the impression of not being fully committed but rather more interested in how he might benefit. That detachment from others' beliefs probably contributed to his newspaper success, perhaps paradoxically, for it allowed him to develop a degree of unconcern about many things he printed. He was therefore willing to publish items from a variety of viewpoints — and he showed a particular openness if the authors were willing to pay. In some respects, his attitude seems similar to the one that later professional journalists developed. Particularly in the 20th century, in part as a result of the influence of objectivity on their perspective on the outside world, journalists often seemed to view other people and events with detachment, as parts of a scene the journalists observed from a distance. Despite his agility in working with other people, Franklin gave the appearance of being somewhat casual, as if he were an aloof spectator who looked at life as a game and could observe even himself as just one of the players.

As most Colonial printers did, Franklin loudly proclaimed his neutrality at the same time that he was promoting the interests of the popular party in Pennsylvania politics. His essential argument was that he could not rightly be criticized for what he printed because it was the nature of his job to print whatever authors gave him. It was a popular principle, recognized by printers and readers alike. Thus, Franklin and other printers argued, they were not to blame for the items they published.

The best-known argument for this policy was Franklin's "An Apology for Printers," published in 1731 in the *Gazette*. Printers, he explained, "are educated in the Belief that, when Men differ in Opinion, both Sides ought equally to have the Advantage of being heard by the Publick.... Being thus continually employ'd in serving all Parties, Printers naturally acquire a vast Unconcernedness as to the right or wrong Opinions contain'd in what they print; regarding it only as a Matter of their daily labour...." The "Apology for Printers" was an accurate statement of the ideal of printer disinterestedness, but it also demonstrated Franklin's dexterity in appealing for the support of subscribers and advertisers. Franklin, however, was certainly not one to remain disinterested on issues. To the contrary, he was energetic in his partisanship. He had, in fact, written his printers' "apology" in response to "being frequently censur'd and condemn'd by different Persons for printing things which they say ought not to be printed."[22]

Along with Franklin, other printers at one time or another found the need to rely on the neutrality defense to appease readers who did not agree with material they had published — or to acquit themselves when readers believed they had not been impartial, as newspapers were expected to be. Even publishers who were clearly biased referred to the concept of neutrality, realizing that they had to justify what they printed. The fact, however, that few newspaper printers gave equal treatment to both sides in arguments, and that many weighted their publications heavily to one side or the other, suggests that their defense of neutrality was not entirely candid. It was a position calculated to shield them from attacks of bias while publishing with bias. Perhaps ironically, the more biased an editor was, the more often he seemed to present the neutrality defense. The reason was that frequent bias called forth frequent criticism, thus resulting in the need for frequent defense.

That cycle can be seen in the case of Thomas Fleet of Boston. There perhaps was no publisher who stated this defense more frequently and ardently than he. An Anglican, he engaged vociferously in the church arguments with the Puritan clergy, and he likewise took pointed stands on political issues. Yet when criticized for the bias in his *Weekly Rehearsal*, he responded that he "declares himself of no Party, and invites all Gentlemen of Leisure and Capacity, inclined on either Side, to write any thing of a political Nature, that tends to enlighten and serve the Publick, to communicate their Productions [to the *Rehearsal*], provided they are not overlong, and [are] confined within Modesty and Good Manners...."[23]

The Great Awakening, that powerful religious movement of the 1740s, brought the argument of newspaper neutrality to the fore. It was the first episode to become an intercolony news event, and it brought out newspaper opinions on conflicting sides. The positions that Fleet took serve as an example of the public argument over newspaper partisanship and neutrality.

Most colonials, who were devout Christians, welcomed the Great Awakening enthusiastically. One publisher who did not was Fleet. He used his newly renamed newspaper, the *Boston Evening-Post*, to support the High Church views of Anglicanism and to criticize the leading evangelist, George Whitefield. In one article, he decried Whitefield as a quack.[24]

When readers condemned Fleet for continually publishing his criticisms, he obviously could not defend himself with the argument that he had simply been printing material from both sides. So at first he appealed to the notion of freedom of expression. "I have never been of any *Company*, Clan or Party, either in Church or State," he claimed, "but wherever I have had a Right to speak or act, have always done it with openness and freedom, according to my own Judgment, and not that of *others*, which may be one Reason why I have had so few hearty friends at this Time.... I have indeed always express'd myself in a free, open and undisguised Manner, as became an *honest* Man, tho' perhaps not as a *prudent* one, as the World now goes."[25]

Only a month later, however, he resorted to the argument that many Colonial printers took up in times of trouble. He said simply that he wished "to be look'd upon only as a Printer, and not as a Party."[26] He was, he insisted, nothing more than a press operator who printed what other people wanted printed. "[A]s I have often declared," he repeated a few months later, "so do I again declare, that I am of no Party, but act purely as a *Printer*...." Since the public viewed printers simply as businessmen, he also explained without apology that he printed anything he thought he could make a profit on, no matter what his opinion of it. Similarly, when criticized for publishing a sermon by John Wesley condemning some of Whitefield's theology and methods, Fleet contended that he had printed Wesley's piece "not because I liked it, but because several Gentlemen of Learning and good Sense ... desired to have it printed, and I had a prospect of getting a Penny by it...."[27]

In response to a Presbyterian minister who did not accept Fleet's explanation that he was a mere printer with no concern for what he published, the irritated Fleet retorted, "I have for a long time observed, that Men who baul out loudest for shutting up the Press, or having it open only for their own Party, are of tyrannical Principles, and Enemies to Liberty both in Church and State, and would be glad to keep the People in the most abject Slavery."[28] Following up on the implication that his own newspaper was open to all views, he added that even Jonathan Edwards, the famous Boston clergyman and a Whitefield supporter, although he was the *"Censurer General of all Europe"* for criticizing newspaper accounts of religion, had never faulted newspapers themselves. If anyone were to blame for what newspapers published, Edwards had said, it was the authors who wrote the articles. Fleet's unpopular stand lost readers, however, and eventually he felt obligated to recant and apologize.[29]

The continuing conflict between readers' expectations and newspapers' practices was apparent elsewhere. The problems that Hugh Gaine, a New York printer, faced were typical. He claimed that he wished to be fair in deciding what to publish in the *New-York Mercury,* and readers criticized him when they did not believe that he had done so. The dilemma for printers like Gaine was especially apparent when readers with a point to argue believed that printers had not given a fair opportunity to their side. Even when printers tried to provide balance, it was difficult to achieve. The difficulties can be seen in a small controversy involving Gaine's refusal to print an essay from two readers about King's College in New York City.

The controversy began when the magazine *Independent Reflector* published arguments about attempts to give King's College a secular bent. Gaine rejected a submission from William Smith Jr. and John Morin Scott, who supported the *Reflector's* position. Thereupon, they wrote him a personal letter critiquing his stated stance of not getting involved in controversial issues. The letter reveals some details of Colonial readers' expectations of newspaper philosophy. Among other things, it equated liberty of the press with neutrality. True press freedom, the authors reasoned, resided with the right of readers to have their writings published and not with the arbitrary authority of printers to determine what should be published. "Your Resolution *not to be any Ways concerned in Disputes,* by which we suppose you mean not to print any Thing in matters of Controversy," they wrote, "is a Resolution that will not only be prejudicial to your Interest, and against the very Design and proper Business of the Press; but is in a very great Degree, an Attack upon its Liberty, which Printers above [all] Men should be sollicitious to maintain and encourage...." But Gaine's refusal to print their essay seemed to them to refute his "Resolution to be unconcerned in Disputes; nor do we accept your promise, as obliging, since you will first print the Attack, but refuse the Answer, unless it should be written

FAIR AND BALANCED • 46

(as you direct) *in a mild manner, and consistent with the Interest of your Calling,* the Judgment of which you reserve only to yourself." As a result, they concluded, "We believe you are averse to Printing any Thing in favor of the *Reflector....*"[30]

Following the letter, Gaine still refused to print the essay, and Smith and Scott gave it to his rival, James Parker of the *New-York Gazette.* Parker thereupon wrote a letter to the *Reflector* chastising Gaine for failing to uphold the newspaper principle of printing all sides. "A PRINTER ought not to publish every Thing that is offered him," Parker lectured Gaine, "but what is conducive of the general Utility, he should not refuse, but be the Author a Christian, Jew, Turk or Infidel. Such Refusal is an immediate Abridgement of the Freedom of the Press. When on the other Hand, he prostitutes his Art by the Publication of any Thing injurious to his Country, it is criminal...."[31]

The whole affair exasperated Gaine, who finally printed Smith and Scott's essay. Along with their letter, though, he ran his own piece accusing them of plagiarizing some of their material from Addison's *Spectator* and then ridiculed them for their "Rage for the *Liberty of the Press,* when its Liberty was never invaded, they having Freedom to chuse two others, Ec....."[32]

More than a year later, Gaine solved the dilemma of deciding which controversial contributions he should publish by printing some debate on King's College after the parties involved agreed to pay him. "During the weekly Publication of the late Papers under the Title of The Independent Reflector," he recalled, "great Complaints were made by my Refusal to publish any Thing that was offered by that Author or his Friends." Since then, however, the controversy, instead of subsiding, had "risen still higher, and become vastly more extensive and interesting." As a consequence, "an almost universal Discontent now appears for want of a FREE PRESS." After getting "many importunate Applications," Gaine had decided to do something to accommodate the arguments in the debate. He explained that he had "... determin'd to give both Parties an Opportunity of being heard thro' his Paper:... Therefore, from this Time foreward, [he] shall lay himself under no Restraints, provided the authors will indemnify him, and deposit a *Quantum meruit* for his Services. The Printer only desires that excessive Heats and personal Reflections may be avoided on both Sides; and that the publick would be pleased to consider him entirely disinterested in all he prints; and that no Man would think him an Enemy to any particular Sect of Religion more than another."[33]

The controversy pointed up the lively debate that was being waged over newspaper principles. Gaine thought that a writer was free to submit his work to any publication, while the printer was equally free to turn down anything he found offensive. Smith and Scott argued that a printer was obliged to print whatever came his way because a newspaper was an agent of popular opinion. Failure to do so, they said, wrenched control of the press from the people, where it belonged, and put it into the hands of a few dictatorial printers. Gaine resolved this particular controversy simply by requiring that writers pay for the cost of printing their compositions. By doing that, he had demonstrated once again the thinking among Colonial readers and some printers that the newspaper was properly an extension of the printing trade.

While such an explanation of the Colonial practice of neutrality may seem simple, the debate over what the proper role of the press should be did not deal in superficialities or crude arguments. It exhibited, instead, reasoning that was as informed as much debate today is. One of the fundamental assumptions was that the press should be closely involved with the concerns of society — rather than being at a professional distance, as it is today. Thus the early press was often integrally involved with public activities. From the beginning of settlement in the New World, American colonists had believed that the printing press was of critical importance. That view was evident in the thinking of the Puritans of Massachusetts, who believed that the individual was the authority in spiritual matters and must, therefore, have the freedom and means to inquire into religious doctrine. They therefore recognized the indispensable nature of the press in making reading material available and in providing a mechanism by which individuals could present their beliefs to others. There were certain bounds beyond which the press was not to go — printing blasphemous material, for example — but even the limitations on the press were signs of the critical importance ascribed to it. The press was also important in political affairs. It served as the prime instrument the key players used in the successive debates over the relationship of Colonial representatives to proprietary and crown officials, the nature of the political and economic association between the colonies and the mother country, and the independence movement in the colonies. In most other areas of life, the press also seemed to play a part, from theological debate to economic policies, cultural manners and daily business transactions.

Because of the crucial role the press played, one of the loudest and longest-running debates was over what the stance of newspapers should be in public controversies — whether they should be neutral or partisan. The answer implicitly was contradictory. As a general principle, the press was to be impartial. However, early Americans also generally agreed that it should be on the side of "right." Thus, Puritans, for example, believed the press should be open to anyone wishing to express his theological views as long as those views did not go to extremes. In political issues, participants accepted the fact that printing opposing views could not be punished by law, but they believed that printers should be responsible enough not to publish dangerous sentiments.

Printers likewise found themselves with divided principles. The concept of neutrality had originated with the perception of the printing press as simply a mechanical device, with the printer merely a businessman who operated the machine and who was hired to reproduce material for members of the public. This tradition in the printing business, which had grown up in the 1600s, was transferred to newspaper printing in the 1700s. Thus, there developed the general concept that newspapers should publish material from a variety of points of view without regard for how the printer personally felt.

Despite that concept, however, most publishers had their personal biases on a variety of subjects, and the columns of their newspapers reflected their opinions. Typically, three-quarters of a newspaper's articles on a controversial issue might be slanted toward the publisher's bias. Opponents of the newspaper's slant generally argued that the proper role of newspapers was to present material that fairly represented a variety of viewpoints. The principle was so generally recognized that editors could not ignore it. Their typical response was to state that they were not personally biased and that they were merely printing what the public brought to them. If only one side provided information, then they could print only one side. That explanation too often conveniently overlooked this chain of facts: (1) most editors did, indeed, publish in favor of one side, (2) they usually were not equally willing to publish submissions from the opposing side, and (3), as a result, contributions they received came predominantly from the side with which they agreed. So their argument that they published whatever they received was artificial because the bulk of the contributions offered was already biased toward the newspaper's view. A reader's complaint was not over the newspaper's printing of arguments by the opposition but rather over its propensity for publishing material on one side only. The editors' explanation was probably transparent to most informed readers. Yet editors commonly used it as a defense.

Clearly, Colonial readers and printers had not worked out a resolution to the issue of newspaper neutrality. They had, however, dealt with it in a way that provided the viewpoints around which the issue would be debated for many years to come.

NOTES

* An explanation of terms is in order here: Printers operated most, although certainly not all, Colonial newspapers and served in the positions that we think of as both editor and publisher. The terms "editor" and "publisher" were not used. Instead, the term "printer" referred to a newspaper's operator. Its use provides some insight into the role that readers expected of the operator. In this chapter, however, we have adopted the modern usages "editor" and "publisher" and use them interchangeably, and we employ the term "printer" to refer to that person only in the modern sense of a printer.

[1]It is certainly possible – perhaps even probable – that the concept of impartiality in the printing trade actually derived from the earlier practice of merchants, who simply sold goods to any customers without regard to the customers' views.

[2]Harris is the subject of a number of brief, mainly encyclopedic biographies. They focus for the most part on his career in England and generally tend to be critical because of his strong anti-Catholic views. Much of the recent distaste for Harris results from his helping to publicize Titus Oates's exposure of the so-called "Popish Plot," a plan in which, Oates claimed, Roman Catholics planned to murder the king, set London afire and massacre its inhabitants. The charges gained wide acceptance, and Oates for a time was a leading public figure. Harris's accounts of the prosecutions and punishments of the alleged plotters may be found in his *Domestick Intelligence*, 7, 14, 17, and 22 July and 31 December 1679. However, although Harris favored the punishments, including some executions, his treatment of them was generally more judicious than that of other newspaper supporters. Typical of the historical treatment of him as an unsavory character is the account by a Tory historian, J.G. Muddiman, in "Benjamin Harris, the First American Journalist," *Notes and Queries*, 20 August 20 1932, 129-33; 27 August 1932, 147-50; 3 September 1932, 166-70; 24 September 1932, 223; 15 October 1932, 273-74. A more balanced, favorable account can be found in Wm. David Sloan, "Chaos, Polemics, and America's First Newspaper," *Journalism Quarterly* 70 (1993): 666-81.

[3]This and the following quotations are taken from *Publick Occurrence*, 25 September 1690.

[4]*Boston News-Letter*, 14 August 1721.

[5]The paper continued to carry that legend during the administrations of Gov. Elizeus Burges (1715-1716) and Samuel Shute (1716-1728), until 11 July 1720, after Campbell had been replaced as postmaster in 1719.

[6]The *News-Letter* of 29 October 1705 had accused the Quakers of misrepresenting conditions in Massachusetts. Campbell promised to the Council of Trade and Plantations in London that in the future he would "carefully forbear reflecting upon those people, who I observe are very well and easily treated by the Government here, and for ought I know are peaceable in their places." Campbell to Wm. Popple, Council of Trade and Plantations, *Calendar of State Papers, Colonial*, Vol. 23 (1706-1708), #510.

In controlling printing, Colonial authorities were acting under the licensing power instituted by James II. After he ascended to the throne in 1685, it became the established policy of the British crown to order Colonial governors to exercise control over the printing press. Thus, all governors received these same instructions: "[F]orasmuch as great inconveniences may arise by the liberty of printing within our said province, you are to provide by all necessary orders that no person KEEP any press for printing, NOR that any book, pamphlet, or other matters whatsoever be PRINTED without your especial leave and license first obtained." ["Licensing of Printing Presses and Printing"], *Royal Instructions to British Colonial Governors 1670-1776*, 2: 495.

[7]His lampoon of the *New-England Courant* on 28 August 1721, for example, turned on the *Courant's* criticism that Campbell was dull.

FAIR AND BALANCED • *50*

[8]*Boston Gazette*, 21 December 1719; 11 and 25 January 1720.

[9]In the *News-Letter* of 4 January 1720, Campbell implied that Brooker was a drunkard, and in the following issue of the *Gazette* (11 January) Brooker said he had been kind in reporting that Campbell had been "removed" from the post-mastership rather than "turned out."

[10]Cotton Mather, 2 May 1706, Kenneth Silverman, comp., *Selected Letters of Cotton Mather* (Baton Rouge: Louisiana State University Press, 1971), 77.

[11]See *Diary of Cotton Mather*, 7 July, 18 August, 17 November 1721.

[12]All but three of the paper's contributors can be identified as Anglicans.

[13]*New-England Courant*, 4 September 1721.

[14]*Boston Gazette*, 15 January 1722. The author probably was Mather Byles, a nephew of Cotton Mather.

[15]9 December 1721, *Diary of Cotton Mather*.

[16]*New-England Courant*, 4 February 1723.

[17]Some historians have argued that Colonial publishers were impartial simply because they wanted to avoid offending customers or government, from which they received their financial support. See, for example, Stephen Botein, "Meer Mechanics' and an Open Press: The Business and Political Strategies of Colonial American Printers," *Perspectives in American History* 9 (1975): 127-225; Mary Ann Yodelis, "Who Paid the Piper? Publishing Economics in Boston, 1763-1775," *Journalism Monographs* 38 (1975); and Lawrence C. Wroth, *The Colonial Printer* (New York, 1931). Such an emphasis on financial concerns as a monolithic explanation of motives, however, defies the reality of human beings as complex creatures with a variety of reasons for most things they do, and it fails to consider the evidence of other factors. It also overlooks the fact that many publishers claimed to be impartial when in fact it was clear that their newspapers were not.

[18]*American Mercury*, 22 December 1719.

[19]*American Mercury*, 16 February 1720.

[20]*American Mercury*, 15 August 1734.

[21]*American Magazine*, January 1741.

[22]*Pennsylvania Gazette*, 10 June 1731. By "apology," Franklin did not mean an expression of regret, but instead a defense or explanation of printers' practices.

[23]*Boston Weekly Rehearsal*, 2 April 1733.

[24]*Boston Evening-Post*, 6 May 1740.

[25]*Boston Evening-Post*, 6 October 1740.

[26]*Boston Evening-Post*, 10 November 1740.

[27]*Boston Evening-Post*, 30 March 1741.

[28]Ibid.

[29]*Boston Evening-Post*, 12 September 1743.

[30]William Smith Jr. and John Morin Scott to Hugh Gaine, 6 April 1753, in Paul Leicester Ford, ed., *The Journals of Hugh Gaine, Printer* (New York: Dodd, Mead & Co., 1902; reprint edition, New York: Arno Press and The New York Times, 1970), 11-2.

[31]*Independent Reflector* (New York City), 30 August 1753.

[32]*New-York Weekly Mercury*, 3 September 1753.

[33]*New-York Weekly Mercury*, 18 November 1754.

CHAPTER 4

The American Revolution and the Death of Objectivity
By Julie Hedgepeth Williams

William Henry Drayton of Charleston, S.C., considered himself a loyal citizen of Great Britain. Like many others, he was British first and a colonist second. Therefore, in the midst of anti-British unrest in 1769, Drayton decided to take a stand.

At issue were the Townshend Acts, passed by Parliament in 1767 to tax American colonists on imported goods, including glass, paper and tea. The acts came close on the heels of the hated 1765 Stamp Act, which taxed printed matter. The colonies had banded together against the Stamp Act, and it had been repealed. Remembering the stamp tax, a group called the General Committee got together to protest the Townshend Acts by boycotting certain British goods. The committee members tried to pressure others into signing a boycott agreement.[1]

The boycott was devastating to merchants who sold such goods, however, and that made Drayton angry. He wrote a retort to people who had signed the agreement. He had "deliberated upon the measure ... from principles of LOYALTY to KING, and RESPECT to the LAWS of THE LAND," and he had decided that people who went along with the boycott were "VIOLATING THE CIVIL LIBERTIES OF FREEMEN, and thereby shaking the CONSTITUTION of their COUNTRY to the very foundations." One faction, he said, was tyrannically dictating what people could and could not buy.[2]

Drayton wanted the piece published in a Charleston newspaper, but Robert Wells wouldn't publish the essay in his *South-Carolina and American General Gazette*. Wells was known as a dyed-in-the-tartan Scotsman[3] who preferred Britain to South Carolina.[4] But Wells was also a good businessman,[5] and he apparently thought publishing Drayton's piece would drive away customers who favored the boycott. Charles Crouch also refused to publish the anti-boycott article. His *South-Carolina Gazette; and Country Journal* had been founded to decry the Stamp Act, so his refusal was hardly a surprise.[6] Finally, Drayton tried Peter Timothy, printer of the *South-Carolina Gazette*. Timothy accepted the piece. He subscribed to a traditional view of newspaper objectivity — that a printer's job was to print whatever any party brought to him. Speaking of himself in the third person, Timothy explained why he had agreed to publish the unpopular opinion:

> He finds himself reflected upon, in the character of a Juryman, as much as others are, in a more exalted Station. The Opinion of the Author [Drayton] no means coincided with his own: But as he has kept his Press *open* to *all Parties* these thirty Years, without permitting his private Interest (which has often suffered) to come in Competition with that of the Public; as the *Liberty of the Subject,* and the Preservation of the *Constitution* depend, very often, in a great Measure, upon a *free* Access to it ... so he flatters himself, that he shall escape the Censure of every Individual, notwithstanding the Publication of this celebrated Performance has been *refused* by the other Printers.[7]

To Timothy, his press was objective — that is, open to all parties. He didn't realize it then, but the days were numbered for that sense of objectivity. As America edged closer to war with Britain, journalistic neutrality got scarcer. Almost from the beginning of the war, printers who supported the rebellious colonists, whom this chapter will call "Patriots," lost their traditional fondness for objectivity. As Patriots saw it, Britain had denied Americans their constitutional rights. To restore those liberties, the Patriot press could no longer be open to the British opinion without stabbing the American cause in the back.

The same reasoning would eventually hold true in the press of the pro-British faction, which will be called "Loyalist" in this chapter. But initially, that faction cried loudly for objective publication. Loyalists berated the Patriot press for curtailing full discussion by both sides. They demanded a fair hearing, saying that freedom of the press lay in its openness — an objectivity that would embrace all sides of the issue. But in the end, even Loyalists were forced by events to shut down debate. By the middle of the war, there was not a neutral newspaper to be found in the newly self-proclaimed United States of America. If a person wanted to read both sides of the story, he had to read two newspapers. Although this may have been an inconvenience for the readers, the end of evenhandedness in the press had far more serious results for the men and women who ran the papers. Had printers been widely accepted as neutral bearers of information from all sides, many careers might have survived the war. As it was, many who were forced to choose sides lost out when the fortunes of war put a paper loyal to one cause in the midst of a town newly overrun by the other side.

Although the word "objectivity" as we know it had not been born yet, printers had a long tradition of practicing a version of objectivity by the time of the American Revolution. Some called it impartiality. Others

The American Revolution • 53

spoke of it as sacrificing their own opinions so others might speak. Still others thought of objectivity in terms of being open to all parties without being influenced by any. An American magazine summed up the traditional view among Colonial journalists when it explained in 1757:

> [W]e would observe once and for all, that we are to be considered merely as Publishers, without giving any Judgment of our own, either one side or the other. And if there be any Persons who dislike the Doctrine or reasoning contained in any such Publications, they will be entitled to a Hearing in their turn.[8]

That view was popular even as the Revolution drew near. John Mein and John Fleeming opened the *Boston Chronicle* with the assurances that the factionalism of the recent Stamp Act was behind them — everyone would be allowed a say in the *Chronicle*. The newspaper's goal, they wrote, was to "be independent — your interest is intimately connected with this noble virtue — if you depart from this — you must sink from the esteem of the public." By encouraging impartiality, they hoped to "throw some light on the complexion of the times."[9] William Rind in Williamsburg, Va., voiced a similar outlook when he commented that his *Virginia Gazette* was "Open to ALL PARTIES but Influenced by NONE."[10] In 1770, James Parker, a New Yorker, ran afoul of objectivity, and he tried to repair the damage by seeking balance. He printed a broadside signed by "A Son of Liberty" who railed against British authority. New York's General Assembly deemed the broadside seditious. So Parker, under pressure from the Assembly, violated the rules of journalism at the time by revealing the author's identity.[11] In doing that, he biased his press against the Patriot faction. He then tried to undo the bias by letting the wronged side have its say in his *New York Gazette or Weekly Post-Boy*. "Attempts to prevent the Liberty of the Press in this Province, will be in Vain, while there is a free Press on the Continent," he wrote.[12] Parker's rival, Hugh Gaine, derided "A Son of Liberty" but did offer to let him respond to criticism.[13] William Goddard founded the *Maryland Journal; and the Baltimore Advertiser* in 1773 on promises that the press would remain free to all sides.[14]

As Peter Timothy put it when explaining that he published any view that came to hand, "I can truly say that the Public Good has ever been the chief Object of my Views — my private Interest has often been sacrificed to it — and I still do, and ever shall, love my Country enough, to sacrifice more."[15] That was in 1772. As tensions heated, however, so did the pressure to choose sides. Every printer felt it. Timothy's response to that pressure, as well as the response of his main rivals in Charleston, the Wells family, illustrates the struggle about objectivity that would ultimately cost both Charleston presses their existence. Impartiality was impossible during the American Revolution, but partiality was also unsustainable in the long run.

The year after his stated commitment to objectivity, Peter Timothy found that he could not remain neutral. In 1773, Parliament passed the Tea Act, which encouraged the consumption of British tea in the Colonies. Opposition to the new law led to additional boycotts and the celebrated dumping of tea into the Boston harbor, known as the Boston Tea Party. Reacting to the incident, Timothy published a political piece predicting America's separation from Britain. Those who refused to stand up for liberty from Britain committed "high treason against GOD," the author said. "By UNITING we STAND, by DIVIDING we FALL!"[16] As a printer who had advocated objectivity, Timothy logically could have printed opposing views and thereby maintained a balance in his newspaper. However, the publication of the piece marked the end of objectivity in Timothy's paper. He became involved in politics, becoming secretary to the Patriot-dominated South Carolina Congress and to the Patriot-backed Council of Safety and other Patriot committees. In time he would be elected a delegate to the colony's Congress.[17] In May of 1775 he pulled the king's coat-of-arms from the flag of his paper.[18] He would no longer step aside personally to let all sides speak. Now he was caught up in Patriot politics, and his press was closed to Loyalists.

Timothy's competitor, Robert Wells, tried halfheartedly to keep his press open to both sides. Wells was known as a Loyalist who gave his sons Scottish educations[19] and insisted that one of them dress in a tartan coat and Scots bonnet to symbolize the connection to Great Britain.[20] Still, Wells had turned down Drayton's piece supporting Britain in 1769. He could not remain neutral in the boycott controversy, however. When boycott sympathizers turned against an aging female merchant for importing banned British goods, Wells took a vehement stand for her.[21]

Briefly, Wells returned to business as usual. While still known as a loyal Briton, Wells sold extracts from "the GRAND AMERICAN CONTINENTAL CONGRESS" in his bookstore through the end of 1774.[22] But when war broke out in 1775, Wells boarded a ship headed for London. He left his press in the hands of his son, John.[23]

John Wells and his father did not see eye to eye on politics. The younger Wells began emphasizing Patriot news in the *South-Carolina and American General Gazette.* He regularly published announcements by Patriot factions.[24] However, Wells discovered, for good and for ill, that many South Carolinians still thought of his paper as Loyalist. The governor gave Wells the text of his speech to King George's Council before he gave it to the other newspapers in town.[25] Shortly thereafter a mob of Patriot hotheads set out looking for trouble at various Loyalist homes and businesses, and they included Wells's shop. As Timothy described it:

The American Revolution • 55

Yesterday evening the Gunner at Fort Johnson (one Walker) had a decent Tarring & Feathering for some insolent speech he had made: there is hardly a street through which he was not paraded or a Tory House where they did not halt.... At Fen. Bull's they stopt, called for Grog; had it; made Walker drink D--n to Bull, threw a bag of feathers into his Balcony, and desired he would take care of it till his turn came; & that he would charge the Grog to the Acct. of Ld. North, finally the wretch was discharged at Milligan's door. The people were in such a humor that I believe there was scarce a [Loyalist] who did not tremble, & Wells had his Shop close shut.[26]

After that, the *General Gazette* quickly shed all remaining traces of its Loyalist past. Wells apparently reasoned that the public did not need to hear the Loyalist side if life and limb were at risk. He signed a commitment to the Patriot faction and began pressuring his Loyalist brother, William Charles Wells, to sign also. William Charles instead went home to Britain.[27] John began publishing Patriot articles, such as *The Duty of Standing Fast in our Spiritual and Temporal Liberties* and *The American Vine*.[28] When the British attempted an unsuccessful siege of Charleston in 1776, Wells fled and hid his press. Eventually the British retreated, and Wells began his newspaper anew, emphasizing his Patriot outlook by taking the king's coat-of-arms out of the *General Gazette's* flag. He bragged about the American victory and the ineffectiveness of the British army.[29] He wrote to a friend that he had made a decision to follow the Patriots' ideals, "& no future Event can ever alter [that decision]. I have ever thought an inconsistent, dubious Character a most contemptable *[sic]* one.... Connected by friendship & even by blood to several who are now our public Enemies, I have been frequently much embarrassed."[30]

Both Wells and Timothy were now Patriots, in both personal life and press. There no longer was a chance of objectivity in the press of Charleston, for the third printer, Charles Crouch, had died.[31]

But taking sides proved to be a dangerous game. Wells got away with it one more time — but then his luck ran out. The British returned to Charleston in 1780, and this time took the city. Wells turned his coat, and his *General Gazette* became once again a Loyalist publication. He restored the king's coat-of-arms to the flag. Americans were now called "rebels" in his paper, and "our" troops were British. "The Loyalists [are] a majority in all places, and [there are] daily accessions to their numbers," he gloated in the newspaper.[32] Wells signed an address praising the British military leader Cornwallis and offering "our joyful congratulations on the total defeat and dispersion of the Rebel army."[33] William Charles Wells returned to South Carolina with the news that he and his brother had been appointed as royal printers. They renamed the newspaper *The Royal Gazette*.[34] They begged for readers to submit essays in favor of loyalty so the Loyalists might "persevere in eradicating every seed of error, that has been sown by the late Tyrants of this Country, and in drawing aside the veil which obstructs the sight of the deluded followers of Rebellion."[35]

Peter Timothy, now a member of the Colonial assembly, had no such option. He shut down his press when the British arrived. The British at first let him go about his life without publishing, but eventually he and other Charleston Patriots were rounded up, held prisoner and marched to the ship *Sandwich* to be banished to St. Augustine in East Florida, which was still a British colony. Timothy and the others were accused of trying "to promote and foment this Spirit of Rebellion," and in fact, Cornwallis suspected them of planning to burn Charleston and massacre Loyalists. When they arrived in St. Augustine, the prisoners had to rent their own houses to be jailed in, at a very high price. Eventually Timothy and the others were freed, but only if they could buy their own passage to Philadelphia. Timothy's family in Charleston was forced to move to Philadelphia at their own expense, too.[36] In the end Timothy decided to start over again in Antigua, where his daughter had property. He was lost at sea.[37] The partisan stance taken by Timothy, then, directly and indirectly cost him everything — his livelihood, his home and eventually his life.

The partisan press, however, flourished in Charleston as the Wells brothers backed the British conquerors. But they, too, soon learned that partisanship carried a high price tag. Cornwallis was defeated at Yorktown, Va., in October 1781, and on July 24, 1782, the *Royal Gazette* ran an alarmed letter to the British commander of Charleston, begging him not to give up. On August 7, however, the *Gazette* published instructions to Loyalists in the city. They were to be evacuated to St. Augustine.

John returned to England, but William Charles took the press with him and started the first newspaper in East Florida. The paper spoke for the refugees in St. Augustine, who were soon forced to move again when Florida was ceded to the Americans. The *East-Florida Gazette* bemoaned the fate of the Southerners who would wind up in chilly Canada and the planters who would soon be farming the "barren soil of the Bahama Islands." Wells begged his readers to try to force the new United States government to come up with some payment for Loyalists' losses. "While they are together they may command some kind of respect and attention, and work upon the fears, if not upon the justice of the nation," he said.[38] The British ceded Florida on September 3, 1783; and John Wells, back from London, packed up the press and moved just where his brother had feared: the Bahamas. There he opened *The Bahama Gazette*, where he spent the rest of his days, never quite happy again.[39]

The experiences of the Timothy and Wells presses showed that partisanship was a requirement during the Revolution, but that the ultimate cost of partisanship was steep. Neither of the Charleston printers could sustain their partisan presses when the tides of war turned against them.

While the Charleston printers were playing out their tragedies in the South, printers elsewhere were also discovering the difficulties of remaining objective during the Revolution. The Patriot Sons of Liberty put pressure on newspaper publishers to skew their content toward the Patriots, prompting pleas from Loyalist publishers for the right to present all sides. James Rivington, a New Yorker who operated *Rivington's New-York Gazetteer*, equated objectivity with the freedom of the press to speak out on any topic. A Loyalist, he took a swipe at the Patriots, who were already turning up the heat against Loyalist printers. His newspaper, he said, would print anything but "acrimonious Censures on any Society or Class of Men." As Rivington put it, "When so many Persons of a vast Variety of Views and Inclinations are to be satisfied, it must often happen, that what is highly agreeable to some, will be equally disagreeable to others."[40] The Patriots were unmoved. Soon Sons of Liberty were trying to compel Rivington to publish only their side of the story. Angrily, Rivington replied that "TRUE SONS OF LIBERTY" would print impartially.[41] Rivington vowed again that he would publish anything submitted to him for the newspaper, "whether of the Whig or Tory flavour."[42]

John Holt, a rival printer who produced the *New-York Journal*, was a Patriot. He denounced Rivington, arguing that unworthy ideas did not deserve publication. Holt said it was his duty to print only what was morally right. "In short, I have endeavoured to propagate such political Principles ... as I shall always freely risk my Life to defend," he said.[43] To Holt, as to many Patriot printers, it was false to publish things one did not believe in.

Some Loyalists defended the idea of an evenhanded presentation. One Loyalist writer argued, "The ears of a genuine son of liberty are ever open to all doctrines; it is his glory to hear them, examine them, to adopt them if they are true, to confute them if they are false."[44] Another Loyalist exhorted people to "[w]ake up, my friends.... See and judge for yourselves."[45]

Despite such pleas, by the time the war broke out on April 19, 1775, most printers had been forced to cease practicing objectivity and to take sides. Rivington, who had tried to present the Patriot and Loyalist sides alike, was one of the first casualties. A Patriot mob rode to his house on a November day and stole his printer's type and other goods. Rivington fled to England.[46]

Rivington returned to New York two years later, this time championing the British cause only and without any pretense of presenting both sides of the story. Objectivity was dead; partisanship was king. His

Gazette covered Connecticut as well as New York; in fact, the posse that routed him to England in 1775 had been from Connecticut. In 1777 when Rivington returned, he was a voice of Loyalism in Connecticut, in direct competition with Thomas and Samuel Green, Patriot publishers of the *Connecticut Journal*. The two sides fought each other with partiality, using unbalanced news coverage in the attempt to aid their respective causes. Each side tried to cast a positive light on its own armies and its own needs and goals, with only occasional nods to evenhandedness.

On September 11, 1777, George Washington's army lost a key battle at Brandywine outside the American capital, Philadelphia. Rivington was jubilant. "[M]ost of the [American] militia returned to their respective habitations with a resolution no longer to take part in the present unnatural rebellion," he gloated. He described the panic among American soldiers. British troops chased them for miles, which "greatly dispirited the enemy." Rivington assured his readers that shortly Philadelphia would fall. Congress had already fled to Bethlehem, Pa., in what Rivington's *Gazette* described as a vain attempt to hide from the inevitable.[47] That was how Rivington told the tale. However, in New Haven, at the Greens' Connecticut print shop, the Patriot printers tiptoed around the disappointing information that the American army had lost so important a battle. Indeed, things would be bleak if the capital fell. The Greens commented on the loss in an offhanded way, blaming it on a piece of bad intelligence. The Americans had expected the attack to come in one location, and instead it happened in another. The Greens' correspondent wrote reassuringly, "I am confident as I am of my own existence that if the attack had been made where it was expected, [British General William] Howe and his army would certainly have been entirely routed." The article added that American troops were hungry because Howe had paid the locals to steal livestock, thus depriving the army of food. Washington, in contrast, was described as almost "more than human" in his positive efforts to rally his men.[48] The discrepancies between the accounts were obvious, and one can only imagine that the truth lay somewhere in between. An objective description of truth did not seem possible.

Slanted news reports continued. When Americans lost a battle at Germantown, outside Philadelphia, on October 4, the coverage from the two sides seemed to be of a different battle. The Americans had attacked Germantown, which Rivington's newspaper decried as "the most daring folly" in "a desperate attempt" to make some gain. The losing Americans, however, were "feeble" in battle, the Loyalist paper scoffed.[49]

The loss at Germantown opened Philadelphia to British soldiers. The *Gazette* was lavish in its praise of the soldiers and in its description of the joy among Philadelphians on the occasion:

The fine appearance of the soldiery, the strictness of their discipline, the politeness of the officers, and the orderly behaviour of the whole body, immediately dispelled every apprehension of the inhabitants, kindled joy in the countenances of the well affected, and gave the most convincing refutation of the scandalous falsehoods which evil and designing men had long been spreading to terrify the peaceable and innocent. A perfect tranquility has since prevailed in the city.[50]

Not surprisingly, the Greens in New Haven had an entirely different view of the British soldiers, who came off as monsters. As the Patriot Greens reported the loss at Brandywine, British troops took over every house in the town, where they pulled their light artillery into people's bedrooms. From there they fired through windows into stubble and hay, which caused a blanket of smoke. Unable to tell where their own guns were firing, the Americans had to retreat. However, as the Greens' correspondent assured readers, all was not lost. Pacifist Quakers, so numerous in Pennsylvania and so committed to avoiding war, had now begun talking about taking up arms against the British conquerors.[51] The British were surely horrible if they could drive Quakers to arms.

The loss of Philadelphia indeed seemed bleak, no matter how much gloss the Patriot printers tried to put on it, but dramatic events were unfolding in New York. On the British side, Gen. John Burgoyne and his men were surrounded and out of supplies. With nowhere to turn, they surrendered at Saratoga on October 17, 1777.[52] The Greens got wind of it by their October 22 issue, in which they announced "public rejoicings, on account of the good news." As details began trickling into New Haven, American forces became more and more heroic in accounts in the *Connecticut Journal*. The American general, Horatio Gates, sent a quick letter detailing the surrender, which found its way to the Greens. However, he could not write more because he had to stop British soldiers from burning towns, a gallant reason that the *Journal* eagerly reported to its readers. The Greens blamed the British for burning the town of Kingston to the ground, and the *Journal* scolded, "Britain, how art thou fallen! Ages to come will not be able to wipe away the guilt, the horrid guilt, of these and such like deeds, lately perpetuated by thee!"[53] A correspondent wrote his impressions: "It was a glorious sight to see the haughty Britons march out and surrender their arms to an army, which, but a little before, they despised and called poltroons [cowards]."[54]

Certainly, the Greens were having a field day with the defeat of Burgoyne. Rivington, however, for the first time since his return to New York, was trying to find a silver lining in the cloud that had suddenly appeared over British fortunes in America. Rivington heard rumors of the capitulation at Saratoga, but he thought that they were too ridiculous to repeat. The story, he said in his newspaper, was a fabrication "with a view to inlist [sic] men; and, to give an air of truth to it, at Elizabeth Town they caused guns to be fired, bonfires to be made, and every other demonstration of joy and triumph." In fact, Rivington said, everyone at the celebration was tipsy from free rum, distributed to all who asked.[55] Certainly the *Loyal Gazette*, as Rivington now called his paper, made the Patriots out to be immoral liars.

Despite Rivington's wishful thinking, rumors persisted. He insisted that he had not gotten "properly authenticated" word on the supposed defeat, so he ignored rumors and waited for word from Burgoyne himself. With hope in his editorial voice, Rivington published a plan for how to treat the rebels when they were ultimately defeated.[56]

Finally, after more than two weeks had passed, Rivington announced the surrender, burying it on page three. He published more stories about the victories at Germantown and Brandywine, however. In fact, in his next two issues he rehashed the battle of Germantown.[57] Saratoga, as he saw it, was a momentary blip in the great march toward ultimate victory.

As a Loyalist, Rivington could scarcely have seen the surrender at Saratoga any other way. He was fighting for the ultimate good as he saw it by slanting his newspaper away from the objective truth in favor of the truth that he wanted to see. Thomas and Samuel Green were just as guilty as Rivington; they did not give their readers a balanced view of affairs because such balance would tend to prejudice readers in the wrong direction, as they perceived it.

The Greens, the Wellses, Peter Timothy and James Rivington were not the only printers who suffered from a lack of objectivity during the Revolution. Margaret Draper, the ardent Loyalist printer of the *Boston News-Letter*, felt it necessary to flee in 1776 with the vanquished British Army, thus ending the first successful newspaper in America, which had started in 1704.[58] John Mein and John Fleeming, who had begun their *Boston Chronicle* so hopefully with their statement of objectivity, were assaulted by a Patriot mob for printing material that damned the Patriot leader John Hancock as an opportunist who used anti-British sentiment for his own gain.[59] Mein fled to England.[60] Fleeming stayed in Boston but was sued by Hancock[61] and again threatened by a mob. This time the mob vowed to kill him. He, too, eventually returned to England.[62] James Johnston, a Loyalist printer in Georgia, had to suspend press operations during the war, but he later started up his paper anew and had a long career in Georgia.[63] On the Patriot side of things, printer James Humphreys Jr. was forced to shut down his *Pennsylvania Ledger* for a year after the British took Philadelphia, and he finally reopened it as a Loyalist organ.[64] Another Philadelphia printer, John Dunlap, a Patriot, had to flee with his press to Lancaster, Pa., where he

The American Revolution • 61

shut down his *Pennsylvania Packet* for three months before he was able to open his shop again.[65] Another Patriot printer, Benjamin Edes, had to flee the British occupation of Boston and issue his *Boston Gazette* from Watertown, Mass.[66] It seems that no printer was able to stay neutral during the Revolution.

Prior to the Revolution, the American press had practiced objectivity as a protection for liberty and a way to guarantee rights for all parties. By the end of the war, however, the new United States was left with a contingent of surviving Patriot printers who thought they had helped turn the tide toward the ultimate victory. As Isaiah Thomas, the Patriot printer of the *Massachusetts Spy*, put it years later when writing the history of American printing, "The history of printing in America, I have brought down to the most important event in the annals of our country — the Revolution.... [T]he press, and particularly the newspapers to which it gave birth, had a powerful influence in producing the revolution...."[67] Thomas was convinced that the press had played a gigantic role in throwing off the yoke of Britain by abandoning objectivity and impartiality in favor of telling what was "right."

Thus, as the American press left the Revolution and headed into the era of building a nation, objectivity was a memory whose death was not deeply mourned. An impartial press was no longer an issue, and a partisan press was being hailed as a conquering hero.

NOTES

[1] William Henry Drayton, ed., *The Letters of Freeman, Etc.* (London: 1771); reprint, Robert M. Weir, ed. (Columbia: University of South Carolina Press, 1977), 10-11.

[2] *South-Carolina Gazette* (Charleston), 14 December 1769.

[3] See ibid., 14 July 1766, 26 March 1772 and 16 August 1773.

[4] Wells wrote an anti-South Carolina poem on 15 April 1773. It is quoted in his daughter's journal. See Louisa Susannah Wells [Louisa Susannah Aikman], *The Journal of a Voyage from Charlestown to London* (New York: New York Historical Society, 1906; reprint, New York: New York Times and Arno Press, 1968), 77.

[5] Lorenzo Sabine, *Biographical Sketches of Loyalists of the American Revolution*, vol. 2 (Boston: Little, Brown, 1846), 406.

[6] *South-Carolina Gazette; and Country Journal* (Charleston), 17 December 1765.

[7] *South-Carolina Gazette*, 14 December 1769.

[8] *American Magazine and Monthly Chronicle* (November 1757): 70.

[9] *Boston Chronicle* (Massachusetts), 21 December 1767.

[10] *Virginia Gazette* (Williamsburg), 14 April 1768.

[11] E.B. O'Callaghan, comp., *Documentary History of the State of New York*, vol. 3 (Albany, 1849-1851), 528-36.

[12] *New York Gazette or Weekly Post-Boy* (New York City), 19 March 1770.

[13] *New-York Gazette and Weekly Mercury* (New York City), 9 April 1770.

14 *Maryland Journal; and the Baltimore Advertiser*, 20 August 1773.

15 *South-Carolina Gazette,* 16 April 1772.

16 Ibid., 3 June 1774.

17 Peter Timothy to Benjamin Franklin, 21 June 1777, in William B. Willcox, ed., *The Papers of Benjamin Franklin*, vol. 24 (New Haven, Conn.: Yale University Press, 1959), 154.

18 *South-Carolina Gazette*, 29 May 1775.

19 William Charles Wells, "Extract Memoir," quoted in Wells, *The Journal of a Voyage from Charlestown to London*, 97.

20 William Charles Wells, *Two Essays: One Upon Single Vision With Two Eyes, the other on Dew* (London: A. Constable and Co., 1818), quoted in Christopher Gould, "Robert Wells, Colonial Charleston Printer," *South Carolina Historical Magazine* 79 (January 1978): 27-8.

21 *South-Carolina and American General Gazette* (Charleston), 15 June 1770.

22 Ibid., 30 December 1774.

23 Wells left for London shortly after 9 June 1775, when the last personal advertisement bearing his name appeared in the *General Gazette*. John Wells continued to use his father's name as publisher, however. See Wells, *The Journal of a Voyage from Charlestown to London*, 61-2.

24 See *South-Carolina and American General Gazette*, 5 May and 9 June 1775.

25 *South-Carolina Gazette; and Country Journal*, 18 July 1775.

26 Peter Timothy to William Henry Drayton, 13 August 1775, "Correspondence of Hon. Arthur Middleton," annotated by Joseph W. Barnwell, *The South Carolina Historical and Genealogical Magazine* 27 (July 1926): 129. Drayton had become a Patriot by this time.

27 William Charles Wells, "Extract Memoir," in Wells, *The Journal of a Voyage from Charlestown to London*, 98.

28 *South Carolina and American General Gazette*, 20 October 1775.

29 Ibid., 2 August 1776.

30 John Wells to Henry Laurens, 28 November 1777, in David R. Chesnutt, ed., *The Papers of Henry Laurens*, vol. 12 (Columbia: University of South Carolina Press, 1968), 107-8.

31 The *South-Carolina and American General Gazette*, 25 August 1775, said Crouch had left via ship for Philadelphia. The ship was lost at sea, according to Isaiah Thomas, *The History of Printing in America* (1810), 2d. edition, ed. Marcus A. McCorison (New York: Weathervane Books, 1970), 571.

32 *South-Carolina and American General Gazette*, 19 July 1780.

33 Ibid., 14 October 1780.

34 Ibid., 24 February 1781.

35 Ibid., 28 February 1781.

36 See David Ramsay, *The History of South-Carolina from its First Settlement in 1670 to The Year 1808*, vol. 1 (Charleston, S.C.: David Longworth, 1809), 371, 444; and "Josiah Smith's Diary, 1780-81," annotated by Mabel L. Webber, *South Carolina Historical and Genealogical Magazine* 33 (January 1932): 3-6, 20; continued in vol. 33 (October 1932): 289; continued in vol. 34 (April 1933): 82. Smith and Ramsay were fellow prisoners of Timothy.

37 Thomas, *The History of Printing in America*, 569.

[38] *The East-Florida Gazette,* quoted in *The South-Carolina Weekly Gazette* (Charleston), 28 June and 12 July 1783.

[39] Thomas, *The History of Printing in America,* 610.

[40] *Rivington's New-York Gazetteer* (New York City), 22 April 1773.

[41] Ibid., 14 July 1774.

[42] Ibid., 8 December 1774.

[43] *New-York Journal* (New York City), 18 August 1774.

[44] *Rivington's New-York Gazetteer,* 15 December 1774.

[45] *Boston Weekly News-Letter* (Massachusetts), 16 February and 2 March 1775. The same author wrote both pieces.

[46] Rivington went into exile in England and detailed the incident upon his return two years later. See *Rivington's New-York Gazette,* 11 October 1777. The newspaper's name had changed slightly.

[47] Ibid.

[48] *Connecticut Journal* (New Haven), 8 October 1777.

[49] *Rivington's New-York Gazette,* 8 November 1777.

[50] Ibid.

[51] *Connecticut Journal,* 15 October 1777.

[52] Technically, Burgoyne signed Articles of Convention, which is not a formal surrender. However, the press of the day called it a "surrender."

[53] Ibid., 29 October 1777.

[54] Ibid., 5 November 1777.

[55] *Rivington's New-York Loyal Gazette,* 25 October 1777.

[56] Ibid., 1 November 1777.

[57] Ibid., 15 and 22 November 1777.

[58] Thomas, *The History of Printing in America,* 175-6. The full name of the newspaper in 1776 was *Massachusetts Gazette and Boston News-Letter.*

[59] *Boston Chronicle,* 24 September 1769.

[60] "Memorial of John Fleeming to Lord North," quoted in O.M. Dickerson, "British Control of Newspapers on the Eve of the Revolution," *New England Quarterly* 24 (1951): 464.

[61] L. Kinvin Wroth and Hiller B. Zobel, eds., *Legal Papers of John Adams,* vol. 1 (Cambridge, Mass.: Belknap Press, 1965), 200.

[62] "Memorial of John Fleeming to Lord North," in Dickerson, "British Control of Newspapers on the Eve of the Revolution,"465.

[63] Thomas, *The History of Printing in America,* 585, and *Gazette of the State of Georgia* (Savannah), 30 January 1783.

[64] See *Pennsylvania Ledger* (Philadelphia), 30 November 1776 and 10 October 1777.

[65] *Dunlap's Pennsylvania Packet or General Advertiser* (Philadelphia), suspended after the 9 September 1777 issue. It reappeared as *Pennsylvania Packet or General Advertiser* (Lancaster), 29 November 1777.

[66] See the *Boston Gazette; and Country Journal* (Massachusetts), 8 January 1776.

[67] Thomas, *The History of Printing in America,* xx.

FAIR AND BALANCED • 64

PART II

The 19th Century:
The Evolution of Objectivity
By Randall Patnode, Donald L. Shaw
and Steven R. Knowlton

In modern journalism we hold objectivity to be among the highest goals of the profession. Young journalists are schooled in what it means to be objective and how adherence to the highest standards of journalistic objectivity contributes to the future of the profession and the good standing of news organizations. In short, the argument goes, objectivity is good as an aspect of journalistic practice, and objective journalism is good for the community. While this book begins by tracing the earliest roots of the idea of objectivity back to the Colonial era, the evolution of journalistic objectivity in a more modern sense — at least in the messages themselves, although not using the word *objective* — can be traced to the 19th century, where evolution was as much a product of historical and technological forces as an ethical and professional goal.

We have to be careful. Present-mindedness tends to confound our understanding of 19th-century objectivity. A message written in the ornate style of Charles Dickens or Nathaniel Hawthorne seems slanted to us 150 years later — all those adjectives, adverbs and long sentences. We are used to Ernest Hemingway and his spare language. We cannot know for certain, but perhaps readers of that period understood words differently, reading Hawthorne as easily as we read Hemingway. Unless an observer of that period commented on bias or tried to horsewhip the editor (which did happen), there is no reason to think that most Americans of the 19th century were aware that they lived amid news bias any more than we feel (generally) we do not. To us, our times are *better*, although we think we see bias in the news on occasion, but perhaps not at the level that led the historian Frank Luther Mott to call the early 19th century "the dark ages of partisan journalism."[1]

There is a history of messages and their evolution, and there is a history of how journalists think about their work. We find in the 19th century evidence that adjectives, adverbs and even verb elements favoring a particular side were being dropped from messages. That is not to say that the press did not engage in biased or sensational stories, which it did, especially during the Spanish-American War, or that the press did not continue to portray sad, happy or scary stories from time to time. Journalism is a rich American literature. Nineteenth-century journalists did not call their work objective. Still, messages evolved, regardless of how journalists or readers labeled them.

The journalistic sense of professional responsibilities also evolved. One can see evidence that what editors and publishers called *independent* in the 19th century was called *objective* in the first half of the 20th century, and *fair* or *balanced* since then. If one discounts the 19th-century tendency to use flowery words, one can argue that American journalists have consistently produced messages that try to inform readers of the plain facts of events, even in a nation that had uncomfortably adopted slavery and drifted toward war.

Objectivity is central to our idea of scientific investigation — that is, we believe that science advances when individuals observe and measure carefully so that whatever is discovered can also be found and measured by someone else. In science, objectivity applies to methodical and established procedures of observation designed to neutralize purely personal or whimsical views. Objectivity is a state of mind. In today's journalism, the end result would be objective messages, as determined by those reading the message.

Some journalists say very simply: objectivity is impossible. Others say that even though objectivity is unachievable, it should nonetheless remain an ideal, a goal to strive for. Some say you cannot be objective, but you can be fair. All agree that objectivity is important, but there is no consensus about when it became central to journalism.

Objectivity is also important to other professions. Doctors are supposed to be able to listen to our bodies or complaints and objectively deduce what is most likely in need of correction. Lawyers are supposed to listen to our problems and determine the best course of legal action for us. In journalism, objectivity is central to what we do, although we define it in different ways.

Journalism historians have argued that objectivity was market-driven in the sense that at the time of the early telegraph, news was most economical if senders telegraphed only the facts. Unnecessary adjectives, adverbs and nouns were expensive to transmit and made some newspaper readers unhappy, so by omitting certain words, the telegraph decontextualized the news by stripping partisanship away from the bare facts.[2] Objectivity, in other words, was technologically driven, according to this argument. The telegraph made bias expensive.

Not everyone agrees with the narrow view that objectivity can be defined in terms of a balance of words and message. From a 20th-century Marxist point of view, objectivity might be seen as a *false consciousness*. That is, the ethical considerations and notions of fairness obscure the real function of objectivity, which is to keep radicalism from

Part II: The 19th Century • 67

reaching a boiling point and upsetting the industrial capital system. In this view, society is essentially a pressure-cooker, and objective journalism allows the system to let off steam occasionally. Thus far the most important call for greater media objectivity and balance has come from the 1947 Commission on Freedom of the Press, an effort financed by the publishing magnate Henry Luce, who clearly had an economic stake in social stability, as did all business owners. The commission stressed message balance and fair news selection more than word choice.

Objectivity also can be considered a process in which the diversity of both message and source is reduced because there is agreement on the facts. Objective messages are more predictable than biased messages. Three reporters covering a city council meeting who produce three objective messages will find that their messages are more similar, in terms of lead topic, inverted pyramid structure and length, than three reporters who make no attempt to be objective or follow any professionally dictated style. The first three reporters may use different quotations and select different angles for the lead, but their articles will have more in common than those in the second group. A lack of diversity in messages may be one reason newspaper circulation was in decline in the late 20th century, since most newspapers looked alike and were different only at the skin-deep (i.e., typographic) level.

A Definition. Objectivity is the absence of bias. Bias, we argue, can occur at four levels. (See figure on page 68.) At the first level are words, typically verbs or adjectives, adverbs and other modifiers, that reflect value judgments on the part of the writer. The second level is within the news story. Here, bias tends to surface in terms of reporting balance. A news story, for instance, could contain neutral words but represent only one side of a story. These two levels are within the control of reporters.

The third level is within the medium — primarily newspapers and magazines in the 19th century. Here bias also is a matter of balance. A newspaper could contain largely balanced news stories but still be biased because the selection of news stories taken together represents only one ideological position or factual perspective. This level is within the control of editors and publishers. Contemporary newspapers are often accused of bias at this third level in their failure to adequately cover minorities, a major charge of the Commission on Freedom of the Press and, in the 1960s, the Kerner Commission.[3]

Finally, bias can occur at the system level when the news media as a group fail to cover an issue or devote a disproportionate amount of space to an issue. In a Marxist view, the capitalist media ignore articles that challenge the dominant economic system. (The same criticism can be made of a Marxist press.) But in modern times, if a newspaper will not cover an issue, perhaps the local radio or television stations, or Internet publications, will — that is, there are many roads to Rome; and objectivity must be considered from a broad point of view. This view holds that at a broad level, a free market system will produce a diversity of messages so public issues are illuminated from all sides.

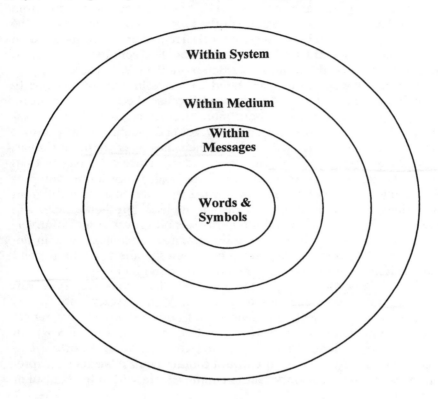

Four Levels of Bias

By the early 19th century, a sufficient number of newspapers and a sufficient mass of audience had formed to create an information system that could support the production of largely objective messages. Several conditions were related to the growth of objectivity.

Faster printing presses, cheaper paper. One reason for the information explosion was the improvement in printing-press and paper-making technology. More information could be reproduced at a faster rate. At mid-century, the introduction of the telegraph pushed this phenomenon further, reproducing and redistributing messages almost instantaneously.[4]

A shrinking news interval. News abundance and cheaper, faster information dissemination combined to shrink the news interval — the period between one news account and the next. The telegraph played a key role in shrinking the news interval and in redefining the news.

The telegraphic report called attention to the issue of time. Pretelegraph reports arriving by the fastest means — private expresses — were typically 24 or 48 hours ahead of the mails. The telegraphic report subdivided the news interval, from the daily cycle of the post office or express deliveries to cycles that could be counted in hours.[5] The division of the news interval into smaller units effectively allowed newspapers to take advantage of economies of scale. Just as the cost/revenue ratio would fall as a paper expanded from weekly distribution to daily distribution, so the addition of extra editions each day put more money in publishers' pockets with a minimal additional cash outlay.

Mass circulation newspapers. With the birth of the penny press in the 1830s, newspapers achieved levels of mass circulation that dictated that these papers tailor their news product to offend the fewest number of people to remain profitable.[6]

Professionalism. Before the Civil War the urban press expanded rapidly, especially in Boston, New York and Philadelphia. As circulation expanded, newspapers hired reporters and developed beats that produced articles on a dependable, daily basis. Beats evolved around the police, the courts, sports and various aspects of government. The *New York Herald's* James Gordon Bennett was a pioneer in this regard.[7] The compartmentalization of job duties helped create specialists, individuals whose value to the news organization depended on their specific in-depth knowledge.[8] Newspapers needed ways to keep themselves filled up, just as modern television does.

Information abundance. In the 18th century, an age of information scarcity, simply gaining access to information was a challenge. People relied on community ties and word of mouth. But by the 19th century, newspapers were gathering and circulating information from a much greater number of sources, including their own reporters and other newspapers through the government-subsidized postal exchange. Simply put, more news was flowing in what the historian Richard Brown calls a shift from information scarcity to information abundance.[9] As a result, editors were able to consider multiple accounts of particular incidents instead of a single view.

A culture of haste. As the historian Daniel Boorstin has noted, speed in all things was prized in the 19th century, including in delivery of the news.[10] When speed was applied to the news, the news language changed — from a slow-to-unfold, discursive style to a more pared-down, efficient one. The need for speedy news delivery also influenced the development of 19th-century journalistic objectivity. Newspapers, if only for the sheer sport of it, sought to deliver the news faster than their competitors, resulting in some wild schemes by newspapers to beat the competition.[11] An objective writing style, aside from being economical when articles were transmitted via the costly telegraph, provided a more efficient means of organizing information and getting it to editors ahead of the competition.

The control revolution. The arrival of information abundance challenged the information consumer. Readers who started getting their news from newspapers and the telegraph needed new rules for validating and absorbing the glut of information, for deciding what to believe and what to ignore. The competitive market that arose in the 19th century provided some of these rules. Information that had fought its way onto the newspaper page could be viewed as more worthy than that which had not. The individual, so critical to initiating news by word of mouth in the 18th century, was replaced in an informational process that the scholar James Beniger describes as the "control revolution," the development in the 19th century of technologies that could handle the speed and volume of goods and information produced by the Industrial Revolution.[12] Also, feedback became important, as editors could tell what readers liked by what sold in the streets.

Circulation-driven newspapers were one such control mechanism. Unlike their predecessors — party newspapers that were sold by annual subscription — the penny newspapers proved their worth on a daily basis, selling on the streets one copy at a time. They provided a feedback mechanism that helped to *regulate* (make regular, make predictable) the news. With an annual subscription to the party press, you bought the fixed ideology of the editor or his patrons. With the penny press, you bought events. Penny newspapers lent themselves to beats and the steady production of news. News was one of America's first mass-produced products — after rifles and clocks, but decades before Fords.

Following Morse's successful demonstration of telegraphic technology in 1844, a group of seven New York publishers banded together to share the costs of gathering information, creating The Associated Press. Soon New York newspapers began to share the same up-to-date stories, even if the stories were short and similar in content. Telegraph operators printed the messages on seven sheets of paper, separated by carbons, and distributed the identical messages to all seven newspapers. The papers could change the wording if needed, by adding, subtracting or other editing; but often the newspapers did not do so.

As several scholars have suggested, the telegraph did more than simply shorten the news article. The study of the coverage of the Mexican War in Chapter 7 suggests that the telegraph specifically affected bias at the word level, paring down news stories to the objective minimum. At the story level, the telegraph put more immediate information into play, providing New York editors with a greater range of viewpoints to include in their accounts. The war reports also hint at other features that would become hallmarks of objectivity, namely an emphasis on facts and a preference for speedy delivery over details.

A study of telegraphic news about presidential elections from 1852

Part II: The 19th Century • **71**

to 1916 found that biased language (mostly adjectives and adverbs) had almost disappeared by the 1880s.[13] However, presidential campaigns were not everyday occurrences, and most news of the period focused on day-to-day events, where a partisan bias was not especially evident.

An aggregate look at a broader range of news articles from the 19th century supports some of the ideas gleaned from the example of the Mexican War. A content analysis of more than 3,000 news stories that appeared between 1820 and 1860 shows that newspapers became more alike — or, put another way, they became less diverse. This development suggests a growing orientation toward objectivity and perhaps shared professional values.[14]

During the years from 1820 to 1860, the nation's newspapers became more balanced in the sources they chose for information. For example, the percentage of stories clipped from other newspapers fell from about 50 percent in 1820 to about 25 percent in 1860. Meanwhile, the percentage of news from local reporters climbed from about 10 percent in 1820 to about 25 percent in 1860. More local news was published, and reports from local reporters and editors replaced clipped news. Telegraph news also displaced some of the clipped news, and the telegraph's style of coverage was different from that of clipped news. By 1860 the world picture that newspapers presented was more balanced from the point of view of sources. Presumably, the individual bias or perspective inherent in one source was offset by another. At any rate, one source did not dominate the discussion.

There was probably also a growing professionalism in newspapers, as local reporters began covering an increasing portion of stories about their own communities. One can hypothesize that news sources were beginning to assume more defined roles, and thus were becoming more consistent and predictable — that is, more guided by professional standards.

Local news articles filed by local reporters became more focused on specific events. An event orientation — as opposed to an issue orientation — is one feature of what we call objectivity. An event-oriented story, for instance, might be an account of a stolen horse, while an issue-oriented story might talk about slavery generally. As newspapers dropped their party affiliations (and the patronage that came with it), they focused on news other than politics. An event orientation was dictated by the market (few readers would reject a factual account of an event as partisan) and by the shrinking news interval (events occurred routinely and continually, while issues tended to evolve slowly).

In addition, a quantitative analysis of a sample of 19th-century newspapers found remarkably little bias, in terms of adjective, adverb and verb usage.[15] Indeed, the 19th century's *dark days* of journalism, heralded by Mott, appears to be mostly myth, if his observations were intended to characterize the press as a whole and not just the party press. Most 19th-century journalists were largely — to use our word — objective in word choice, although many would have regarded themselves as independent. That is, they reported on events of the day with relatively little editorializing, and they became more fact-oriented as the century wore on.

American journalism appears to have gone through three phases in which the responsibility for determining bias shifted from the message originator to the audience. First was what one could call the craftsman phase, up to the first half of the 19th century, in which lone editors produced small-circulation publications that more or less reflected their own views. Their tools were words and message elements.

The second phase was the professional phase, in the second half of the 19th century, a period that saw the segmentation of job responsibilities. Here, responsibility for eliminating bias shifted to the organization, mainly in the role of the editor. This *all-seeing* individual considered not only individual messages but the publication as a whole. Editors were able to select among messages. Of course, publishers such as William R. Hearst and Joseph Pulitzer still wielded great power over their news organizations and sometimes used that power to influence news messages.

The most recent phase in the evolution of journalistic objectivity, mainly a phenomenon of the 20th century and the early 21st, might be called the cultural phase. The responsibility for evaluating bias has somewhat shifted from message maker to audience. The audience is expected to use the variety of media that modern technology allows and that, in many cases, large corporate news structures produce. Audiences have not been shy in taking this responsibility, as when the Democratic presidential candidate Adlai Stevenson called the press one-sided (i.e., Republican) in the 1952 campaign.

In the 19th century (and even 18th century) printers, editors or publishers were more likely to call themselves independent than objective. Independent meant that newspapers were not reflecting any particular partisan point of view (such as favoring the Democratic Party or Liberty Party) or political issue (such as being abolitionist or pro-slavery). While newspapers did not always put political labels in their mastheads, many did support or oppose one cause or another. In the Revolution, New York's James Rivington and Boston's John Mein tried to balance information between the Patriot and Loyalist sides, without success[16] By the early 19th century, more newspapers became independent as the news evolved into a broadly marketed product. News transmitted over the telegraph tended to be stripped of excess words, such as adjectives, to focus just on the facts, so messages were evolving, too, regardless of whether editors and publishers saw themselves as independent or — more recently — as fair or balanced or objective. By the 20th century, the ethics that guided professional newsgathering began separating from the newspaper's political stance. A newspaper could be pro-Democrat or pro-Republican on its editorial pages (and in its name) and yet still claim to be objective in its reporting.

One can argue that local reporters in the 19th century began to imitate the stripped-down telegraph messages, thereby allowing a more pared-down version of writing to replace more colorful writing.[17] But journalism was influenced by more than technology. The 19th century German historian Leopold von Ranke believed that history would reveal itself if one could just discover and correctly order the facts because there was an underlying dynamic in history, just as there was in star patterns and — more disputed — in Charles Darwin's theory of human evolution.

• • •

The Chapters Ahead

This book makes the transition from the period of proto-objectivity by considering a transitional figure of the first quarter of the 19th century, an era often overlooked in accounts that leap straight from the Revolution to the dawn of Benjamin Day's *Sun* in the 1830s. Carol Sue Humphrey, in *Chapter 5*, focuses on Hezekiah Niles and his *Weekly Register*, which sought to provide a new type of news source. Niles was determined to present the news without partisan political comment, something that none of his contemporaries thought possible. Although not completely successful, Niles tried to bring objectivity to the reporting of the news by no longer obviously using it to gain political ends.

Chapter 6 looks into material more identified with the 19th century: the transition from the partisan,to the penny press. Hazel Dicken-Garcia argues that journalistic standards in that era are integrally related to cultural contexts. She discusses how shifting notions of the press' role, function and purpose in the 1830s related to the development of a standard that came in later years to be called objectivity. What did people expect of journalism, and how could those expectations be fulfilled? From the penny press era onward, readers increasingly seemed to expect information more than partisan rhetoric from the press — and thus some standards were needed to ensure that the information was reliable and useful. One standard or concept that eventually came to be called "objectivity" increasingly gained substance in the era, although the term was not used in the penny press era.

After the telegraph began to be used to transmit news, professional standards for news began to change. In *Chapter 7*, Professors Patnode and Shaw analyze the coverage of the Mexican War in the middle of the 19th century and conclude that there does appear to be a connection between the growth of the writing style we consider objective and the de-

FAIR AND BALANCED • *74*

velopment of both the telegraph and the wire service, which relied on telegraphic transmission, even before the changes that many have noted during the Civil War.

Another way to follow the development of the writing style we associate with objectivity in the 19th century is to examine the coverage of three cholera epidemics in New York City in 1832, 1849 and 1866. In *Chapter 8*, David T.Z. Mindich breaks substantial new ground, concluding that as the medical treatment of the disease became less grounded in philosophy and religion and more based on empiricism and other elements of the modern scientific method, so, too, the news coverage became more objective.

In *Chapter 9*, Elliot King looks at the second newspaper revolution of the century, in the 1880s and 1890s, and into the first 15 years of the 20th century, a period that included the sensationalism known as yellow journalism. Although the developments discussed in earlier chapters led to the growing popularity of an objective writing style during this period, King argues that editors and publishers used truth and accuracy as tools to achieve political ends. Leading journalists did not shy away from advocating and agitating for specific political positions. Many publishers saw that advocacy as a primary responsibility of journalism and marshaled verifiable, objective facts toward that end.

NOTES

[1] Frank Luther Mott, *American Journalism: A History, 1690-1960* (New York: Macmillan, 1962).

[2] One study of the Wisconsin press found evidence that local political reporters seemed to imitate national wire copy because news bias – operationalized mostly to mean adjectives and adverbs – dropped out of local copy after it already had dropped out of the wire copy. Wisconsin editors called for reporters to be objective at state conventions when they already were, perhaps not realizing it. See Donald L. Shaw, "News Bias and the Telegraph: A Study of Historical Change." *Journalism Quarterly* (Spring (1967): 3-12, 31.

[3] Commission on Freedom of the Press, *A Free and Responsible Press* (Chicago: University of Chicago Press, 1947).

[4] Wm. David Sloan, ed., *The Media in America: A History*, 6th ed. (Northport, Ala.: Vision Press, 2005), 132.

[5] For a more complete discussion of the news interval, see Menahem Blondheim, *News Over the Wires: The Telegraph and the Flow of Public Information in America, 1844-1897* (Cambridge, Mass.: Harvard University Press, 1994).

[6] Gerald J. Baldasty, *The Commercialization of News in the Nineteenth Century* (Madison, Wis.: University of Wisconsin Press, 1992). Modern editorial cartoonists find there is external and internal pressure to trim off bold statements as the number of papers that publishes them grows, a modern version of the old argument that Associated Press copy had to be neutral to satisfy its many newspaper clients. See David Shaw, *Press Watch: A Provocative Look at How Newspapers Re-*

port the News (New York: Macmillan, 1984), 233-57.

[7] John D. Stevens, *Sensationalism and the New York Press* (New York: Columbia University Press, 1991).

[8] Sloan, *The Media in America*, 131.

[9] Richard Brown, *Knowledge is Power: Diffusion of Information in Early America, 1700-1865* (New York: Oxford University Press, 1989), 286.

[10] Daniel J. Boorstin, *The Americans: The National Experience* (Sphere Books: London, 1988), 97.

[11] Victor Rosewater, *History of Cooperative News-gathering in the United States* (New York, London: D. Appleton and Co., 1930).

[12] For a full discussion of the importance of feedback mechanisms during the Industrial Revolution, see James R. Beniger, *The Control Revolution: Technological and Economic Origins of the Information Society* (Cambridge, Mass.: Harvard University Press, 1986).

[13] Shaw, "News Bias and the Telegraph."

[14] Data for the following conclusions come from an earlier study by one of the authors, which involved a content analysis of 3,273 news stories appearing in 67 newspapers from around the country. See Donald Lewis Shaw, "At the Crossroads: Change and Continuity in American Press News 1820-1860," *Journalism History* 8:2 (Summer 1981): 38-50, and "Some Notes on Methodology: Change and Continuity in American Press News 1820-1860," *Journalism History* 8:2 (Summer 1981): 51-53, 76.

[15] See Shaw, "At the Crossroads."

[16] See Chapter 4 in this book; also Sloan, *The Media in America*, 57-8.

[17] Shaw, "News Bias and the Telegraph."

CHAPTER 5

Objectivity During the Early Republic

By Carol Sue Humphrey

One important part of the development of objectivity appeared in the pages of *Niles' Weekly Register*, published in Baltimore, Md., from 1811 until the Civil War. Hezekiah Niles, publisher and editor of the *Register* from its inception until his retirement in 1836, was a transitional figure who represented a departure from the highly partisan press of the first quarter of the 19th century. He sought to present the truth about every issue, regardless of his personal opinion.

Historians have long debated when "objectivity" became the guiding watchword for journalists. Most have said that the move toward objectivity occurred either during the 1830s and 1840s, with the rise of the penny press, or during the Progressive Era of the 1920s, with its emphasis on applying the scientific method to the social sciences, including journalism. However, elements of what became objectivity can be found as early as the American colonial period, as the previous chapters in this book have documented. Journalists in the early 19th century were clearly aware of the principle. A few were definitely progressing toward putting it into practice. Hezekiah Niles was one of them.

Niles believed that people discovered truth through exposure to as much information as possible, and he sought to provide his readers with as many details as he could pack into the pages of his weekly publication. He never hesitated to express his own opinions about issues in his editorials, but he worked diligently to present accurate reports of the details of events and the various opinions of the people involved. As a result, *Niles' Weekly Register* proved to be a "national news magazine of exceptional quality and integrity," which "provided its readers with the best available review of the American political and economic scene," from the War of 1812 to the end of the Age of Jackson in the 1830s.[1] By 1823, the paper circulated to all 24 states, the District of Columbia and several territories and foreign countries. Congress bought 10 copies for the use of its members, and the federal government sent copies to all overseas representatives.[2]

Niles would not have used the term "objectivity." However, he

Objectivity During the Early Republic • 77

would have understood many of its aspects because he sought to eliminate political bias as much as possible from his publication. He sought to be fair to everyone by presenting information about all sides of any issue.[3] He believed that readers could then reach impartial, truthful conclusions. For example, in December 1823, he published the text of President James Monroe's annual message to Congress, containing what later became known as the Monroe Doctrine. Niles declared that "instead of ... attempting to explain what the President means, the readers of this work are referred to the message itself, in a belief that the document may be understood without the aid of editorial interpretations. I would only invite a careful perusal of it."[4] He clearly believed that people were capable of reaching their own decisions if given all the necessary information, and he sought to do that. For Niles, then, objectivity, as an ideal, consisted of equal treatment and balanced coverage. Although not always successful in his efforts to attain this goal, he set a high standard for himself and others to follow and thus helped push the American press toward a more evenhanded approach, and thus toward objectivity.

The newspapers of the early republic fell short in terms of a modern definition of fairness or objectivity. In fact, they frowned on it. Such editors as Benjamin Russell, William Duane and others did not consider objectivity a goal for which they should strive. To the editors and publishers of the early 1800s, newspapers served one primary purpose: to promote the goals of particular political parties. Although not quite as vociferous in their attacks as their predecessors, newspaper producers of the early 1800s continued the tradition established by the early partisan editors of the 1790s, such as John Fenno and Philip Freneau. To support their parties, they berated the policies and leadership of the other factions. So issues of accuracy, balance or objectivity were meaningless. Editors and authors were deliberately one-sided, filling the pages of the daily and weekly newspapers with attacks on the political opposition and accusing opponents of all sorts of evil plots and schemes. To do less, argued the Federalist editor William Cobbett, would be to allow a newspaper to become "an instrument of destruction" to all that was good.[5] Upon starting *Porcupine's Gazette and Daily Advertiser* he proclaimed, "Professions of impartiality I shall make none." Any editor who "does not exercise his own judgment, either in admitting or rejecting what is sent to him," he claimed, "is a poor passive fool, and not an editor."[6]

The historian Wm. David Sloan has explained the reasoning of these editors this way: "Even to consider impartiality, some editors argued, was dereliction of duty. The editor of *The Portfolio* in Philadelphia stated adamantly that 'he will not publish an impartial paper.' Neutral men, he said, 'cry amen to every creed, and venture on all sides, without being trusted by any.' Similarly, the editor of the *Baltimore American and Daily Advertiser* announced that he would declare himself openly in support of 'the principles of Republicanism' and in opposition to 'toryism and royalty.'"[7]

The editors, Sloan continues, "were publishing during a time of what they believed were important political questions. They would have failed in their devotion to truth and in their duty to serve the best interests of their country had they not stood up for their political convictions. 'Objective' news reporting would not have been enough. Advocacy of a cause was imperative."

Despite such denunciations of impartiality, Sloan explains, it is evident from them that the *idea* that newspapers should be impartial did circulate among Americans. If the idea were not current, there would have been no reason for editors to argue against it. Clearly, the concept was one that in earlier times had become expected of newspapers. Thus, the editors' arguments against impartiality provides "negative evidence" that the concept was a strong one that they had to deal with.

With the passage of time and the clear stability of the new government of the United States established under the Constitution, some editors moved away from the partisan view of how the press should operate. Foremost among them was Hezekiah Niles. He was born in 1777 in Chadd's Ford, Pa., after his parents had fled their home in Wilmington, Del., in hopes of escaping the approaching British Army. Niles grew up in Wilmington but went to Philadelphia in 1794 to learn the printing trade from Benjamin Johnson. He returned to Wilmington in 1796 to enter the printing and bookselling business and went into partnership with several different people in the late 1790s and early 1800s. In 1805, he first tried his hand at publishing a regular weekly publication, establishing the literary magazine the *Apollo or Delaware Weekly Magazine*. It lasted less than a year. Following its failure, Niles moved to Baltimore, where he would live the rest of his professional life. From 1805 to 1811, he published the *Baltimore Evening Post*, a Republican paper. He sold the *Post* in June 1811 and, two weeks later, issued the prospectus for the *Weekly Register*.[8]

Niles' Weekly Register first appeared in Baltimore on Sept. 7, 1811. Under the editorship of Niles, it contained documents, speeches, letters and government papers concerning all the major political issues of the day. It also included history, biography, geography, manufacturing, agriculture and a "neat summary of the news."[9]

Niles always sought to preserve an accurate record of all the major issues of the day. He actively sought to present a balanced view of the various political debates, stating that "by the insertion of original and selected essays on both sides of great national questions, we shall feel it our duty to preserve a history of the feelings of the times on men and things."[10] By carefully selecting what he published in the *Register*, Niles earned the respect of most of the politicians of his day and

Objectivity During the Early Republic • 79

achieved his own personal goal of being known as "an honest chronicler."[11] The pages of the *Register* still provide the best single record of the events of the early 19th century.

Niles, however, hoped to do more than just provide an accurate historical record. He criticized his colleagues for failing in what he perceived to be the proper role for newspaper editors to play. "The newspapers of the day," he wrote, "devoted to party and partizans, seldom dare to 'tell the truth, the whole truth, and nothing but the truth." [12]

For Niles, the failure to print information on all sides of a controversy constituted a misuse of the power and influence that naturally fell to editors of the regularly published media. He intended to go beyond the contents of the typical newspaper to provide his readers with all the information they needed to make informed decisions:

> Under the general head of POLITICS shall be inserted essays and discussions, original and selected, on all matters of a public nature deemed interesting to the generality of the readers of the REGISTER. It shall be open to all parties, temper, moderation, and dignity being preserved. Selections will be made with justice and impartiality, so that the public reason may fairly discern the merit of a case in controversy.[13]

Niles planned for the *Register* to be different. It was not "intended for electioneering purposes."[14] Rather, he desired "to print a work useful to all, rather than promotive of the interests of a part."[15] He hoped that his publication would be above party and could concentrate on the needs and interests of all the citizens of the United States: "Its politics shall be American — not passive, not lukewarm, but active and vigilant, not to support individuals, but to subserve the interests of the people, so far as he shall be able to discern in what their interest lies."[16]

Niles identified his own political affiliation in the first issue: he was a Democratic Republican. However, he believed that such identification should not overly influence his newspaper. He concluded that "there are good and bad men in both the great political parties which serve the people of the United States; there are republicans who are not federalists, and federalists who are not republicans — there is a difference between name and deeds." For Niles, all should have the right to discuss their ideas because that was the only way "that truth may be discerned."[17]

Enabling his readers to seek the truth proved to be the guiding principle for most of what Niles published. In seeking to provide information about any given issue, he hoped "that the matter may be fairly argued, devoid of personalities and indiscriminate censures."[18] Furthermore, he promised to present all sides of an issue fairly. "Whatever may be our private opinions, we never will make ourselves liable to the charge of suppressing, or neglecting to insert, any official paper belonging to any series of them laid off for the Register. All or none, is our motto."[19] Furthermore, he declared that "every effort shall be made to ascertain the truth, and it shall be inserted with fairness and impartiality, affect whom it may."[20] He promised that "the editor of the Weekly Register will constantly endeavor to give his numerous readers a true statement of things as they are. Party feelings shall not induce him to violate truth. He wishes his paper to be a record of facts; and, so far as it is possible to ascertain them, so it shall be; let them operate to the praise or disparage of whom they may."[21]

Niles's emphasis on the need for truth and accuracy led him to have a low opinion of many of his fellow newspaper editors. He declared that "the poor printers who are obligated to support this great man or oppose that, are to be PITIED. It is their vocation. Their poverty but not their will consents and they disseminate poison for subsistence."[22] For Niles, such activity was distressing and misleading: "This work shall not become the partizan of James Madison, DeWitt Clinton or Rufus King. The editor would play a higher game."[23] He stated firmly that he would never allow his newspaper to come under the influence of any politician:

> So long as the editor owns a press, it shall be kept free from passion and party — it never shall be knowingly used for the purpose of exalting one man or set of men, or for depressing another, or for the promotion of any local or sectional interest whatsoever — it shall never be encumbered by the advisements of bashaw-like persons on any subject, and the truth shall be told, when it is needful to speak it.[24]

For Niles, the decline of excessive partisan politics would lead to truth and happiness, and he believed such a change was coming after the War of 1812: "We have more nearly perfect peace and comfort than, perhaps, any people ever enjoyed — party has lost its fervor, and our citizens have both leisure and inclination to seek truth, unprejudiced."[25] Sadly, Niles was disappointed.[26]

By desiring to see an end to party strife, he did not want all disagreements to end. He agreed with a correspondent to the *Register* in 1817 who declared that "for the good of our glorious forms of government, neither of us, probably, would wish to see the whole nation think alike, and follow, like mere automata, all sorts of public measures; but let us, if possible, make this necessary contest good natured, charitable, and gentlemanly."[27] He worried that a "state of apathy" would result from the decline in party politics.[28] What concerned him was not the fact that there were differences of opinion — he disliked the electioneering and distrust that led to all sorts of conflicts and personal attacks. He

Objectivity During the Early Republic • 81

urged his readers to take seriously their personal participation in the political system of the United States:

> Go to the polls with the same deliberation that you go to church, with hearts devoted to good purposes. Give your suffrages to no man as your representative who solicits them at grog-shops and taverns, who descends to amuse you by singing songs or telling stories. The person that is mean enough for this, will surely seek his own interest at your cost. Reject those who are fond of much speaking — who can make a speech at any time: one thinking man is worth a gang of them.[29]

To avoid such problems in his own newspaper, Niles sought to concentrate on issues and policies and avoid personalities. He declared that "the proprietor of a press stands as a sort of centinel, and he must not cry 'all's well,' when an enemy is within reach of his point, without being thought a traitor. We have no choice about men — we do not care who it is that makes or executes the law, provided it is good in itself. We have nothing to gain or lose by a change of persons — the congressman and the common laborer are equal in our eyes, if each performs his part honestly."[30] During the more than 20 years in which Niles edited the *Register*, the journal never endorsed or opposed any political candidate. On one occasion, he came close to opposing a candidate when, in 1812, he urged DeWitt Clinton to run for vice president and wait four more years before running for president. However, he qualified his statement with a comment that such would be good "if so long the present power predominates."[31] He did not assume that one particular political party would definitely stay in power because he recognized "the honest difference of opinion, between the two great political parties, which divide the republic."[32] Although he personally supported one party over another, he tried to present the ideas of both in the pages of his newspaper.

In covering political issues, Niles's policy was "measures, not men." He worked diligently to avoid personal attacks upon political candidates or government leaders. He sought to present all sides of any national question "to preserve a history of the feelings of the times on men and things."[33] Also, he wanted his readers to make up their own minds about issues facing the nation.

Numerous examples of how Niles reported various political issues could be mentioned, but only a few will be considered here. In the years after the War of 1812, the *Register* covered the various revolutions in Latin America. Niles generally supported the efforts of the Spanish colonies to break away and become independent, but he also recognized the potential impact on the United States if a larger war should result. In the spring of 1818, he published in detail several Congressional speeches that either supported or opposed giving aid to the revolutionaries to the south. Of particular interest was the oration by Henry Clay of Kentucky calling for the appointment of a minister to Buenos Aires. Niles declared that the speech would "command attention, even from those who may not approve of the proposition." Several weeks later, he printed the rebuttal of John Forsyth of Georgia.[34]

During the debate over Missouri and slavery, Niles published many of the Congressional debates, being sure to include speeches from all sides. He also published numerous committee reports from Congress and news articles and editorials from other newspapers dealing with the issue of whether Missouri should be admitted into the Union. Resolutions that took strong stands on one side or the other appeared following their official adoption by the various state legislatures. After the debate reached its conclusion, Niles said he hoped that his efforts had been satisfactory:

> We have now inserted all that we design to give place to, of the speeches in congress, on the Missouri question. It has cost much time and attention to make the selection which we have — the purpose was, to avoid a repetition of the same arguments and present a full view of the subject, on both sides of the question. How far we have succeeded in this, our readers will determine.[35]

During the 1820s, Niles provided extensive coverage of the electoral disagreements that took place in the national arena. Following the election of 1820, he decided that the Congressional caucus was not a representative method for nominating the president, and he began to speak out against it. He declared that the caucus was "not only injurious, but absolutely dangerous to the liberties of the country.... I would rather learn that the halls of congress were converted into common brothels, than that caucuses of the description stated should be held in them; I would rather that the sovereignty of these states should be re-transferred to England, than that the people should be bound to submit to the dictates of such an assemblage."[36] Even so, Niles printed a series of resolutions and comments both opposing and in favor of the Congressional caucus throughout 1823 and 1824.[37]

As the election of 1824 approached, and it became clear that the nominee of the caucus would not automatically be elected, Niles sought to provide his readers with enough information about the various candidates to enable them to make informed decisions when they voted. Beginning on April 5, 1823, he started a series of articles on the candidates, or at least "the only persons who are seriously spoken of just now." Included in his list were John Quincy Adams of Massachusetts, John C. Calhoun of South Carolina, Henry Clay of Kentucky, William Crawford of Georgia and Andrew Jackson of Tennessee. Throughout the

Objectivity During the Early Republic • *83*

course of the campaign, Niles printed a vast amount of specific information about the candidates, resolutions from legislatures and various other groups in support of a particular candidate, editorials from newspapers all over the country supporting this or that person and all sorts of other materials dealing with the issues of the presidential election.[38] But he never stated a preference, declaring that he planned to vote as he thought best, and he urged all of his readers to do the same.[39]

Because of the lack of a clear winner in the Electoral College in 1824, the House of Representatives had to choose the next president. Niles traveled to Washington and watched the balloting in person. John Quincy Adams was elected, but not without controversy. As charges of a "corrupt bargain" between Adams and Henry Clay, speaker of the House, surfaced in the newspapers, Niles dutifully reprinted charges and countercharges from both sides of the controversy. Following Adams's inauguration in March 1825, the discussion continued as the supporters of Jackson continued to assert that their candidate had been cheated out of the presidency. Letters, speeches and other newspaper articles and editorials appeared from March through May of 1825. Niles made sure that he presented both sides in full. In a sense, the campaign for the election of 1828 began in 1825, and he provided balanced and detailed coverage of all the issues. But his coverage proved unusual among the news publications of the day because Niles refused to publish the personal attacks against the characters of Adams, Clay and Jackson that appeared in most of the other newspapers of the time. As the contest drew to a close in 1828, Niles bemoaned how far the two sides in the election had gone in the hopes of winning victory. The campaign had been "severe and ruthless" with "a more general grossness of assault upon distinguished individuals than we ever before witnessed."[40]

The presidential election of 1832, which centered around the issue of rechartering the 2nd Bank of the United States, also produced balanced coverage in the pages of the *Register*. Niles printed various speeches and resolutions supporting both candidates, Henry Clay and Andrew Jackson. He also provided detailed coverage of the national nominating conventions, which were used by both parties for the first time to choose their candidates for president. He published a variety of predictions from all across the country as to who would win the election. But he continued to defend his own coverage of politics and to worry about the impact of party electioneering on the future of the country:

> In this ardent controversy, which has cast out, we think, a larger amount of gross and rude, and strange and curious matter than any previous one, we have endeavored to render justice to men and their motives, generally — and, while standing free from assaults upon individuals, have seldom used hard words, even when, without any just reason, assailed. We have not entered into personal

electioneering, though supporting, (and in strict conformity with the original prospectus of this work), certain *measures* of lofty interest, or regarded essential to the welfare of the people of the United States — such as a protecting tariff, internal improvements, and a sound national currency, under the *restricted* new charter proposed for the bank of the United States.... But, as before observed, the ballot boxes may have decided every question of this sort, and it will become all parties to reconcile themselves to results — as well as they can and this maxim recommended to others, we shall strive to practice ourselves, in all moderation, and with a decent respect for the opinions of others, while maintaining our own.[41]

By and large, Niles succeeded in his efforts to be fair to all opinions. He published Congressional speeches that dealt with all sides of any controversy that arose and sought essays to support the varying views on any given issue. His own editorials often supported one side of a controversy, but he tried diligently to assure that ideas and views other than his own were presented in the pages of the *Register*. However, his objectivity did slip whenever he dealt with several issues that he felt particularly strongly about. The issues about which he could not be totally fair were the tariff, banking and Great Britain.

Throughout his years as editor of the *Register*, Niles strongly supported the adoption of a protective tariff to encourage American manufacturing. He printed statistics and information related to the growth of industrial output and encouraged citizens to buy American products to encourage economic growth. Following the War of 1812, he published a variety of material discussing the need to support American industry. He urged the development of a true protective tariff system to enable American factories "to meet, on equal grounds, the more wealthy and older institutions of Europe." Furthermore, if the United States would "protect the manufacturers for the present, ... in a little time, they will protect themselves and us."[42] Niles argued strongly for protection because he believed that industry and manufacturing were essential for economic growth and success. For him, such economic development was essential for American stability, and he argued for such ideas throughout his editorial career. In 1831, he urged voters to support the economic future of the United States as Niles envisioned it:

I ask you not to vote for this man or that man, or any particular man, but this I exhort, and entreat you to do — by all that is good for the nation, by all that is beneficial for yourselves, to give your suffrages to no human being who does not stand broadly pledged, manfully and honestly "committed," and unquestioningly devoted, to the preservation of the AMERICAN SYSTEM, the fountain of public wealth, the guarantee of private comfort, proclaiming plenty

Objectivity During the Early Republic • 85

and securing peace, offering relief to the opposed of all nations, and *establishing the independence of these United States.*[43]

Niles tried to be fair in his coverage of economic issues, printing reports of free trade conventions and other opponents of the tariff. However, he doubted that free trade actually existed anywhere, and he continually sought to urge his readers to support the use of tariffs by the United States to ensure economic stability and independence.[44]

While strongly supporting the adoption of a protective tariff in 1816, Niles was quiet when Congress adopted a charter for the 2nd Bank of the United States the same year. He did comment that he thought the bank unnecessary, but said very little else. However, by 1818, he was so distressed over the entire issue of banking that he felt it necessary to discuss it. He described banking as a "demoralizing and pernicious business" and "the 'Pandora's box' that is to fill the republic with all sorts of moral and political diseases."[45] When criticized for his comments, Niles replied: "I wish it clearly understood, that a special enmity against the bank of the United States, or any other bank, had not led me to the subject that now engages my attention. 'I owe ill will only to ill conduct,' and am doing what I believe is my duty. If I am mistaken, the people will forgive me — if I am right, they will support me in a well-intended effort to redress their grievances. I am myself but incidently interested."[46] But after a year of attacking banks, Niles decided that he had said enough: "We think that we have done our duty, and believe that a spirit is roused that will reform the evils which press upon the people; and are desirous of devoting a part of our attention to other matters of moment."[47] He found it difficult to print anything positive about the banking industry immediately following the War of 1812, but he did cease the discussion when he believed that the people had enough information to make a fair decision. He even came to support the Bank of the United States by the time Andrew Jackson became president.

The same could not be said concerning Niles's attacks on the British. Although most of his comments appeared during the War of 1812, Niles never had anything good to say about Great Britain or the British people. He believed that the British hated the United States and sought to destroy the young country in any manner possible.[48] Furthermore, the British were "more barbarous and cruel than ... any other people," a fact that explained why they were at war with so many countries at once in the 1810s.[49] In 1813, he described England as "the common robber, the man-stealer, the scalper of women and children and prisoners, the incendiary and the ravisher ... the enemy of our fathers, and our present unprincipled foe ... the cause of every war that has afflicted the civilized world for fifty years past, the common pest of society and plague of the earth ... the cold-calculating assassin of thirty millions of people in *India*, the ferocious murderer in Ireland, the minister of famine and pestilence in America ... the most profligate and corrupt government in the universe ... a government so polluted, so gangrened with every abomination, that it must perish of its own action, sooner or later.... [A] nation red to her arm-pits in the blood of innocents."[50]

As far as Niles was concerned, the British were to blame for the War of 1812. His major complaints against the British on the part of Americans dealt with issues on the high seas, particularly the impressment of American sailors by the British Royal Navy. He strongly urged American leaders to settle for nothing less than retribution for these wrongs: "Accursed be the American government, and every individual of it, who by the omission or commission of any thing, shall agree to make peace with Great Britain, until ample provision shall be made for our impressed seamen, and security shall be given for the prevention of such abominable outrages in future."[51]

Beyond the issues of trade and freedom of the seas, Niles agreed with many Americans when he stated that the British also sought to stir up trouble on the frontier by inciting the Indians. He believed that this situation would improve once the United States had declared war on Britain:

> In the event of a declaration of hostilities against England, and the prospect of it daily increases, every 'savage' in alliance with that 'magnanimous' nation may be expected to 'unbury the tomahawk.' But even in this we shall have a change, perhaps in the end, for the better: the line will be drawn between open enemies and pretended friends — the savages will receive a summary punishment, while just retaliation shall correct the proceedings of their abettors. We have had but one opinion as the cause of the depredations of the Indians — which was, and is, that they are instigated and supported by the British in Canada, any official declaration to the contrary notwithstanding. As it was in 1776 and in 1791, so it is now.[52]

Even after the War of 1812 ended in 1815, Niles said Americans had to be diligent because British plots had not ended with the signing of the peace treaty. In November 1815, he urged Congress to rearm because British officers were in American seaports, making maps and preparing for further military action.[53] As late as 1817, he urged diligence because of "the miserable shifts of the British ministry to keep up 'their system,' by herds of spies and informers, sham-plots and the like."[54]

Although Niles blamed the British for bringing on the War of 1812, his dislike for Great Britain went beyond the issue of the military conflict. At the heart of his hatred for the British lay a deep distrust of kings and monarchical government:

Objectivity During the Early Republic • 87

As an "American" I am a constitutional enemy of these men; I believe the whole business of "kingcraft," a horrid knavery, and that the present kings and princes of Europe are among the most "rascally members of creation." A reference to facts — an observance of their proceedings, will shew what they are; and, when I have occasion to speak of them, I will endeavor to press upon others the sovereign contempt I have for them. The common mind is too easily led to a veneration of monarchy and aristocracy; and, unfortunately, too many of our books (written by "British" authors,) are calculated to cast false lights upon them. I cannot any more believe that a man is born "royal" or "noble" (in the "true" meaning of the words) because his supposed father is called a king or a lord, than that a man must be a horse if the place of his birth were a stable. The talk about "divine right," "legitimate sovereign," &c. with which too many in the United States endeavor to mislead the public mind, is a kind of treason against humanity — they are all "Usurpers" — power alone constitutes their right; all other pretension is a barefaced cheat. I have no commiseration for them. I am glad that some have felt a portion of the suffering they heaped on the heads of the people.[55]

Such strong comments often produced reactions from readers of the *Register*, for clearly Niles lost his desire to be fair and impartial when he discussed anything to do with the British. However, he did not apologize. Rather, he defended his actions. In 1813, he stated categorically that "though we would not knowingly insinuate a falsehood, or distort a fact, we cannot, dare not, will not, stand with our arms folded, 'neutral and insensible.' By diligent investigation, truth shall be ascertained, and faithfully recorded in the 'Events of the War' — yet we will use our best efforts to rouse and encourage our fellow-citizens to such deeds of patriotism as may lead to a glorious termination of the controversy, so far forth as the same shall be in our power. Our country, the best and most happy in the world, requires this of all who breathe its free air and partake of its manifold blessings."[56]

This search for truth guided all of Niles's actions in his weekly publication. Even when he was not successful, he perceived this goal as the only one possible for a good editor. In 1820, he summed up his views on what an editor should do to best serve his readers by talking about what he had tried to do in his own publication:

While, with great freedom, the editor has expressed his own opinions on some of the leading topics of the day, he has been careful not to offend by rudeness, or impeach men's motives who had the same right to determine on things that he himself exercised; and the selected articles on those subjects have been chosen with the sole

FAIR AND BALANCED • 88

view of giving the best intelligence on the matters at issue. As, for instance, a speech in congress on one side of a question, has never been inserted without its opposing argument on the other, if to be obtained; and we believe that the editor of a journal refused justice to his readers, when he pursues a different course.[57]

Throughout his career as an editor, Niles sought to do "justice to his readers" by presenting them all the facts available so that they could reach their own conclusions about what constituted the truth.

Niles's efforts to present all the facts in his *Register* laid the groundwork for future developments in American journalism. Much of the commercial value of the penny papers, which began right at the end of Niles's editorship of the *Register*, resulted from the ability of their editors to present factual, honest news stories about local, national and world events. Niles's emphasis on complete information, rather than on partisanship and opinion, provided the basis for this change as he showed that it was possible to publish a successful newspaper based upon fair and thorough reporting.

NOTES

[1] John Thomas Guertler, "Hezekiah Niles: Wilmington Printer and Editor," *Delaware History* (Spring/Summer 1976): 37.

[2] Norval Neal Luxon, *Niles' Weekly Register: News Magazines of the Nineteenth Century* (Westport, Conn.: Greenwood Press, 1947), 8.

[3] Scholars today, making a comparison to modern media, usually describe the *Register* as a news magazine. Niles, however, perceived it as a newspaper, and that term will be used in this chapter.

[4] *Niles' Weekly Register* (Baltimore, Md.)., 6 December 1823, 209. *Niles' Weekly Register* will be identified as *NWR* in the remaining footnotes.

[5] *Porcupine's Gazette* (Philadelphia), 5 March 1797.

[6] Ibid.

[7] Wm. David Sloan, "The Party Press, 1783-1833," in *The Media in America: A History*, 6th ed. (Northport, Ala.: Vision Press, 2005), 75. The newspaper quotations are from the *Independent Chronicle*, 7 August 1798, and the *American and Daily Advertiser* (Baltimore), 16 May 1799.

[8] Guertler, "Hezekiah Niles," 37-53; Luxon, *Niles' Weekly Register*, 17-23.

[9] *NWR*, 7 September 1811, 2.

[10] Ibid., 1.

[11] Quotation from *Henry VIII* 4.2.69-72 by William Shakespeare – part of the masthead of the *Register* during its first year of publication.

[12] *NWR*, 7 September 1811, 2.

[13] Ibid.

[14] Ibid., 1

[15] Ibid., 8.

[16] Ibid., 3.

[17] Ibid.

[18] Ibid, 8.

[19] *NWR*, 21 December 1811, 296.

[20] *NWR*, 25 February 1815, 401.

[21] *NWR*, 24 October 1812, 128.

[22] *NWR*, 16 October 1819, 97.

[23] *NWR*, 24 October 1812, 128.

[24] *NWR*, 14 April 1821, 97.

[25] *NWR*, 9 August 1817, 369.

[26] *NWR*, 19 February 1825, 386.

[27] *NWR*, 12 July 1817, 310.

[28] *NWR*, 28 April 1821, 132.

[29] *NWR*, 20 February 1821, 391.

[30] *NWR*, 25 August 1821, 401.

[31] *NWR*, 6 June 1812, 235.

[32] *NWR*, Preface to Volume II (March-August 1812).

[33] *NWR*, 7 September 1811, 1.

[34] *NWR*, 24 March 1818, 121-30; 18 April 1818, 156-65.

[35] *NWR*, 26 August 1820, 449.

[36] *NWR*, 26 January 1822, 338-9. This was very strong language for someone who hated England as much as Niles. See below for further discussion of his attitude towards Great Britain.

[37] See, for example, *NWR*, 26 July 1823, 322-5; 20 September 1823, 40-1; 11 October 1823, 81; 1 November 1823, 131-3, 137-9; 8 November 1823, 145-6; 27 December 1823, 258, 260; 3 January 1824, 273, 281-4.

[38] *NWR*, Volumes XXV through XXVII, September 1823 to February 1825.

[39] *NWR*, 6 September 1823, 3.

[40] *NWR*, 13 September 1828, 33.

[41] *NWR*, 3 November 1832, 145.

[42] *NWR*, 24 February 1816, 437-47.

[43] *NWR*, 9 July 1831, 327.

[44] *NWR*, 15 October 1831, 129, 135-41; 22 October 1831, 156-8; 29 October 1831, 166.

[45] *NWR*, 28 February 1818, 1.

[46] *NWR*, 7 March 1818, 17.

[47] *NWR*, 16 January 1819, 385.

[48] *NWR*, 10 September 1814, 1.

[49] *NWR*, 2 September 1815, 2.

[50] *NWR*, 30 October 1813, 144-5.

[51] *NWR*, 18 April 1812, 119.

[52] *NWR*, 7 March 1812, 5.

[53] *NWR*, 4 November 1815, 169.

[54] *NWR*, 30 August 1817, 3.

[55] *NWR*, 28 September 1811, Supplement, 70-1.

[56] *NWR*, 6 March 1813, 1.

[57] *NWR*, 26 August 1820, 449.

CHAPTER 6

The Transition from the Partisan to the Penny Press

By Hazel Dicken-Garcia

Seventy-eight years after the penny press began, Charles G. Ross, in what may be the first use of the word "objectivity" in journalism, wrote in a 1911 textbook that "[n]ews writing is objective to the last degree, in the sense that the writer is not allowed to 'editorialize.'"[1] No form of the word has been found in early American sources, and this nearly century-old use of "objectivity" as the opposite of "editorializing" is narrow compared with today's use. Although its meaning remains open to interpretation, "objectivity" is more than a mere separation of fact from "bias" and values. Today, we might define it as unbiased accurate reporting of verifiable facts with detachment and completeness in a manner that is fair, balanced, thorough and clearly separate from the reporter's views and opinions.

None of today's ideas about objectivity were generally accepted in the journalism of the early 19th century. Concepts associated with objectivity — such as impartiality and the use of reliable facts — had been acknowledged for generations, as earlier chapters in this book have shown. However, before the penny press appeared in 1833, words like "journalist" and "reporter" were rare, and "printer," "mechanic," "printer's apprentice," "printer's devil" and "editor" dominated the journalism lexicon. "[N]o such profession as 'Journalism'" existed before 1827, a witness to the era wrote, and "judgment of the value or knowledge as to the effective arrangement of news were then unknown qualifications." Publications "were mere personal or political organs, and aimed to influence public opinion by arguments — not to enlighten ... with facts." [2] A January 1803 *Wasp* editorial illustrates the point. Harry Croswell wrote of agony over filling "one little paper" with lies on behalf of a party, speculating that a rival editor managed to do it from habit. But Croswell said he could not acquire the habit and "therefore must give up the idea of becoming a Democrat."

Objectivity would have had difficulty existing in a journalism that served political factions engaged in no-holds-barred partisan debates, but Croswell's putting truthfulness above party loyalty here foreshad-

From the Partisan to the Penny Press • 91

owed — just as Hezekiah Niles, as shown in the previous chapter, had done — a journalistic shift favorable to its development after 1833. Did the penny press journalists, however, discuss and apply concepts now associated with objectivity? Although many sources deal with the dramatic changes across penny press history, from 1833 until Civil War conditions inflated prices after 1860, few relate them to journalistic standards. Detailing the shift from the political to the information model, this chapter emphasizes context, especially preconditions for the development of an objectivity standard: press purposes, models, notions of journalistic responsibility and work routines.

Much literature suggests that the penny press quickly supplanted partisanism with independent, objective reporting. This, however, assumes that journalism could represent only partisanism or nonpartisanism, that nonpartisanism equaled the adoption of objectivity as a standard, that independent journalism is synonymous with objective journalism and that the conditions fostered objectivity. And it neglects then-current and precursor notions about journalistic responsibility, including the very purposes and development of journalism, press models, notions of responsibility and work routines.

At the broadest level, journalistic standards flow from societal purposes for communication systems. Those purposes embody beliefs about national character, goals, values, the individual's role and relationship to government, as well as the source, substance, role and interrelationships of knowledge, truth and power and how they are attained and used — and particularly how truth is manifest. Central are beliefs about communication — what it does, can and should do, and how — and about information — what is needed and how it is gathered, exchanged and presented. A perceived press purpose to promote debate fosters concern about substance, for example, and this dominated the early American press. But a perceived purpose to convey information fosters concern about presentation quality and connects the penny press and objectivity.

The purpose of the party press was to advance one's party. So objectivity, balance and even accuracy were irrelevant. Francis Preston Blair's career and Andrew Jackson's presidency best exemplify this model while, ironically, marking the shift away from it. After the journalists Blair and Amos Kendall led a campaign to elect Jackson in 1828, he rewarded both with political appointments, installing Blair with a state-of-the-art printing press and pointedly "inviting" government workers to subscribe to the new *Washington Globe*.[3] In 1829 *National Journal* editors listed 40 journalists Jackson had appointed to political office and, in 1832, the *National Intelligencer* editors listed 57 appointed to federal positions.[4] Although New York City was the nation's journalism center, Blair, in Washington, D.C., was the journalist to reckon with — or so it seemed.

But a new press model emerged during Jackson's presidency, as Americans' collective assumptions about society, individuals and information underwent a major transformation. People increasingly saw the purpose of the press as conveying news and information about events and institutions, so how information was presented became more important than party battles.

The party newspapers, which a contemporary, James Parton, later called "cumbrous, heavy, solemn," reflected class differentiation; "respectable" people would have thought "hawking" a cheap newspaper in the streets in "competition with cakes and apples" to be "unspeakably absurd."[5] But in late 1833, with Jackson firmly ensconced in his second term, the hawking of the *New York Sun* on the streets of Manhattan signaled a change in journalism in almost every way.[6] "When the respectable New Yorker first saw a penny paper, he gazed at it (I saw him) with ... mingled curiosity and contempt," Parton wrote.

The founder of the *New York Sun*, Benjamin Day, eschewing partisanship, developed a street circulation system and a per-line advertising rate that, combined with aiming content and cost at the mass public, demonstrated a way to put newspapers on a sound financial basis. Instead of the polemical essays that marked the party press, the content of the *Sun* was concise, interesting and entertaining. The journalism historian Frederic Hudson, himself a journalist during the penny press era, wrote in 1872 that the *Sun* had assisted "in the great revolution of the press ... ultimately throughout the world; and it still lives. It helped to make newspaper readers."[7]

Whereas the party press reflected assumptions that power lay with such groups as political parties and the business sector, penny press journalism assumed that individuals needed information for living in an ever-more-complex society. Beginning with the election reforms of the 1820s and the Jacksonian view that anyone could hold public office, the expansion of democratic principles to encompass the political abilities of all citizens implied a greater public need for information. The historian Carol Sue Humphrey has pointed out that increasing literacy rates encouraged newspaper reading and that newspapers, because of their availability, became an increasingly important source of knowledge, especially for political affairs.[8] Much of the population lacked empowerment before the election reforms began in the 1820s, but the penny press came on the heels of those reforms and aimed at active participants in the political system.

The information model brought attention to the public's right to know and the watchdog role. To serve and champion individuals, this model argues, the press must monitor public institutions and expose abuses. The concept of the public's right to know about abuses in order to be able to correct them evolved from notions of the press' right to inform — as illustrated by a Massachusetts judge's statement in 1822 about the press' right to bring "government, magistracy, and individuals, to the bar of public opinion," which would "certainly be highly serviceable to the public."[9] More people became newspaper readers, and the growing recognition of the press as providing information for use in improving life and defending the public's rights brought awareness of, and connection with, the community, nation and world. The increasing citizen participation and the growing expectations of the press fueled impatience with content that fell short and led to calls for responsibility.

Stress in the penny press on information and the individual[10] had implications for development of objective reporting as new kinds of criticism bred new concepts of responsibility. Indeed, unsettling kinds of news provoked the clearest early expressions about press responsibility. Reporting crime, sex, violence, "lowly" individuals and the seamier side of life belied tradition. Critics opposed all such reporting, saying printing "private" matters rendered the press indecent and immoral — especially abhorrent because people believed the press existed to ennoble humankind — and covering "lowly" members of society trivialized the news and the press' vast potential.

Thus, the information model highlighted the values of accuracy and utility and prompted criticisms of inaccuracy, triviality and poor taste. The old practice of editors' mutual insults illustrates the point. Party editors' mutual verbal assaults were a natural consequence of the early role of the press: persuading readers included destroying opponents' credibility, taking to the extreme Madison's notion that anyone seriously arguing a position expects and *"intend[s] to excite ... unfavorable sentiments,"* and "[s]ome degree of abuse is inseparable from the proper use of everything" — especially the press.[11] But in the new era, editorial insults wasted valuable news space, and readers demanded that they end. In effect, partiality, a natural product of the party press function, was illogical and superfluous in the new model.

Whereas earlier concerns about responsibility had correlated with partisan opinions, penny press editors treated a broader range of subjects. Although they published their own views, just as party press counterparts had, the editors' experience in advocating party interests was translated later into advancing their convictions on any pet cause. Soon after the founding of the Philadelphia *Public Ledger* in the 1830s, for example, Russell Jarvis said an editor held "a post of high responsibility," and his "purpose ought to be to instruct, to improve the world; not *to take it as he finds it,* and ... direct it to his own views or private interest." An editor's duty was "to assail prejudices," to correct them, "not to flatter, for the purpose of profiting...." It was to "hold up folly and vice to ridicule and scorn; not to treat them tenderly [because] they have money" just to buy patronage.[12] James Gordon Bennett's announcement of the *New York Morning Herald* on May 6, 1835, illustrates the emerging notions of responsibility — couched in familiar images: "We shall endeavor to record facts on every public and proper subject, stripped of verbiage and coloring, *with comments when suitable, just, independent, fearless, and good-tempered* [emphasis added]."

Thus, old and new concepts of responsibility merged as an older emphasis on press implications for society at large overlapped the discussions of new matters that became important to developing notions relevant to objectivity: attention to facts, "coloring" (what we would now call bias), "good-temper" (taste); independence, detachment and balance. The foundations of these concepts, although shaped by the information model, lay in prior standards.

Among the preconditions for objectivity's development, cultural influences intertwined with perceived press purposes to produce ways of thinking about journalism. In the party press era, Americans, caught up in partisan conflicts, asked if one could treat the political opposition impartially, so pre-penny-press journalists used the term "impartiality" in a way that seems to embody the core idea of what is called "objectivity" today. Similarly, the meaning of the word objectivity has roots in the turn of the 20th century, when it emerged, particularly in the preoccupation with the scientific method and the realism movement's questioning of subjectivism.[13] Thus, the terms impartiality and objectivity are not equivalent, but they reflect prevailing values of their eras — plus shadings accumulated through usage.

Impartiality, the primary journalistic standard discussed, was perhaps the most important forerunner of objectivity because of its apparent meaning of equal treatment of opposing parties.[14] Madison wrote in 1828, for example, that "one-sided" publications meant the "best minds" might "be filled with the most gross and injurious untruths" because people reading "erroneous statements … without any exposure to their fallacies" would be deluded.[15] Condemning one-sided content, a writer to a 1798 Vermont newspaper said people inevitably took on the prejudice they were constantly exposed to, and they had no access to the truth if they read only a partisan paper.[16] And a newspaper prospectus in 1800 promised fairness and impartiality.[17] One finds the word impartiality rarely in the 1830s.

In addition to broader purposes as shapers of journalistic standards, other significant preconditions are the perceived concrete purposes tied directly to concepts of news, news values, work routines and the reporter's role. Indeed, objectivity depends on these. A 1971 book says that objectivity is inseparable from a reporter's attitude toward it as a goal. The authors cited one perspective that said objectivity, although not always achieved (indeed, rarely is achieved), would be attainable if the reporter tried "to be fair, accurate, balanced, dispassionate, uninvolved, unbiased, and unprejudiced." Attitude makes one "an objective reporter," the authors wrote.[18] The penny press introduced news values

From the Partisan to the Penny Press • 95

of proximity, prominence and human interest and defined the reporter's role, which developed significantly over the next 30 years — but did the role impose obligations to be objective as understood today? Discussions at the time considered newspaper content as a function of editors' roles, not reporters'. The journalism traits drawing the most attention to reporters developed appreciably only later: eyewitness reporting, interviewing and using multiple sources, among others. Even bylines were rare before the Civil War, and attribution was still barely visible by the end of the century.[19]

A glance at early 19th-century newspapers shows that they aimed to fulfill the familiar press purposes of providing news, opinion and entertainment, but hardly a trace of much that is now commonplace: background, follow-up and investigative reporting, and, on the opinion side, interpretation, commentary and analysis. As the penny press began, the editorial page had not developed, and news was just becoming predominantly event-oriented. Hudson wrote that the *Sun's* "early numbers" had "no editorials ... no opinion."[20] Parton, who witnessed the introduction of the penny press and later called it the most momentous event in the nation's first 70 years, treated news as a novelty: "That part of the newspaper which interests, awakens, moves, warns, inspires, instructs and educates all classes and conditions of people, the wise and the unwise, the illiterate and the learned, is the NEWS!" The penny press "brings the *Course of Events* to bear on the progress of every individual."[21]

The reporter's very arduous work of simply getting the story probably crowded out any thoughts beyond immediate tasks. How much did work routines include verifying facts, when there was no rapid transportation to speed to scenes of breaking news or telephones to track leads and consult from the "field"? As the 19th century began, there were no trains, telephones, ballpoint pens or even lead pencils to foster communication among the new nation's approximately 200 newspapers. Setting type for two pages took 16 hours; putting inked type on paper required 13 manual operations; two people working together could print only 240 pages per hour — and then a page had to dry before the back could be printed on. Steam-driven presses appeared in the mid-1820s and the first miles of railways in 1830, when approximately 1,200 newspapers existed. Although the telegraph arrived in 1844 and the number of publications increased to more than 4,000 by 1860, journalists did not use multiple sources and rarely used the telegraph. How could articles provide "balance" before journalists valued multiple sources — or could readily get access to them? More basic, were the penny press reporters' views of their work conducive to the abstract thought required for being "objective?"

Clues about the work routines and views of reporters — who might have provided the most insight about the standards applied in their work — are elusive. The earliest set of reporters' rules found dates from 1862.[22] Most journalists lacked formal education and, since the focus of the occupation was on becoming an editor, reporters probably gave little attention to "policy" matters like standards. Indeed, because the reporter's role and the event-orientation of news were developing, work routines probably lacked refinement — and attention to abstract principles.

At a philosophical level, the belief that truth would emerge in the clash of ideas in the public sphere probably inhibited the development of standards as known today. In 1828, Madison wrote that "truth would always have a fair chance" if "every newspaper, when printed on one side, should be handed over to the adversary, to be printed on the other, thus presenting to every reader both sides of every question." And "where the press is free," contradictions in "rival or hostile papers" must always control the effects of published "falsehoods and slanders."[23] As newspapers brought ordinary individual's lives into public view and event-reporting increased chances for witnesses to events to see inaccuracies in news accounts of those events, faith in the "self-righting" process declined. Indeed, historically, objectivity became important as questions grew about the marketplace-of-ideas theory.

Brian Thornton reports one aspect of significance for the development of objectivity: two-thirds of the letters to the editors of four 1830s newspapers emphasized truth as important.[24] But most significant, perhaps, was the emerging concept of "balance," the responsibility to present all sides of issues. In 1837, the editor of the *New York Evening Post*, William Cullen Bryant, wrote that the "right to discuss freely and openly, by speech, by the pen, by the press, all political questions, and to examine and animadvert upon all political institutions," were "so clear and certain, so interwoven with our liberties, so necessary, in fact, to their existence," that anarchy and despotism would rule without them.[25] And Jarvis wrote that an editor who would be "frightened from his duty by the cry of *stop my paper*," or who would "withhold one stroke of the lash from any back that deserves it, in the hope of obtaining an advertisement or a subscriber, is a venal pandar": "his services are for sale to anybody or any cause and the highest bidder may obtain him."[26]

The editor of the *New York Tribune*, Horace Greeley, wrote in 1841 that he sought a "happy medium between these extremes" of partisanship and nonpartisanship, from which a journalist could freely "advocate the principles and commend the measures" of any party he chose, while also frankly dissenting from it on particular questions and "even denounc[ing] its candidates" if they lacked ability and integrity.[27] This concept of balance can be traced from the impartiality standard around 1800. For example, a 1798 writer to a Vermont newspaper suggested that editors suppress their own political opinions, read

From the Partisan to the Penny Press • 97

at least one outstanding paper of each party, and publish equal amounts — in quantity and quality — of thoughtful, decent articles from both sides, avoiding "squibs, and ... rancorous party trash."[28] In 1828, Madison wrote that the only solution to a "biased" press he could see was for each party to present views on the same issues in the same newspapers.[29]

At least one allusion to the idea of conflict of interest appeared in the 1820s.[30] It hardly implied today's meaning, but an allusion in 1841 did: an editor said "the [political] appointment of an editor, publisher, or other person interested in a newspaper, is unjust and impolitic...." More to the point, the editor Samuel Bowles III eloquently editorialized in the 1850s for "independent" journalism, asserting that people were realizing that a party newspaper could not be honest.[31] Many, of course, date the emergence of "objective" journalism from Henry J. Raymond's 1851 founding of *The New York Times* and the well-known promise to "get into a passion as rarely as possible," but the same prospectus made clear the newspaper's politics.[32] Explicit or implicit allusions to these concepts — balance, conflict of interest, independence, etc. — remained exceedingly rare in antebellum America. And Raymond, Greeley and other editors kept partisan associations throughout the era and beyond. These seeds of standards were nevertheless crucial to the development of objectivity.

Although the penny press journalists did not separate opinion strictly from news, partisanship gradually became relegated to a large category called bias, which implies a journalistic failure to fulfill the information role. Concern about bias culminated in the creation of the journalistic standard of objectivity amid American preoccupations with scientific methods, which were assumed to be a reliable means to eliminate bias. Thus the shift from the political to the information model paved the way for developments ultimately culminating in a standard called objectivity.

NOTES

[1] Charles G. Ross, *The Writing of News: A Handbook* (New York: Henry Holt, 1911), 20. Quoted in Harlan S. Stensaas, "The Rise of Objectivity in U.S. Daily Newspapers, 1865-1934." Presented to the American Journalism Historians Association, St. Louis, October 1986.

[2] W.F.G. Shanks, "How We Get Our News," *Harper's New Monthly Magazine* 34 (March 1867): p. 512.

[3] William E. Smith, "Francis P. Blair, Pen-Executive of Andrew Jackson," *Mississippi Valley Historical Review* 17 (March 1931): 543-6; William E. Smith, *The Francis Preston Blair Family in Politics*. 2 vols. (New York: Macmillan, 1933); Elbert B. Smith, *Francis Preston Blair* (New York: Free Press, 1980).

[4] James E. Pollard, *The Presidents and the Press* (New York: Macmillan, 1947),

161; Ronald Shilen, "The Concept of Objectivity in Journalism in the United States," Ph.D. diss., New York University, 1955, 39-40; Smith, "Francis P. Blair...," 70.

5 James Parton, *The Life of Horace Greeley* (New York: Mason Brothers, 1855),141-2.

6 For an excellent account of the penny press, see Susan Thompson, *The Penny Press* (Northport, Ala.: Vision Press, 2004). She reasons that "the authority of the correspondent overpowered any professional ideal of objective or non-intrusive reporting. The separation of news articles from editorials became clearer by the 1850s, but purely objective news reporting never emerged as a clearly stated professional ideal" (p. 200).

7 Frank M. O'Brien, *The Story of The Sun: New York: 1833-1928* (New York: D. Appleton and Company, 1928), 1-88; Frederic Hudson, *Journalism in the United States From 1690 to 1872* (1873; reprint ed., New York: Haskell House Publishers, Ltd., 1968), 420.

8 Carol Sue Humphrey, *The Press of the Young Republic, 1783-1833* (Westport, Conn.: Greenwood Press, 1996), 135-6.

9 *Trial: Commonwealth vs. J.T. Buckingham, on an Indictment for a Libel, from the Municipal Court of the City of Boston, December Term, 1822* (Boston, 1822), 53.

10 Hudson, *Journalism in the United States...*, 426-7.

11 Virginia General Assembly, House of Delegates, *The Virginia Report of 1799-1800 Touching the Alien and Sedition Laws* (New York: DeCapo Press, 1970), 226-7; Leonard Levy, ed., *Freedom of the Press from Zenger to Jefferson* (Indianapolis: Bobbs-Merrill, 1966), 216.

12 Hillier Krieghbaum, *Facts in Perspective*, (Englewood Cliffs, N.J.: Prentice-Hall, 1956), 19.

13 Shilen, "The Concept of Objectivity in Journalism in the United States"; John Higham, *History: Professional Scholarship in America* (Baltimore: The Johns Hopkins University Press, 1990), 92-4.

14 Donald Stewart, *The Opposition Press of the Federalist Period* (Albany: State University of New York Press, 1969), 28, citing the Poughkeepsie, N.Y., *American Farmer*, 29 October 1799.

15 Madison to N. P. Trist, dated Montpelier, Virginia, 23 April 1828, quoted in Frank Luther Mott and Ralph D. Casey, eds., *Interpretations of Journalism*, New York: F.S. Crofts, 1937), 113-4.

16 Stewart, *The Opposition Press of the Federalist Period*, 28, citing the Peacham, Vt., *Green Mountain Patriot*, 6 April 1798.

17 Quoted in "The *National Intelligencer* and Its Editors," *Atlantic Monthly* 6 (October 1860): 477.

18 John C Merrill and Ralph L. Lowenstein, *Media, Messages and Men: New Perspectives in Communication* (New York: David McKay Co., 1971), 228-41.

19 Lynn Groth, "The Journalistic Standard of Attribution: An Historical Study of the Change in Attribution Practices by Journalists Between 1890-1924," M.A. thesis, University of Minnesota, 1989.

20 Hudson, *Journalism in the United States From 1690 to 1872*, 420.

21 Parton, *The Life of Horace Greeley* , 137-9.

22 George Henry Payne, *History of Journalism in the United States* (New York:

D. Appleton, 1925), 251-3.

[23] Madison to N.P. Trist, dated Montpelier, Va., April 23, 1828; quoted in Mott and Casey, *Interpretations of Journalism*, 113-4.

[24] Brian Thornton, "Humbug, P.T. Barnum and Batmen on the Moon: Editorial Discussion of the Moon Hoax of 1835," paper presented to the Association for Education in Journalism and Mass Communication (AEJMC), New Orleans, August 1999, 11-2.

[25] Jeffrey B. Ruttenbech, "Partisan Press Coverage of Anti-Abolitionist Violence – a Case Study of Status Quo Journalism," paper presented to AEJMC, San Antonio, Texas, August 1987.

[26] Krieghbaum, *Facts in Perspective*, 19.

[27] Quoted in Francis Brown, *Raymond of the "Times"* (New York: W.W. Norton, 1951), 25.

[28] *Green Mountain Patriot* (Peacham, Vt.), 6 April 1798.

[29] Madison to N.P. Trist, Montpelier, Va., April 23, 1828; quoted in Mott and Casey, *Interpretations of Journalism*, 113-4.

[30] *U.S. Telegraph*, 6 and 14 February 1826.

[31] *Chicago Tribune*, 3 July 1841; *Springfield Republican*, 30 September 1858.

[32] Brown, *Raymond of the Times*, 98-101.

CHAPTER 7

Objectivity and the Mexican War
By Randall Patnode
and Donald L. Shaw

The coverage of the Mexican War (1846-1848) by two newspapers — one in New York and the other in New Orleans — provides some insight into the forces at work on 19th-century objectivity. The role of the telegraph was particularly important. For the first time, the telegraph was available for newspaper use in covering a war. It specifically affected bias at several levels. At the word level, it helped pare down news stories to the objective minimum. At the story level, the telegraph put more immediate information into play, providing New York editors with a greater range of viewpoints to include in their accounts. The war reports also hint at some of the other features that would become the hallmarks of objectivity, namely an emphasis on facts and a preference for speedy delivery over detail.

The Mexican War came barely 13 years after Benjamin Day launched the first penny newspaper in New York City and only two years after Samuel F.B. Morse sent his first telegraphic message to Washington, D.C. Editors in New York, the nation's information hub, and New Orleans, the main collection point for news about the Mexican War, were particularly aggressive in covering the conflict. The New Orleans *Daily Picayune* sent five reporters to Mexico to chronicle the conflict, while the *New York Herald's* James Gordon Bennett stationed a reporter in New Orleans to send back news reports by the fastest means possible.[1] Of course, New Orleans was closer to the war than was New York. The closest telegraph terminal to New Orleans was in Philadelphia. (The telegraph reached New Orleans in 1848, after the war was over.)

News reports from the battlefields were typically sent by ship to New Orleans, then by ship from New Orleans to Mobile, Ala., and by horseback from there north to Philadelphia. From there, messages were telegraphed to New York. Although the telegraph is the main focus of this study, other indicators of growing objectivity surface in news reports of the Mexican War.

The *Picayune* was very much a regional paper covering an issue of both regional and national importance, and other newspapers, particu-

Objectivity and the Mexican War • *101*

larly those in New York, relied on the *Picayune* for information about the war. The *Picayune's* war coverage was more personal, more anecdotal, more linguistically rich than the *Herald's* because it relied on the unmediated reports of its own correspondents, George Wilkins Kendall and C.M. Haile, among others.[2] In addition to reporting breaking news, Kendall and Haile sent back long, discursive dispatches; some were about the effects of the war on the local inhabitants, some recounted stories about local customs, and occasional pieces were little more than travelogues. Their reports were often limited to specific events in specific locales, but their information contained great detail and depth.

By contrast, readers of the *New York Herald* learned of the war's events from a variety of sources — including Kendall and Haile secondhand — courtesy of the clipping exchange system.[3] New York editors were at the center of the country's information market and had available to them a wide range of news sources, mainly clipped stories from newspapers on the Gulf Coast, which were the first to receive news from the front. A battle in Mexico might be observed by correspondents for a half-dozen newspapers. Their accounts would flow back to their hometown papers, and from there to the New York papers. The *Herald* might pluck one or two of these accounts to run following the latest dispatch from the battlefield. Often the *Herald* also attached to the top of a clipped or telegraphed story a summary of reports from several sources, as the following excerpt, taken from 12 paragraphs total, illustrates:

> By the Southern mail yesterday afternoon, we received full files of the New Orleans papers to the first of May, inclusive. We give from our New Orleans papers, everything that relates to the state of affairs on the Rio Grande. It will be seen that the intelligence of the Mexican troops crossing the Rio Grande, was communicated verbally by the captain of a vessel, and that it was discredited by some of the papers in New Orleans.
>
> We also received from Philadelphia, at 10 o'clock, yesterday, a telegraphic despatch, with this news from the army on the Rio Grande, which immediately [was] published.[4]

In a sense, the news in New York regressed to the mean. The reader's understanding of events in Mexico presumably became an average of all accounts.

The *Herald's* composite accounts from a variety of sources provided a broader but less personal view of the war. New York editors during the Mexican War were not necessarily seeking greater objectivity in providing these balancing accounts of the war, but the effect was probably there. New Yorkers, by virtue of being at the center of the nation's information flow, were exposed to a wider view of the war from a greater number of sources. Editors were making choices in the Mexican

War, and individual reports were less important than they had been in the American Revolution. This composite of news — in our view, at least — probably served the diverse nation's nationalistic drive better than the more personalized journalism that ushered in the 19th century or characterized Revolutionary War coverage. Powerful voices are needed to give birth to a nation, but temperate, measured discourse is what holds a nation together.

The broader perspective brought by information abundance was offset by the attenuating effects of technology. With the arrival of the telegraph, attribution changed or was dropped. Detail and context were omitted, and opinion was stricken. On May 1, 1846, even before war had been officially declared, the *Picayune* ran a 730-word story headlined "LATER FROM THE ARMY! Col. Cross Murdered! — His Body Found!" The story made its way by ship to Mobile, Ala., and then north by horseback to Philadelphia, where it was telegraphed to the *New York Herald*. The *Herald* ran its 288-word account of the incident — clearly based on the *Picayune's* story — on May 9. It differs from the *Picayune* report in several respects. This difference is illustrated in the following two excerpts. The first is taken from the *Picayune's* story of May 1, which totaled 730 words. The second excerpt is from the *Herald's* telegraphic version of May 9, which had a total of 288 words.

The brig Apalachicola, Capt. Smith, arrived at this port yesterday from Brazos Bay, whence she sailed on the 24th ult., and reports that on the 22d she left Point Isabel, where Major Thomas, the acting Quarter Master, informed Capt. Smith that the body of Col. Cross had been found about four miles from Gen. Taylor's camp on the Rio Grande. From the wounds on the body it seems evident that he was killed by a lance.

It was further reported that a person in Matamoras had acknowledged that he was the murderer, and had the watch and clothing of Col. Cross in his possession.

Gen. Taylor, it is reported, had made a formal demand for the murderer....

We have just received from Philadelphia, the following Telegraphic despatch, with later news from the army on the Rio Grande.

Colonel Cross has been murdered, and his body found.

Three vessels have arrived at New Orleans, bringing later information from the army.

The body of Colonel Cross has been found about four miles from General Taylor's Camp. — From the wounds upon the body it appears he had been killed by a lance. Report says a man in Matamoras has acknowledged the deed.

Objectivity and the Mexican War • 103

General Taylor had made a formal demand for the murderer. The body was stripped, and in an advance state of decomposition.....

In the telegraphic version, the *Picayune's* attribution is dropped, the locus of the information shifts from Mexico to Philadelphia, and human sources are replaced by an inanimate electrical device, the telegraph. The telegraphic version of the story is also shorter by more than half. The telegraph story essentially is a rewrite of the original, and it consequently achieved greater economy of language. The telegraph message cut out much detail.

The *Herald's* version of the story omits the *Picayune's* references to rumors regarding the size of the Mexican force and the difficulty in determining the actual number (2,000). It leaves out an excerpt from an officer in Taylor's camp, who reports that the Americans "had not retired one foot from the bank of the river, nor does the General [Taylor] mean to do anything that can look like it.... Our flag waves over the waters of the Rio Grande, and we have a fixed battery of 18 pounders that can 'spot' anything in Matamoros." The telegraph story refrains from referring to the report of Colonel Cross' death as "melancholy news," as the *Picayune* does. Such news, among other factors, led President James K. Polk to ask Congress to declare war on Mexico.

The *Herald* used a similar "boiling down" process to condense Polk's May 11, 1846, call for a declaration of war. The original address to Congress — approximately 4,000 words — was reduced to a 413-word telegraphic message. The telegraphic version appeared in the *Herald* only hours after the president spoke, with the complete text of his speech running in the *Herald* on May 12. Aside from its brevity, the telegraphic report is notable for its absence of direct quotations and the way in which it coolly objectified the president's views. After a long paragraph in which it recounted Polk's version of the events leading up to the declaration, the dispatch, in an approach typical of modern objectivity, reported on the functional intent of the president's speech: to recommend a declaration of war and to call for volunteers. Here is the complete telegraphic version of Polk's address from the *Herald*:

We have received an important communication by the telegraph, announcing that the President sent a message to Congress, at 12 o'clock yesterday, in which he stated that all attempts to bring our relations with Mexico to a peaceable termination had failed, and announcing that the two countries were at war.

The president, in his message, after referring to the various injuries received at the hands of Mexico, recapitulates the efforts made during the past year to effect a settlement by negotiation, and also the recent occurrences on the Rio Grande. He states that previous to the appointment of Mr. Slidel, in October last, the inquiry was made — through our consul at Matamoras — whether a minister from the United States would be received by the Mexican government, and an affirmative answer given on the condition that the American naval force should be withdrawn from before Vera Cruz; that President Herrera was anxious to receive Mr. Slidel, but was prevented by the events of the day in Mexico; that on the accession of Paredes, Mr. Slidel was instructed to again present his credentials, which Paredes declined receiving; that Texas having in 1836 asserted the Rio del Norte as her boundary, the American army was ordered thither from Corpus Christi, because of the greater facilities there for obtaining supplies; that on the 12th ult. Gen. Ampudia notified the American General (Taylor) to retire from his position — which notification was repeated by Gen. Arista, on the 26th, with the addition that he considered hostilities commenced — and thence ensued the further difficulties already known to the public: that Gen. Taylor had made a requisition upon Louisiana and Texas for troops, and had also invoked the further aid of the General Government. The President concludes by recommending a declaration of war by Congress, and asks authority to call out a large body of volunteers for twelve months' service, and that appropriations be made for supplies, etc.

In the Senate, after the reading of the message, a spirited discussion ensued, in which Mr. Calhoun took an active part. He insisted that, according to the constitution of the United States, no war existed; that a collision had probably taken place; but that nothing short of a proclamation by Congress, to that effect, would put the two countries at war.

In the House, a bill authorising the President to raise volunteers, and making appropriations, was immediately introduced, and it was expected the question would be taken before adjournment.

Left out of the telegraphic message was Polk's more impassioned rhetoric — with references to "grievous wrongs," "outrage and extortion," "insults" and "patriotism" — that readers would have discovered only if they read the complete transcript the following day. Here are some selected excerpts from Polk's address:

The existing state of the relations between the United States and Mexico, renders it proper that I should bring the subject to the consideration of Congress. In my message at the commencement of your present session, the state of these relations, the causes which led to the suspension of diplomatic intercourse between the two countries in March, 1845, and the long-continued and unredressed wrongs and injuries committed by the Mexican Government on citizens of the United States in the person and property, were briefly set forth....

... The grievous wrongs perpetrated by Mexico upon our citizens throughout a long period of years remain unredressed, and solemn treaties, pledging her public faith for this redress, have been disregarded. A Government either unable or unwilling to enforce the execution of such treaties fails to perform one of its plainest duties.

Our commerce with Mexico has been almost annihilated.... [O]ur merchants have been deterred from prosecuting by the system of outrage and extortion.... Had we acted with vigor in repelling the insults and redressing the injuries inflicted by Mexico at the commencement, we should doubtless have escaped all the difficulties in which we are now involved....

... Mexico has passed the boundary of the United States, has invaded our territory and shed American blood upon the American soil....

... [W]e are called upon by every consideration of duty and patriotism, to vindicate, with decision, the honor, the rights, and the interests of our country.

In its speedy delivery of an abbreviated version of Polk's message, the telegraph rendered the slower, complete version less newsworthy. A great many readers knew all they needed to know from the telegraphic version of the story. Polk's complete address was old news. In this regard, the *Herald* competed with itself for timely news, and one way to win such a race was to eliminate the time lag by de-emphasizing old news. The *Herald* and other newspapers continued throughout the war to print the longer, discursive versions of articles that arrived after the telegraph dispatches, but these articles were typically tacked onto the end of more timely stories and were given less typographic emphasis. It was something like waves in the ocean, with a new wave passing smoothly over the old one as it slides back to sea, facts always content to ride over the froth of context and details.

The 19th-century news system, in objectifying news stories and reproducing them many times over via the wire services, may have had its greatest effect on journalism by turning the news into a commodity, a thing to be bought and sold. A commodity, by its nature, is objectified. It is stripped of its many qualities and boiled down to its essence so it may be easily traded, like corn or crude oil. A commodity can be categorized. It is gradable and portable, and it exists in sufficient quantity to support a market. By the 1840s, these features were becoming apparent to the front-line journalist. Daniel H. Craig, a pioneer of the wire services and a European correspondent for the *New York Herald*, col-

Commodity fetishism?

lected a bonus of $500 for each hour that his European dispatches preceded receipt of the same news by the *Herald's* New York competitors. Craig later declared that in earning his bonus he came to view news as nothing more than "a string of onions."[5]

Objectified, commodified news was often news without context. Stripped of surrounding cues, the news became inert. Objectivity turned the reader's attention to the event, focusing on the moment rather than the meaning. The race to be first with the news tended to objectify information by turning it into entertainment, something to be enjoyed momentarily, then discarded. Financially speaking, objectified news benefited the provider of the information more than the consumer. News that could be timed and counted was news that could be packaged and sold to ever larger, undifferentiated audiences that were becoming more important in the age of feedback. Objectified news also had the advantage of absolving newspapers of responsibility for their views. Readers could hold newspapers harmless because the newspapers added no value statements to their messages.

NOTES

[1] Tom Reilly, "The War Press of New Orleans," *Journalism History* 13: 3-4 (1986): 86-95; Susan Thompson, *The Penny Press* (Northport, Ala.: Vision Press, 2004), 128-9.

[2] Fayette Copeland, *Kendall of the Picayune* (Norman: University of Oklahoma Press, 1943).

[3] Richard Kielbowicz, *News in the Mail: The Press, Post Office, and Public Information, 1700-1860s* (New York: Greenwood Press, 1989).

[4] 10 May 1846.

[5] Menahem Blondheim, *News over the Wires: The Telegraph and the Flow of Public Information in America, 1844-1897* (Cambridge, Mass.: Harvard University Press, 1994).

CHAPTER 8

The Rise of Journalism's Scientific Mindset, 1832-1866

By David T.Z. Mindich

Between 1832 and 1866, the cultural landscape of the United States was transformed. Medicine, art, literature, the social sciences and journalism shifted during this period from a paradigm combining religion and philosophy to one of science. "The world has grown tired of preachers and sermons," wrote one late-19th-century observer. "[T]o-day it asks for facts." Another, the scientist and philosopher Herbert Spencer, wrote that "objective facts are ever impressing themselves upon us."[1] An example of the new "scientific" way of thinking was the evolving medical response to three New York City cholera epidemics, in 1832, 1849 and 1866. The responses in 1832 and 1849 were based on superstition, religious beliefs and random experimentation. By 1866, doctors relied on data gathering and the scientific method to combat the disease. This chapter examines objectivity as an outgrowth of the journalistic response to the epidemics and the relationship between science and journalism during this period.

Objectivity took a giant step toward its modern form in the middle of the 19th century with journalists' growing reverence for facts and the growing belief that the world was knowable and namable. That change in perspective reflected a shift from a mainly religious frame to one of science.[2] From the 1830s, which saw the birth of the nonpartisan penny press, to the 1860s, objectivity developed in steps: detachment and nonpartisanship in the antebellum period, the inverted pyramid during the Civil War and empiricism from roughly 1832 to 1866.[3]

This chapter begins by looking at the medical and journalistic response to the 1832 and 1849 cholera epidemics. Then, in the context of the journalistic response, it examines the abundant changes in American society and culture as a whole. Finally, it returns to cholera and shows how medicine and journalism dealt with the epidemic of 1866. Together, these changes reflected a new way of thinking, a new scientific approach shared by the medical and journalistic communities. While the medical response to the cholera epidemics has been discussed at length in historical literature, notably in *The Cholera Years*, by Charles

Rosenberg, the link between the cholera epidemics and journalism has never been explored.

Cholera first appeared in America on the dirty, pungent, impoverished streets of New York City in 1832. The first successful explosion of the penny press was also on these same streets, just about a year later. While contrived historical coincidences are frequently proposed, the confluence of cholera and journalism, from the birth of penny papers in New York City through the 1860s, was no coincidence. The spread of cholera across the United States, by rail, wagon and steamer, paralleled the spread of news by the same means. The disease, which is conveyed by drinking water polluted with human excreta, thrived in cramped cities. The penny papers also found a haven in the cities, where news, too, could be spread and consumed easily from door to door. By the 1860s, the medical profession, using scientific method, data gathering and technology, defeated cholera on the streets of New York City. Technology and science also helped to propel American journalism toward objectivity.

Cholera first came to New York in July 1832. Before it had abated in late August, more than 2,200 deaths had been reported, which means that more than 1 percent of New York's inhabitants had been killed in less than two months.[4]

The central belief of the medical profession, duly reported in the newspapers, was that the disease sprang from atmospheric conditions, rather than from contagion. This was based on a philosophical, not an empirical, view of the disease. According to Rosenberg, "'empiric' was — as it had been for generations — a synonym for quack." One doctor, for example, upon seeing a cluster of cholera cases, thought that only contagion could explain the outbreak, but because he could not reject other causes, he thought that it would be unphilosophical to accept the possibility of contagion.[5]

The newspaper coverage of the 1832 outbreak reflected the view that the atmosphere played the biggest role, but it also reflected a disregard for scientific method and logic. The *Courier and Enquirer* tried to calm readers' fears (often addressing merchants who might be scared to travel to New York) by discussing the atmosphere. Before the extent of the cholera epidemic was apparent, the *Courier and Enquirer* announced that the city would be spared. "The purity of the atmosphere — the beauty of the weather for several days past was never surpassed," explained the paper's editor, James Watson Webb, in an editorial.[6] Less than three weeks later, however, the paper took solace in a seemingly contradictory sign: "A very severe thunder storm passed over the city yesterday morning, which will, we hope, have the effect of purifying the atmosphere."[7]

While the *Courier and Enquirer* did not accept the possibility of contagion, the atmosphere was not the only cause discussed. Panicked New

Journalism's Scientific Mindset, 1832-1866 • 109

Yorkers wanted guidance in avoiding the disease, and the *Courier and Enquirer's* pages were filled with preventative advice. One doctor who had suffered from cholera himself, Dr. De Kay, wrote to the paper to warn of "excess in diet, exposure to night air; fear, anxiety, &c."[8] Other reports warned against cold feet ("keep on your flannels"), fruits and vegetables.[9] Cucumbers were constantly cited as culprits ("take care of *cucumbers"*), leading one skeptical doctor to call cucumbers "the 'mad dog' of all our fruits.... [N]one is more abused, more slandered."[10]

Perhaps even more than the *Courier and Enquirer* realized, its ideas of cause and cure were wrapped up in its religious notions of morality and its view of the sizable destitute population of New York. "Drunkeness [sic], intemperance, dissipation and all their attendent [sic] evils," wrote the *Courier and Enquirer*, "are so many inducements for cholera attacks.... Be temperate."[11] The newspaper's point of reference seemed to be biblical notions of plague. A lead story sounds almost like a line from Exodus: "This pestilence, which walketh in darkness, continues its ravages among us, and is daily sacrificing hundreds of victims to its unmitigated fury."[12]

If God is at the bottom of the cholera epidemic and God is just, the syllogism goes, his victims must be culpable. Authorities proposed a day of "fasting and humiliation," which the *Courier and Enquirer's* editorials heartily endorsed, to purge the city of its sins.

The *Courier and Enquirer* printed a series of cures, including one that advocated the immediate application "to the epigastric region 20 or 40 leeches according to the severity of the case."[13] "The means used for my recovery," wrote the evangelist Charles Finney in remembering his own experience with cholera, "gave my system a terrible shock, from which it took me long to recover."[14]

The city's next great cholera epidemic was in the summer of 1849, when it claimed more than 4,000 New Yorkers. The 1849 epidemic stood between those of 1832 and 1866, both temporally and in terms of the relative sophistication of the response, as an investigation of the *New York Herald* during the epidemic reveals.

From 1832 to 1849, many of the existing notions about the disease remained the same, including many of the ideas about the cause as well as the level of invasiveness in the cures. Rosenberg found that the atmosphere was still considered the big culprit in 1849, and the *Herald* bears this out. "The return of electricity to the atmosphere," wrote James Gordon Bennett, "has had on the whole, a favorable tendency."[15] Cases were still attributed to things like drunkenness, national background, filth, fruits, exposure to the sun and "offensive effluvia" from soap factories.[16] The biblical tone of 1832 was also present in 1849, with Bennett thanking Providence for a relatively short mortality list.[17] Also remaining from 1832 were the contradictions found in the newspaper columns. One week after cautioning readers about the relationship between cholera and alcohol, the *Herald* praised a cure of "laudanum [an opium tincture] ... camphor ... cayenne pepper ... ginger ... peppermint ... put into a quart of French brandy."[18] Still, in 1849, medicine shared with newspapers an inability to understand cholera's cause, prevention or cure; the news was still operating without the necessary facts it needed to help its readers make decisions.

Although it came too late to help the victims of the 1849 epidemic, the medical response to cholera was making gains in Europe. One London anesthetist, Dr. John Snow, had, in fact, discovered the cause of the disease and began publishing his findings in a British journal in 1849. Snow theorized correctly that cholera was spread through water contaminated by infected excreta. In 1849, Snow's theory was just one among many. In 1854, when a cholera epidemic hit London, he was able to prove his theory. Through extensive data gathering and analysis, the type of empirical research so suspect in 1832, Snow proved that the customers of the water company that received its water from the lower Thames, south of where London dumped its sewage, were at a much greater risk than the customers of the former.[19]

In 1849, U.S. doctors and journalists still had no notion of how cholera was transmitted. And as in 1832, the New York doctors did little but harm, with some of their more creative "cures" ranging from tobacco smoke enemas to electric shocks and immersion in ice water.[20]

An inchoate yet palpable respect for data and scientific inquiry is nonetheless apparent in the pages of the *Herald* during this time. It is no surprise that Bennett's *Herald* was highly critical of the medical profession (his *modus operandi* was unrelenting attack of everyone and anyone), but it is interesting that the focus of his criticism reflects a concern for empiricism and science. The *Herald* angrily presented evidence that not "a single ... physician or student of medicine had made his appearance at any of the cholera hospitals for the purpose of observing and investigating the disease."[21] Columns of statistics, with lists of everything from mortality rates to national origin and age of victims, and comparisons of the 1832 and 1849 epidemics, appeared regularly in the newspaper. There were even charts analyzing the correlation between the virulence of the disease and the average outdoor temperature, from which the *Herald* concluded that the statistics did not support a causal relationship.[22] This attempt to conduct scientific inquiry also reflected the paper's impatience with doctors for not finding a cure and for their indelicate experimentation: "The cholera is a most terrible infliction; but bad doctors and bad drugs are worse," one editorial announced.[23]

The mortality rate did not change significantly from the 1832 cholera epidemic to that of 1849. But in 1866, the medical response was able to cut the rate by 90 percent.[24] Paralleling this shift were fundamental changes in the way journalists practiced their craft, changes that were reflected in the coverage of the epidemics.

Journalism's Scientific Mindset, 1832-1866 • *111*

Changes in the practice of journalism took place in mid-century as newspapers became more of a mass medium. By the end of the Civil War in 1865, newspapers had seen monumental changes since their penny progenitors. In essence, urban papers had grown from small operations to large businesses with large staffs in various departments. The *Herald, Times* and *Tribune* went from four pages to eight every day, and they increasingly contained timely news from around the nation and Europe. Circulation boomed. Literacy reached 94 percent in the free states by 1860, and school enrollment went from fewer than 50 percent of the children in 1850 to 72 percent in 1860.[25] Simple innovations such as gaslight had profound consequences for people.[26] People also became increasingly confident about their doctors and the scientific and medical professions in general. The two greatest innovations of 19th-century surgery were born: anesthesia and antiseptics.[27]

At the same time, religion was being replaced in the minds of many by a reverence for empiricism. Some penny newspapers saw themselves as a part of this shift. "Books have had their day," Bennett's *Herald* screamed, "the temple of religion has had its day. A newspaper can be made to take the lead of all these in the great movements of human thought."[28] The content of newspapers was becoming more and more secular and factual. All the penny papers read in this study asserted their own nonpartisanship, factuality and accuracy, while few routinely asserted specific religious beliefs. The "dynamo," Henry Adams wrote at the turn of the century, had replaced the "Virgin" as the central metaphor for power.[29]

The middle of the 19th century saw not only the decline of the religious paradigm, but also the birth of "realism" as an artistic form. In 1839, Louis Daguerre discovered a way for images to be stored on metal plates. By 1850, the public was increasingly interested in what was seen as the "true" representation of life, and photographs were quickly replacing painted portraits as the preferred method of capturing reality.[30] If photography helped to bring an appreciation of "reality" to the United States, this was never more true than the photographic exhibitions of the Civil War, which, according to the *New York Times*, virtually "brought bodies and laid them in our door yards and along streets."[31]

During the middle of the 19th century, a new secular, empirical and scientific world view replaced religion and non-empirical philosophy in many areas of intellectual life, and had an effect on journalism. Darwin's *The Origin of Species*, a forceful argument for a scientific world view, was published in 1859. Karl Marx's scientific analysis of European society and politics reached American news consumers through the hundreds of articles and editorials he wrote during the 10 years (1852-1862) that he was employed by Horace Greeley as a European correspondent for the *New York Tribune*.[32] Herbert Spencer's attempt to draw sociology into the sciences, *Principles of Sociology*, did much to shape that profession; Spencer's work was discussed in newspapers and serialized in *Popular Science Monthly* (1874).[33]

Baconism, the belief that reality could be understood through the "collection, classification, and interpretation of facts," came to dominate the professions of sociology, political science and economics.[34] These changes in the social sciences paralleled the rise of objective notions in journalism: empiricism, data gathering and the scientific method. And the advent of the telegraph helped journalists and news consumers put a lasso around the believable world.

In 1835, a newspaper hoax about "man-bats" on the moon could still rouse a group of Ivy League scientists from their perch in New Haven; verifying or disproving it would take more than a month, as ships carried letters to and from London.[35] But by 1866, with the birth of the trans-Atlantic cable, the moon story's sources could have been checked and disproved in a matter of hours. The telegraph had extended what one historian has called the "awareness of the impossible."[36]

"What has become of space?" the *New York Herald* asked in 1844, the telegraph's first year. Providing its own answer, the paper announced that it had been "annihilated."[37] In 1844 the annihilation of space meant mainly a faster reporting of events. In the years that followed, however, space was annihilated by what a number of critics refer to as the commodification of news by the telegraph and the press wire services. With the founding of the Associated Press in 1848, Wolff in 1855 and the Reuters news service in 1858, a number of companies sought to market news as a salable commodity. James Carey wrote that telegraphic news demanded a "'scientific' language," stripping news of "the local, the regional and colloquial."[38] Other studies confirm this, and while the inverted pyramid form was not standard until the end of the century, researchers have discovered a decline of bias in news after the mid-19th century, especially in news sent over the wires.[39]

In the middle part of the century, in order to sell to newspapers of different political positions, the wire services had to repress partisan signals to produce a commodity palatable to all.[40] By the late spring of 1866 (the time of the next major cholera epidemic in New York), the wire services and newspapers had discarded much of their partisan flavor, as Lawrence Gobright, the Washington agent for the Associated Press, explained: "My despatches are sent to papers of all manner of politics, and the editors say they are able to make their own comments upon the facts which are sent to them.... I ... try to be truthful and impartial. My despatches are merely dry matters of fact and detail."[41]

Gobright's "dry" and bland gruel, without the spice and piquancy of partisan criticism and local dialect, had helped to produce a unified journalistic voice, a scientific voice and a faith that reporters could actually write to *everyone* and be understood by all.

Journalism's newly scientific approach can be seen in the coverage

Journalism's Scientific Mindset, 1832-1866 • *113*

of the cholera epidemic of 1866, when newspapers reported on the bureaucratic machine the city mobilized to muscle out the disease with science and technology. The Registrar of Vital Statistics put out statistics and corresponding charts, including the "New York Mortality Table," breaking down all diseases by deaths per week and ward, listing the sex, nativity and age of the victims.[42] Weekly reports of the Sanitary Police listed things like the number of outhouses cleaned. There were no mentions of the atmosphere — the officials may have been too busy to worry about the weather.

As it did during the Mexican War and especially the Civil War, the telegraph played a major role in the dissemination of information in the summer of 1866. The Atlantic Cable, completed at the height of the 1866 epidemic, brought cholera news from Europe, while in New York the cholera cases were reported to police precincts and then telegraphed to the Sanitary Superintendent, who in turn dispatched his Inspectors.[43] News reports of cholera were telegraphed from city to city and overseas as well.

If the organizing principle of the 1832 and 1849 newspapers' coverage of cholera was the atmosphere, God and sin, that of 1866 was much less lofty. It would not be too much to say that the newspapers' chief concern shifted from God and air to outhouses. Column after column in the three major New York dailies discussed, usually without the least mention of sin or God, the best ways to disinfect privies.[44] The *Times* reported that all doctors now agree that "the excreta, and especially the rice-water discharges of cholera patients are at least one means of propagating the cholera-poison and they urge ... disinfection ... of all privies, water-closets, and cess-pools connected with the sick."[45]

Rosenberg explained that arguments in medical journals based on philosophical arguments had given way to ones based on "statistics and disciplined observation."[46] That can be said of the newspapers as well, which resembled medical journals in their scientific language. In an article in the *Tribune*, a writer described the "pathognemonic [sic] characteristics of the disease": "Violent purging and vomiting, rice-water dejections, cold tongue, muscular cramps, and collapse,"[47] a description based on empirical evidence more than on religious notions. Similarly detailed and scientific were the descriptions of how to disinfect privies and clothing, with exact measurements of disinfecting agents provided for readers.

The attacks on doctors seen in newspapers in past epidemics were gone in 1866. In fact, the information that newspapers reported to the public came increasingly from doctors serving as designated sources of authority. Reporters got much of their news from organized and tightly controlled sources. "The records in the office of the Registrar of Vital Statistics show ...," began one report in the *Times*.[48]

Many of the shifts described in this chapter can be found in a single

FAIR AND BALANCED • *114*

paragraph, a lead of an inverted pyramid article in the *New York Tri-bune*: "The officers of the Board of Health, yesterday, took charge of the premises No. 14 Cherry St., thoroughly disinfected them and burned that portion of the clothing of the deceased, John Fitzgerald, which had been soiled by dejections during his illness."[49] The article conveys the organization of the medical community, an understanding of how cholera is conveyed and a concern not with religious issues, but with empirical investigation and concrete action to stop the spread of the disease.

Just as the transportation revolution was at the bottom of the spread of both journalism and cholera in New York in 1832, the epidemic of 1866 saw another confluence of forces: the first successful trans-Atlantic cable and New York's last major cholera epidemic. The ascendancy of science and the growing understanding that empiricism could be both possible and profitable were at the bottom of both developments. Once again, New York was frightened by the ships filled with cholera-stricken Europeans. But in 1866 doctors and journalists knew what to do, and the 90 percent decrease in mortality from 1849 to 1866 shows that the world had changed.

From 1832 to 1866, journalism and the wider culture had moved from a religious and philosophical paradigm to one of empiricism and the scientific method. More and more people, including journalists, had moved their gaze from the heavens to the privies, from the Virgin to the dynamo. The objective paradigm had advanced significantly, both in science and in journalism.

NOTES

[1] David Shi, *Facing Facts: Realism in American Thought and Culture, 1850-1920* (New York: Oxford University Press, 1995), 69.

[2] The best work on the change in perspective is Harlan Stensaas' *The Objective News Report: A Content Analysis of Selected U.S. Daily Newspapers for 1865 to 1954* (University Microfilms International, 1987). He concluded that the most important factor in the increase in objectivity during the period was "a basic shift in Western culture and thought which may be labeled 'Secularization.'"

[3] David T. Z. Mindich, *Just the Facts: How "Objectivity" Came to Define American Journalism* (New York: New York University Press, 1998).

[4] *Morning Courier and New-York Enquirer* (hereafter referred to as the *Courier and Enquirer*), 30 August 1832, p. 3; Charles Rosenberg, *The Cholera Years: The United States in 1832, 1849, and 1866*, (Chicago: University of Chicago Press, 1987), 90. In his *Memoirs of Rev. Charles G. Finney, Written By Himself* (New York: A.S. Barnes & Co., 1876), Finney, the evangelist, writes of seeing five hearses pull up at once, to five different doors on his street (p. 320).

[5] Rosenberg, *The Cholera Years*, 79.

[6] *Courier and Enquirer*, 7 July 1832, p. 2.

[7] Ibid., 26 July 1832, p. 2.

Journalism's Scientific Mindset, 1832-1866 • 115

[8] Ibid., 18 June 1832, p. 2.

[9] Ibid., 16 June 1832, p. 2.

[10] Ibid., 27 June 1832, p. 2.

[11] Ibid., 26 June 1832, p. 2.

[12] Ibid., 25 July 1832, p. 2.

[13] Ibid., 21 June 1832, p. 2.

[14] Finney, *Memoirs*, 320.

[15] *New York Herald*, 23 July 1849, p. 3.

[16] Ibid., 5 July 1849, p. 1; 10 July 1849, pp. 1 and 2; 15 July 1849, p. 3; and 17 July 1849, p. 3.

[17] After this report, however, the number of cholera deaths rose exponentially. *New York Herald*, 1 July 1849, p. 3.

[18] *New York Herald*, 15 July 1849, p. 2.

[19] John Snow, *Snow on Cholera, Being a Reprint of Two Papers by John Snow, M.D. Together With a Biographical Memoir By B.W. Richardson, M. D. and an Introduction By Wade Hampton Frost, M.D., Professor of Epidemiology, the Johns Hopkins School of Hygiene and Public Health* (New York: Commonwealth Fund, 1936), 63-75; Rosenberg, *The Cholera Years*, 193-4.

[20] Rosenberg, *The Cholera Years*, 152-3, 161. The homeopathic doctors were an exception to this, for while their cures did little good, they were not nearly as dangerous as the standard medical cures.

[21] *New York Herald*, 27 July 1849, p. 3; 8 August 1849.

[22] Ibid., 21 August 1849, p. 3.

[23] Ibid., 12 August 1849, p. 3.

[24] Rosenberg, *The Cholera Years*, 209.

[25] James M. McPherson, *Ordeal by Fire: the Civil War and Reconstruction* (New York: Knopf, 1982), 24; Charles Sellers, *The Market Revolution: Jacksonian America, 1815-1846* (New York: Oxford University Press, 1991), 369.

[26] Jack Larkin, *The Reshaping of Everyday Life: 1790-1840* (New York: Perennial Library, 1988), 142-3.

[27] Ira Rutkow, *Surgery: An Illustrated History* (St. Louis: Mosby-Year Book Inc., 1993), 321-35. The hospital was Massachusetts General.

[28] Quoted in Willard G. Bleyer, *Main Currents in the History of American Journalism* (New York: Houghton Mifflin, 1927), 191.

[29] Henry Adams, *The Education of Henry Adams*, Edited by Ernest Samuels (Boston: Houghton Mifflin, 1973), 379-90. Adams, writing in the third person, recalls visiting the Great Exposition of 1900 in Paris, where he stood before huge steam and electric engines: "to Adams the dynamo became a symbol of infinity. As he grew accustomed to the great gallery of machines, he began to feel the forty-foot dynamos as a moral force, much as the early Christians felt the Cross. The planet itself seemed less impressive, in its old-fashioned deliberate, annual or daily revolution, than this huge wheel, revolving within arm's length at some vertiginous speed....Before the end, one began to pray to it" (p. 380).

[30] Michael J. Carlebach, *The Origins of Photojournalism in America* (Washington, D.C.: 1992).

[31] *New York Times*, 20 October 1862, p. 3.

[32] Janet E. Steele, *The Sun Shines for All: Journalism and Ideology in the Life of*

Charles A. Dana (New York: University of Syracuse, 1993), 35; J. Herbert Alt-schull, *Agents of Power: The Role of the News Media in Human Affairs* (New York: Longman, 1984), 90-7; Robert C. Tucker, ed., *The Marx-Engels Reader* (New York: W. W. Norton, 1978), 294-300.

[33] Mary O. Furner, *Advocacy and Objectivity: A Crisis in the Professionalization of American Social Science, 1865-1905* (Lexington, Ky: University Press of Kentucky, 1975), 32.

[34] Ibid., xii, 14 and 35.

[35] In 1818 a trans-Atlantic crossing was a least 22 days. In 1838, steamships began making the voyage; and one, in 1839, made the trip in thirteen days. Mitchell Stephens, *A History of News* (New York: Viking, 1988), 226. In the *New York Times*, the "Atlantic cable" was announced 30 July 1866, p. 1.

[36] Lucien Febvre, quoted in Stephens, *A History of News*, 126. Stephens argues that literacy and printing had been limiting monsters and make-believe since at least the 1400s. Walter Lippmann's introduction to his seminal *Public Opinion* contains an interesting discussion of a tangential, yet related topic: the relationship between "the world outside and the pictures in our heads." In this section of his book, Lippmann discusses the fate of a group of island-bound Europeans at the start of the First World War who did not yet know that they were enemies at war. "There was a time for each man when he was still adjusted to an environment that no longer existed." (p. 3).

[37] Stephens, *A History of News*, 226.

[38] James Carey, "Technology and Ideology: The Case of the Telegraph," *Prospects* 8 (1982): 310. Carey also discusses the emergence of "Standard Time" in the 1870s, which sought to replace the local, erratic times with a system that divided the country, and later the world, into time zones, yet another example of the submergence of the local.

[39] See especially Donald L. Shaw, "News Bias and the Telegraph: a Study of Historical Change," *Journalism Quarterly* 44 (Spring 1967): 5-11.

[40] Stephens, *A History of News*, 259; Carey, "Technology and Ideology...," 302-25.

[41] United States House of Representatives, Judiciary Committee, "Telegraphic Censorship," 37th Congress, 2nd Session: Report 64. 20 March 1862, 1-14.

[42] *New York Times*, 8 August 1866, p. 3; 1 August 1866, p. 3; 9 August 1866, p. 3; 2 June 1866, p. 6.

[43] Rosenberg, *The Cholera Years*, 206; *New York Tribune*, 2 July 1866, p. 3.

[44] Rosenberg, *The Cholera Years*, 230. The *New York Times'* coverage seems more secular and less subjective than that of the *Tribune* and *Herald*, which often tried to deny the severity of the epidemic (*New York Tribune*, 10 August 1866, p. 5). The *Herald* even went so far as to suggest that any coverage of the epidemic was alarmist (*Tribune*, 4 August 1866, p. 3; *New York Herald*, 1 July 1866, p. 3).

[45] *New York Times*, 1 July 1866, p. 3. In *The Cholera Years*, Rosenberg explains that by 1866, "few intelligent physicians ... doubted contagion" (p. 195).

[46] Rosenberg, *The Cholera Years*, 198.

[47] *New York Tribune*, 2 July 1866, p. 3.

[48] *New York Times*, 8 August 1866, p. 3.

[49] *New York Tribune*, 1 June 1866, p. 3.

CHAPTER 9

Objectivity During a Clash of Titans, 1883-1915

By Elliot King

In many ways, the period from 1883 through the first two decades of the 20th century represents the second great revolution in American journalism. Although mass newspapers embraced some of the values typically associated with "objectivity," such as accuracy and truthfulness, they had not shed their political character. News columns were not always filled with neutral, evenhanded reporting of newsworthy events, but with reporting designed to achieve specific political or social ends. The nascent value of journalistic objectivity was in competition with another important value of journalism: that the press had the duty to be politically active, to lead popular opinion, to originate causes and to achieve political ends.

In the same way as the *New York Herald* and the *New York Sun* achieved exponential gains in circulation in the 1830s, newspapers in the 1880s and 1890s, led by the *New York World* and *New York Journal*, also increased their circulations by a factor of 10. Moreover, the number of pages printed daily expanded significantly, as specialized sections for sports, material of interest to women, comics and other information were added. The layout and presentation of the newspaper changed as banner headlines with bold type came into vogue. Newspapers became an increasingly effective advertising medium, particularly for retailers, and advertising consequently became an increasing important revenue stream. Moreover, in size, scope, appearance and reach, newspapers at the end of the 19th century were very similar to newspapers of today.

By the 1880s, American journalism recognized the principle that newspapers should be impartial, balanced and factual. They did not always achieve such an ideal, especially in political matters, but by the 1860s the journalistic mindset leaned toward what later came to be known as "objectivity." Toward the end of the 19th century, though, newspapers — far from retreating from a partisan approach to the coverage of politics — in some ways became more involved and more politically aggressive than before. The major newspapers were closely identified with major political parties. They routinely crusaded to accomplish political goals and routinely attacked politicians from the opposing political party, accusing them of corruption. As news reporting became a more important aspect of newspapers, the attacks on political opponents moved from Page 4, which was usually the place where editors expressed their opinions, to the news columns and headlines on Page 1.

Why did newspapers maintain their involvement with partisan political activities even as they pursued larger readerships? Editors and publishers believed that it was the role of newspapers to be politically involved. Leading public opinion; safeguarding the public welfare, serving as the public's watchdog and protecting party principles were central elements in the mission of newspapers at that time. Editors and publishers thought that it was their role to give expression to the voice of the people and to lead, not follow, public opinion.[1] Newspapers that were not politically active were seen as derelict in their duties. Theodore Roosevelt observed that the editor "wields great influence; and he cannot escape the responsibility of it." In short, as Michael McGerr writes in *The Decline of Popular Politics*, publishers and editors did not want to run away from their politics; they embraced them.[2]

The notion of objectivity in journalism — that is, among other things, the idea that news reporting should be neutral, nonpartisan, balanced and evenhanded — competed with the value of political engagement. Editors and publishers around 1900 conceived of journalism as a combination of partisanship, accuracy and truthfulness. They tried to achieve their political objectives through "crusades," coverage of political controversies, and the presentation of the news. Newspapers' political allegiances determined how they handled all of these practices.

It is convenient to mark the beginning of the second revolution in American journalism with Joseph Pulitzer's purchase of the *New York World* in 1883. Pulitzer set the rhetorical tone for the period. Even though he relinquished his hands-on control of the *World* in the early 1890s, he was still the most admired journalist of the era as late as the 1930s. And Pulitzer was very clear about what he believed was the mission of a newspaper. The *World*, noted James Barrett, a former managing editor, was not just a newspaper, but a public institution that was committed to fighting for progress and reform. Pulitzer believed that the domain of the journalist was not only gathering and distributing news, but also the advancement and promotion of the public welfare. In 1884, shortly after Grover Cleveland's election, Pulitzer proclaimed, "The *World* is as great a public trust as the presidency."[3]

Journalism's job, Pulitzer argued, was to lead. Its mission was to supply society with the ammunition to fight its seven deadly enemies: inaccurate information, injustice, special privilege, corruption, public plunder, demagoguery and inertia. After blindness forced him to give up day-to-day operating control of the *World*, the main question Pulitzer asked was in what ways was the *World* promoting progress and reform, combating injustice and corruption, stimulating public opinion and defending the public welfare. His main concern was to prevent the editors at the *World* from becoming satisfied with merely printing the news.[4]

Other publishers and editors echoed Pulitzer's sentiments. The *World's* primary competitor was the *New York Journal* under the leadership of William Randolph Hearst, who argued that "whatever is right can be achieved by an awakened and informed public opinion." Newspapers should not inquire whether a thing can be done but determine whether it should be done, he contended, and then, through the exertion of focused publicity, public opinion will see that it is done.[5] Hearst's right-hand man, Arthur Brisbane, defended so-called "yellow journalism," the sensational journalism of this period that is often seen by scholars as a nadir of sorts in American journalism because of its lack of objectivity. He said, "Yellow journalism is war, war against hypocrisy, war against class privilege and war against the foolishness of the crowd that will not think and not use the weapon that it holds — the invincible ballot."[6]

Indeed, looking back, many observers of journalism disapprovingly argue that the sensationalism of the *Journal* and others pushed the United States into the Spanish-American War in 1898. In a typical observation, Edwin Emery wrote:

> Certainly the excesses of yellow journalism and the reflections of the doings of the most guilty of the newspapers in the other press of the country, played an important part in the country's decision to go to war.... The situation was one in which journalist excesses and outright war propaganda could be effective... enough newspapers were willing to provide the alleged justification for the war to come.[7]

The accuracy of that assessment is in doubt.[8] But Hearst himself was proud of the *Journal's* behavior. In the middle of the conflict, the *Journal* crowed, "How do you like the *Journal's* war now?"[9] Hearst asserted that the force of the newspaper was the greatest force in civilization. Under the republican form of government, he observed, newspapers form and express public opinion, suggest and control legislation, and declare wars. In fact, he added, newspapers control the nation because they represent the people.

Pulitzer and Hearst were expressing widely held views of the time. Milton McRae of the Scripps McRae chain recounted that he had bought a newspaper in Columbus, Ohio, after a local minister convinced him that journalists had more power to serve common people than did ministers from their pulpits. McRae also asserted that the Scripps family's greatest contribution to journalism was the training of young men in the ideals of public service, as exemplified by journalism. E.W. Scripps himself said that he had only one journalistic principle: to make it harder for the rich to grow richer and easier for the poor to keep from growing poorer. When William Nelson, a bridge builder, bought the *Kansas City Star*, he said that he had bought the newspaper not to make money, but to serve his community.[10] Clearly, newspapers were seen as great actors on the public stage. Reporters, editors and publishers had the same responsibility as preachers and politicians to shape society according to their vision of progress.

On the other hand, the newspapers that abandoned an active role in politics were open to criticism. In 1923, for example, Oswald Garrison Villard, a former editor of the *New York Post* and editor of the *Nation*, harshly chided the *New York Times* and the *New York Herald Tribune* for being so committed to the status quo that they could no longer claim to be the originator of causes. Villard linked their abdication of the role of championing causes to a general subordination among newspapers of "journalistic public service to sordid money making." He blasted the *New York Times* and its publisher, Adolph Ochs, for not crusading for political ends. He wrote, "Those seeking a better world knocked in vain at Ochs' door." Women, land and tax reformers, and even Jews were turned away, he wrote, noting Ochs's refusal to publish a report of a pogrom in Poland, even though the *Times* accepted the report as an advertisement. Though Ochs claimed to be impartial, Villard maintained that impartiality was not independence. The *Times* was a class journal (meaning it catered to the upper class), Villard argued, and "no journal exceeded it in disseminating falsehoods, misrepresentations and half truths." Nor could the *Times* claim to be an originator of causes, he said.[11]

Others also saw the *Times's* refusal to play a more dynamic role in public life as a failing of the newspaper, not a strength. The writer Silas Bent said: "When Mr. Ochs bought the *Times*, its only claim to fame was that, a half century before, it had helped to crush the corrupt Tweed ring in Tammany. It has never exposed nor crushed any corruption since Mr. Ochs took charge." Bent argued that if a newspaper was not willing to fight corruption and champion unpopular views, it was not entitled to First Amendment protection.[12]

How could editors and publishers shape public opinion? The very politically oriented editors and publishers were fierce advocates of accuracy, fairness and completeness. They contended that these values did not contradict a commitment to partisan activity, but rather supported it. Indeed, even Hearst, the epitome of the partisan newspaper proprietor, issued instructions to all his newspapers to be fair and impartial in the news columns and to give unbiased coverage of all creeds and parties. Moreover, looking back at the success of the *Journal* in the first years of his ownership, Hearst argued that the paper had gained readers at the rate it had because "the news is reliable and delivered with dispatch."[13]

Pulitzer and Hearst demanded accurate information because it strengthened the effect of editorials on public opinion. Strong arguments relied on accurate information. If the news was wrong, the independence and integrity of the newspaper would be compromised. This was one of the reasons that Pulitzer set up his Bureau of Accuracy and Fair Play.[14]

With this twin commitment to accuracy and political aims, crusading journalism — reporting geared toward achieving a specific political goal — moved to the front page starting in the 1880s. As E.W. Scripps, the proprietor of one of the first newspaper chains, told Will Irwin, a leading reporter: "The headlines are our editorials. Give me the right hand column front page and I won't care what they put on the editorial page."[15]

The insight that the front page was more powerful than the inside editorial page was clear to observers as early as 1881, when Charles Dudley Warner pointed out that editors expected to form public opinion not so much by their arguments as by the news they chose to present. He might have added that how editors and publishers chose to present the news was significant as well. The most dramatic example of the new form of presentation came in the days before the election of 1884, when Pulitzer spread an eight-column illustration of the "Feast of Belshazzar," denouncing a fund-raiser for the Republican candidate for president of the United States, James Blaine, across the front page of the *World*.[16]

While the editorial page continued to be significant, it was not nearly as significant as the front news section. But the amount of space devoted to politics in general grew in proportion to the growth of the newspaper.[17] And the news columns became the tool that editors used to achieve their political ends and to attack their political foes.

Crusading was one vehicle by which newspapers attempted to achieve political ends through news reporting. In a crusade, a newspaper would latch onto a particular political issue and attempt to achieve a specific political outcome. The newspapers of William Randolph Hearst regularly crusaded to achieve political ends.[18] Soon after he assumed control of the *San Francisco Examiner* from his father in the middle of the 1880s, Hearst began to attack the major political force in California, the railroads. He also attacked the party bosses rewriting the San Francisco city charter and the local water companies. Municipal utilities were a favorite target of Hearst's. In 1899, the *Journal* fought the Ramapo Water Company's effort to control New York City's water supply, and in the summer of 1900, Hearst attacked the so-called ice trust, which was formed when several ice companies merged to form the American Ice Company. The *New York Journal* revealed that Robert Van Wyck, the first mayor of Greater New York, and his brother held $400,000 in stock in the American Ice Company. Hearst applied to the New York State attorney general and others to have it dissolved as a threat to the life and health of the residents of the city. Eventually, in part because of Hearst's pressure, New York City was forced to cancel its contracts with the company. In 1899, Hearst won an injunction preventing the Board of Aldermen from giving the Nassau Railroad the right of way to 40 miles of streets, a deal that would have cost the city $10 million.

The *New York World* was also an aggressive crusader. Among its most notable efforts was the revelation that a commission created by the State Legislature to supervise the installation of underground telephone and telegraph wires was to be paid for by the telegraph company itself. It also opposed the high cost of milk, demanded city fire protection for tenement dwellers and agitated for a public parks program and against substandard housing.[19] In 1905, the *World* exposed corruption in the insurance industry.[20] The crusade began on Feb. 12, when a *World* reporter, David Ferguson, wrote an article detailing an internal squabble between the president and vice president of the Equitable Life Insurance Company. The president, James Alexander, was ready to retire but did not want to turn the company over to the vice president, James Hyde — the son of the founder — who was mainly known as a socialite. The company had only $100,000 in capital stock, but it controlled assets worth $500 million. Hyde's control of the stock gave him control of the company. Alexander wanted to "mutualize" the company and give the right to vote for directors to the policyholders.[21] The squabble revealed the double-dealing rife at the company. For example, one board member, Jacob Schiff, was also a director of the firm of Kuhn, Loeb, which had sold $22 million in bonds to the Equitable, which was called the largest financial institution in the country. In the deal, Schiff was potentially both the buyer and the seller of the bonds, though he denied any wrongdoing.[22]

Eventually, the *World* called for an investigation of the entire insurance industry. The governor of New York responded by asking the State Superintendent of Insurance to investigate. The *World* printed a leaked report of the investigation, and eventually a State Senate committee was appointed. Charles Evans Hughes served as counsel. Throughout the committee's work, David Ferguson was at Hughes's elbow, and a series of laws regulating the activities of insurance companies was eventually passed.

These crusades should not be mistaken for good-government, nonpartisan campaigns. Politically oriented crusades should be seen in sharp contrast to the do-gooder social service campaigns that newspapers also conducted.[23] In most political crusades, newspapers attacked politicians from the opposing political party (or from a different wing of their own party). Newspapers from the same party or faction often did not join in the attack, or defended those being criticized. As significantly, political crusades were conducted in the news columns as com-

A Clash of Titans, 1883-1915 • 123

binations of news and commentary. The success of a crusade depended on accurate reporting, but crusades were carried out to achieve specific political ends.

While crusades are the most obvious example of how newspapers used news for political purposes, newspapers also reported the same news differently. The particular slant was influenced by the papers' political orientations and leanings. The difference is epitomized in the coverage of the gas trust and a franchise bill in New York City in December 1896 and the investigation of William Lorimer in Chicago in 1910. Neither of these events is remembered in the annals of journalism as major turning points. Instead, these stories should be read as typical business-as-usual examples of reporting.

By 1896, the question of whether municipalities should own their own utility companies had long been on the public agenda. Many cities around the country had already moved to municipal ownership.[24] On Dec. 5 and 6, 1896, the *New York Journal* began what it called a crusade for cheaper gas in New York City. Offering a detailed analysis of the operations of the Consolidated Gas Company — which represented several companies providing gas to New York City and which Hearst described as the gas trust — the *Journal* argued that New Yorkers should pay no more than $1 per 1,000 cubic feet of gas. On the following Wednesday, the City Board of Alderman met and took two actions. They established a committee to investigate the possibilities of municipal ownership of the gas company. And they awarded a franchise for the provision of gas to a company called the Consumer Fuel, Gas, Heat and Power Company. The *Journal* claimed that the aldermen had acted in response to its pressure.[25]

The following day, the *Journal* ran an analysis of the franchise just awarded. It noted that the Consumer Fuel Company had just been organized and was not yet registered in the appropriate business registries. Nobody knew who the real principals behind the company were. Moreover, the city would receive only a franchise fee of $15,000 and 30 cents per foot for pipeline laid. In return, the company was supposed to deliver gas for 40 cents per 1,000 cubic feet and invest $50,000 annually in pipelines. But, the *Journal* noted, the fine print of the franchise did not require the company to build new lines. Nor did the award require the company to provide more expensive illuminating gas. It had to provide only lower-grade cooking and heating gas. If it leased existing lines, Consumer Fuel could reap rich financial rewards. Moreover, if it chose, the company could sell its sweetheart franchise to another party at a profit — a franchise that the president of the Board of Aldermen argued was worth $10 million. The *Journal* cried foul.[26]

At that point, the *Journal* swung into action. Trumpeting that "While others talk, the *Journal* acts," it filed suit to win an injunction prohibiting the awarding of the franchise.[27] When the injunction was granted and the Board of Aldermen indicated that it would retract the bill rather than attempt to override a veto from the mayor, the *Journal* boasted that the aldermen had "yielded to the *Journal*." The newspaper printed on its first page the front page of the suit it had filed and the front page of the court order. The *Journal* claimed that it had won a great victory against an effort to bilk the city out of a franchise worth $10 million.[28]

The mayor of New York City was from the reform wing of the Republican Party, having been elected on a good-government ticket in 1894. The Board of Aldermen was dominated as well by Republicans, though not reformers. The *Journal* was a fiercely Democratic paper and played the story as a contest in which the Democratic *Journal* was defending the public interest against the board. But the story appeared very differently in the pages of the *New York Post*, a newspaper associated with the reform wing of the Republican Party, and the *New York Tribune*, a mainstream Republican newspaper.

The *Post* started coverage of the gas trust on Dec. 8, when it noted deep inside the newspaper that the Board of Aldermen had established a committee to investigate municipal ownership of the gas utilities.[29] The next day, it reported that Mayor William L. Strong, the reform mayor, planned to veto the bill awarding the franchise to the Consumer Fuel Company and that the corporation counsel, the city's lawyer, had issued an opinion that awarding the franchise was beyond the authority of the Board of Aldermen. It also noted that the award had "given rise to talk about boodle,"[30] the common word for corruption. On Dec. 11, the *Post* reported that the mayor had asked the corporation counsel to get an injunction against the award; it noted that although the mayor planned to veto the bill, the board might have enough votes to override the veto. If the injunction was denied, the newspaper added, the mayor planned to prohibit the commissioner of public works from issuing the necessary permits.[31] On Dec. 12, in a Page 1 article, the *Post* observed that although the Consumer Fuel Company was of "doubtful" origin, many of the people associated with it were respectable. It also printed a spirited defense of the current administration's success in improving municipal services, compared with the corrupt regime that had preceded it. On Dec. 14, also on Page 1, the *Post* reported that the bill had been recalled and that its proponents had "backed away from Mayor Strong's proposed veto." In this version of events, the *Journal* had played no role whatsoever; the reform mayor, who was supported by the *Post*, had taken the lead in defending the public interest.

The *New York Tribune*, a mainstream Republican newspaper whose publisher was the Republican candidate for the vice presidency of the United States in 1892, had yet a different view and a different way to report these events. Largely uninterested in the whole affair, in an editorial on Dec. 9 the newspaper opined that while the gas companies

A Clash of Titans, 1883-1915 • 125

could undoubtedly sell gas more inexpensively than they were, it was not clear that municipal ownership would be better. The city should wait for the committee authorized by the Board of Aldermen, a committee led by a regular Republican who would soon be named district attorney, to investigate the issue and report.[32] The *Tribune* did not mention that the mayor had vetoed the franchise award to Consumer Fuel until Dec. 11, when it included that information at the bottom of a long article on Page 4 describing the views of the chairman of the newly established municipal gas committee. The next day, the *Tribune* argued that while the aldermen had perhaps not been acting in the public interest when they had awarded the franchise to Consumer Fuel, perhaps they had been. The investigation by the municipal gas committee would reveal the truth.[33] The story never made the front page of the *Tribune*. It was as if nothing very newsworthy had happened.

These kinds of sharp differences in view and presentation were common. Newspapers that were aligned with one party attacked politicians either from an opposing party or from a different faction of their own party, typically accusing them of corruption or criticizing them to achieve specific political aims. In an example from 1910, the Republican *Chicago Tribune* accused Democratic state lawmakers in Illinois of being bribed to appoint William Lorimer as a United States senator.[34]

At first glance, this episode appears to support that idea that newspapers were "objective." After all, Lorimer was a Republican, and the *Tribune* had long been associated with the Republican Party. It can be better understood, however, as a demonstration of the complexity of the political landscape. Lorimer had risen from being a streetcar conductor to becoming a Republican Party boss, and he was a prime enemy of the *Tribune*, which was associated with a competing wing of the party.[35] The *Tribune* and the equally Republican *Chicago Daily News* had clashed with Lorimer on a wide range of issues. The *Daily News* described him as an "enemy of good popular government."[36] Lorimer, in turn, accused both the *Daily News* and the *Tribune* of not paying their property taxes and bilking the school fund.[37]

Lorimer was elected to the U.S. Senate on the 95th ballot with Democratic support after five months of deadlock and deliberation. The *Tribune's* reporting on the incident started on April 10, 1910, when a legislator confessed in its pages to accepting a bribe in exchange for his support of Lorimer. He also accused the Democratic leader of the Legislature with heading up the bribery operation.[38] Later the *Chicago Record Herald* reported that the general manager of the International Harvester company admitted that he had been asked for a contribution of $10,000 to a $100,000 fund to ensure Lorimer's election. He also revealed the names of other members of the bribery committee. The word was that a juror had been bribed. The *Tribune* offered $5,000 for evidence that would lead to the conviction of the conspirators.

Under this public pressure, the U.S. Senate opened its own investigation and on July 14, 1912, voted to unseat Lorimer. The *Tribune* saw the expulsion as its vindication. Lorimer saw his expulsion as the evidence of the power of his political enemies — Lawson, Stone, McCormick, Patterson, Noyes and Hearst, all editors and publishers of major newspapers — to sway public opinion.[39] While Chicago Republican reform newspapers and the Democratic newspapers did attack Lorimer, the *Chicago Inter Ocean*, the regular Republican newspaper, supported him until the end.

According to the general notions about the development of the press, overtly partisan activities would seem to have been counterproductive in the years from 1883 to 1915. After all, the newspaper business became much more competitive, and hundreds of new newspapers were established to compete for millions of new readers. In 1880 there were between 843 and 971 daily newspapers in the United States. By 1909, there were 2,400 to 2,600 daily newspapers, about 600 to 800 more than exist now. In 1880, there were approximately 3.5 million daily newspaper readers. By 1919, that number had soared to 33 million.[40]

To attract as many readers as possible, newspapers, according to the conventional wisdom, should have been as inclusive as possible. Newspapers that supported the Democratic Party could not expect to attract Republican readers, and vice versa. Consequently, business imperatives would dictate that newspapers should tone down their political involvement. In short, they should have become evenhanded and politically neutral.

This was not the case, however. Neither publishers nor editors saw a contradiction between partisan political activity and large circulations. To the contrary, they saw political activity as complementary to large circulations, and large circulations were desirable because they increased a newspaper's social and political influence as well as its financial independence. And the publishers and editors thought that such large circulations could be built through vigorous political activity.

The most articulate proponent of this viewpoint was Joseph Pulitzer. To be of real value and of real service to the public, Pulitzer argued, a newspaper must have a large circulation for two reasons. First, with a large circulation, its news and comments would reach a wide audience. Second, a large circulation would help attract advertising, which would lead to the increased revenue that would in turn mean even greater independence.[41]

Pulitzer believed that the circulation growth of the *World* depended not only on the quality of the front page but also on Page 4 — the editorial page — as well. He told his private secretary that the *World* owed its success "not only to its news... but to its principles and convictions." In 1884, as the circulation of the *World* grew, Pulitzer credited its principles as much as its news and features for its success. He used the *World*

A Clash of Titans, 1883-1915 • *127*

to sell his politics, and he believed that his politics sold the *World*.[42]

Pulitzer's great rival, William Randolph Hearst, attributed the immediate success of the *New York Journal* to its enterprising efforts to gather news, its top-rate editorial staff and its outspokenness "in its opinions, taking the side of the public interest as against special interests, such as those of the trusts." Later, Oswald Villard would assert that editorials had commercial value by showing that a newspaper was put out by people with brains. Thousands of people read the *Boston Globe* for the editorials of Uncle Dudley, he asserted, although they did not like the rest of the newspaper.[43]

The publishers were not fooling themselves with that perspective. Newspaper performance indicates that papers made huge circulation gains when they found themselves in the heat of political battle. Although Hearst's business manager suggested that it would be financial suicide for him to support William Jennings Bryan in 1896, since Free Silver, one of Bryan's primary positions, was unpopular in New York, and Hearst himself believed that he had little to gain and everything to lose by a Bryan endorsement, it turned out that the opposite was true. From Oct. 13 to Oct. 27, 1896, the *Journal* gained 90,495 readers; and on Election Day it sold more than 1.5 million newspapers, a figure unheard of in journalism until that point. That figure included sales of the *Morning Journal*, the *Evening Journal* and a German-language version of the *Journal* that Hearst had inherited.[44]

The results were even more dramatic during the crisis leading up to the Spanish-American War. From Jan. 9, 1898, to Feb. 18, 1898, the average daily sales of the *Journal* soared from 416,885 to 1,036,140. As Commodore George Dewey approached Manila Bay, the circulation of the *Journal* reached 1.6 million on May 2, 1898.[45] In 1900, when Hearst started up the *Chicago American* to support Bryan's second run for the presidency, he immediately built a circulation of 300,000, setting off a fierce and often violent circulation war with other established newspapers.[46]

Hearst was not the only publisher who profited by politics. In fact, the hotter the political controversy, the better the sales. In 1896, when the *New York Post*, whose circulation seldom topped the 20,000 mark, published a pamphlet of its editorials attacking the Democratic platform, it sold nearly two million copies. Of the 10 days when the *New York Sun* had its top circulation numbers, eight were linked to elections.[47] The inescapable conclusion is that partisan political activity helped newspapers gain readers.

But economic benefits were only one reason newspapers remained politically committed. More important, publishers, editors and reporters remained politically active because that is what they felt they were supposed to do. A newspaper was considered to be a public trust that had the responsibility to lead public opinion. To discharge those re-

The conversion factor? Did NPs feel that accurate info would change minds, gain partisans?

sponsibilities, newspapers had to be partisan champions.

The record indicates that in the period from 1883 to 1915, newspapers were fully engaged in partisan political activity. Leading newspapers actively crusaded for the political goals they supported. They undertook these activities unhesitatingly and with enthusiasm, often bragging about their involvement and their successes. The editors and publishers who dominated journalism from 1883 to 1915 believed that it was the role of newspapers to fight corruption, to lead public opinion and to fight to implement their political values. Political involvement was business as usual because editors and publishers believed that political involvement was within the mission of their newspapers. In fact, political activity was at the center of that mission.

In addition, based on circulation figures, it appears that readers shared that point of view. The greatest leaps in circulation came when newspapers were intensely involved in heated political campaigns. Partisan politics was good for business. While partisan, newspapers had the power to fight party bosses. They could carve out their own power bases within the fragmented political structure of the time.

In contemporary journalism, the notion of objectivity has the idea of nonpartisan reporting embedded within it. But other values now associated with "objectivity" — such as accuracy and truthfulness — were significant in the period from 1883 to 1915. The reason they were important, however, was that accurate and truthful reporting made partisan political reporting more effective.

NOTES

[1] W. A. Swanberg, *Citizen Hearst* (New York: Bantam Books, 1963), 120.

[2] James Pollard, *The Presidents and the Press,* (New York: MacMillan, 1947), 594; Michael McGerr, *The Decline of Popular Politics* (New York: Oxford University Press, 1987), 110.

[3] James Barrett, *The End of the World* (New York: Bobbs Merrill, 1931), XIV, 96.

[4] Ibid., XIII, 121.

[5] Roy Littlefield III, *William Randolph Hearst and His Role in American Progressivism* (Landham, Md.: University Press of America, 1980), 44.

[6] Michael E. McGerr, *The Decline of Popular Politics: The American North, 1865-1928* (paperback ed.; Oxford University Press, 2002), 127.

[7] Edwin Emery, *The Press and America: An Interpretative History* (Englewood Cliffs, N.J.: Prentice Hall, 1962), 431.

[8] W. Joseph Campbell's *Yellow Journalism: Puncturing the Myths, Defining the Legacies* (Westport, Conn.: Greenwood Press, 2001) debunks several prominent myths of the yellow press, including its impact on starting the war.

[9] *New York Journal,* 8 May 1898, p. 1.

[10] Milton McRae, *40 Years in Newspaperdom* (New York: Brentano's, 1924), 33-4, 207; Oliver Knight, ed., *Scripps, I Protest* (Madison: University of Wiscon-

sin Press, 1966), 271; Oswald G. Villard, *Some Newspapers and Newspapermen* (New York: Alfred A. Knopf, 1923), 213.

[11] Villard, ibid., 11; James L. Baughman, *Henry Luce and the Rise of the American News Media* (Boston: Twayne Publishers, 1987), 56.

[12] Silas Bent, *Strange Bedfellows* (New York: Horace Liveright, 1927), 247, 249.

[13] Ibid., 41; *New York Journal*, 28 September 1897, p. 3.

[14] Littlefield, *William Randolph Hearst...*, 14.

[15] Will Irwin, *The Making of A Reporter* (New York: G.P. Putnam's Sons), 165.

[16] *New York World*, 30 October 1884.

[17] In a typical four-page newspaper, in addition to political reporting and political commentary on Page 4, there was an eclectic mix of business, foreign and local events and literary articles. Straight domestic political coverage did not represent more than about 25 to 35 percent of the total mix, which is similar to the percentage it represents today.

[18] The material on Hearst is drawn from Swanberg, *Citizen Hearst*, 29, 56; and Littlefield, *William Randolph Hearst...*, 5-6, 63-71.

[19] McGerr, *The Decline of Popular Politics*, 125; George Juergens, *Joseph Pulitzer and the New York World* (Princeton N.J.: Princeton University Press), 280; Littlefield, *William Randolph Hearst...*, 10.

[20] The characterization comes from Alfred M. Lee, *The Daily Newspaper in America* (New York: Macmillan, 1937), 645. The story is drawn from Barrett, *The End of the World*, 196-203.

[18] *New York World*, 13 February 1905, p. 1.

[22] *New York World*, 15 February 1905, p. 1.

[23] The social service crusades in the next two paragraphs are culled from Barrett, *The End of the World*, 78; Alfred Lee, *The Daily Newspaper in America*, 633; James M. Lee, *The History of American Journalism*, (Garden City, N.Y.: Garden City Publishing Co. 1917), 357; Swanberg, *Citizen Hearst*, 121; Elmer Davis, *A History of the New York Times* (New York: New York Times Co., 1921), 340.

[24] *New York Journal*, 19 December 1896, p. 8; 20 December 1896, p. 10.

[25] *New York Journal*, 9 December 1896, p. 1.

[24] *New York Journal*, 10 December 1896, p. 1; 11 December 1896, pp. 7, 11.

[27] *New York Journal*, 13 December 1896, p. 1.

[28] *New York Journal*, 16 December 1896, p. 1.

[29] *New York Post*, 8 December 1896, p. 9.

[30] *New York Post*, 9 December 1896, p. 3.

[31] Ibid.

[32] *New York Tribune*, 9 December 1896, p. 5.

[33] *New York Tribune*, 12 December 1896, p. 6.

[34] This story comes from Lloyd Wendt, *Chicago Tribune: The Rise of a Great Newspaper* (Chicago: Rand McNally, 1979), 368-70.

[35] Joel Arthur Tarr, *A Study in Boss Politics: William Lorimer of Chicago* (Urbana: University of Illinois Press, 1971).

[36] *Chicago Daily News*, 14 July 1912, p. 4.

[37] *Chicago Daily News*, 11 July 1912, p. 1.

[38] Associated Press in *Chicago Daily News*, 8 July 1912, p. 3.

[39] *Chicago Daily News*, 11 July 1912, p. 3.

40 Alfred Lee, *The Daily Newspaper in America* , 717-27.

41 Juergens, *Joseph Pulitzer and the New York World*, 16.

42 Ibid., 50; McGerr, *The Decline of Popular Politics*, 110.

43 Quoted in Willard Bleyer, *Main Currents in the History of American Journalism* (Boston: Houghton Mifflin, 1927), 362; Villard, *Some Newspapers and Newspapermen*, 104.

44 Littlefield, *William Randolph Hearst...*, 34.

45 This is based on the *Journal's* own reporting. When circulation began to climb, Hearst would publish the previous day's circulation figures.

46 Swanberg, *Citizen Hearst*, 236; Wendt, *Chicago Tribune*, 353.

47 Allan Nevins, *The Evening Post: A Century of Journalism* (1922; New York: Russell and Russell, 1986), 501; Edward P. Mitchell, *Memoirs of an Editor* (New York: Charles Scribners Sons, 1924).

PART III

The 20th and 21st Centuries: What's in a Name?
By Randall Patnode, Donald L. Shaw and Steven R. Knowlton

In the 20th century, journalists began thinking of what they did as a profession, and started using the term "objectivity" when talking about professional standards. While education and professional associations gave the profession more cohesion and encouraged adherence to high standards, it faced new pressures — from more sophisticated advertising and new business models for journalism, from politicians who found ways to manipulate the press, and from great moral crusades and social movements. The certainty that once came with the term objectivity gave way to doubts and ambivalence as critics attacked the term's underpinnings, pointing out that it is impossible not to bring one's own background and experiences to the reporting or editing of a story and that such psychological baggage is sure to subtly undermine the most conscientious journalist's attempt to be objective. In response, many journalists stopped using the term *objectivity*, but maintained adherence to its synonyms: fairness, balance, evenhandedness. The modern journalist recognizes that while the individual will never be objective, in the sense of being a blank slate, a journalist can and should aspire to objectivity in professional work, and that an awareness of one's own predispositions helps one ward off bias and come close to attaining the goal of objectivity. So even as journalism has been transformed by new technologies, with the development of broadcasting in the 20th century and the arrival of the Internet near the end of the century, the concept of objectivity remains an ideal.

If yellow journalism in the preceding era showed some signs of becoming objective, but never truly did, then the muckrakers who came shortly afterward were perhaps more objective than they are generally thought to have been. Facts demonstrated their power in the first decade of the 20th century when Ida Tarbell's study of John D. Rockefeller revealed the details of how one could grasp power, and Lincoln Steffens used documents and interviews to show how some American cities were corrupted.

By the early 1920s, Walter Lippmann's talent in journalism surfaced in his book *Public Opinion*, shortly to be followed by *The Phantom Public*.[1] In these books Lippmann identified the power of the press to spotlight issues, and he expressed serious reservations about the ability of members of the public to sort out facts by themselves. In Chapter 11 of this book, Barbara Kelly presents a forceful argument that objectivity became the cornerstone of journalism during this period. It served as one of the dominant journalistic paradigms of the era. Journalists, like social scientists, began to approach their work in a self-consciously objective fashion. They assumed that facts could be separated from opinion, as was true in science. Practitioners of many social sciences borrowed the techniques of bench science in the post-World War I years, and journalists did, too. The world of the 1920s was a bewildering place. The government was vastly more complex than it had been a generation before — the muckrakers who had cried for reform had done their work well. Freud had convinced the world that the human mind was not nearly the ultimate rational machine that the Enlightenment had described, and the new business of press-agentry had made it even less likely that everything was what it seemed. The best solution possible, Lippmann and many others argued, was reliance on the best evidence to form logical conclusions: fact-based thinking.

This faith in facts was reflected in journalism education. Leon Nelson Flint wrote one of the first book-length studies of journalistic ethics,[2] while Sigma Delta Chi in the 1920s adopted a code of ethics that emphasized facts over opinion.

But within a generation — and, as a closer examinatiion will reveal, even sooner than that — there appeared a counterargument. In the 1930s, Professor Curtis MacDougall wrote the first journalism text that used interpretative journalism in the title, suggesting that facts alone were not enough.[3] Immediately after World War II, the famous Hutchins Commission on Freedom of the Press ignited a debate about objectivity and fairness when it argued that the press had a positive obligation not only to provide a full account of the day's events, but to also put those events "in a context which gives them meaning." Facts alone — even undisputed facts, even facts based on the best evidence — were not enough. That debate has continued to the present, when many observers argue that objectivity is a goal that is impossible to achieve. Many audience members are not as willing to accept the objective findings of journalists compared with that of other scientists because they know too much about the topic, or they think they do.

The journalists who carefully select and balance the news, using neutral word choices and professional standards, are as objective as any other social scientists. In different contexts, both John Milton and John Stuart Mill said the truth would emerge, not from a single voice, but from different arguments colliding. To bring that emerging truth to *objectivity vs. economics*

Part III: The 20th and 21st Centuries • *133*

fruition requires the audience to do something that is beyond the control of journalists: to listen, to watch and to read widely, and to reason conscientiously.

•••

The Chapters Ahead

In *Chapter 10*, Bruce Evensen argues that Progressive-era muckraking was hardly as antithetical to objectivity as so many contemporary critics have assumed. Muckrakers, rooted in the Enlightenment belief that rational audiences could be trusted with political information, held that democratic republicanism was possible only when journalists gave readers the news they needed to know so they could make informed judgments in their personal and public lives. The journalistic passion to personalize the predicaments of society's most vulnerable was a strategy the muckrakers used to arouse action by the private citizen and the public agency. The moral force of these writers came from the descriptive, not the prescriptive, aspects of their writing. That made their inquiry an ally, not an enemy, of objectivity.

Objectivity had become entrenched as a journalistic standard by 1920, Barbara Kelly writes in *Chapter 11*. In the period between the two world wars, the industrialization of the newspaper business speeded up. At the same time, journalists increasingly began to demand greater respect for themselves and their craft. Their attempt to claim professional status used the same approach as those practiced by the other service occupations: academic standards, a code of ethics, formal associations and peer review. These steps were a corrective reaction, as journalists disassociated themselves from the sensational and narrative style that had gone before.

The next three chapters deal with topics that stretch across broad periods, looking at the issue of objectivity in light of the effects of market research and advertising, the development of academic journalism education, and the advent of broadcasting.

Adding to the mix in the early years of the 20th century was a new phenomenon driven neither by partisan advocacy nor by the idealism of enlightened democracy, but rather by advertising. Mass-market advertisers wanted reliable information, not only on how many readers a magazine had, but, more important and far more difficult to ascertain, on who those readers were — on their tastes, what they wanted, how much money they had to spend and which goods and services they were most likely to spend it on. In *Chapter 12*, Douglas Ward examines this often-overlooked area of journalism in the early 20th century. On the advertising side, he focuses on the Curtis Publishing Company, publisher of the *Saturday Evening Post* and a major innovator in readership surveys. And on the editorial side, he introduces a young graduate student named George Gallup, who refined some of these emerging techniques and applied them to the editorial side for the purpose of helping editors give readers what they wanted.

Journalism developed its own specialized literature and curriculum within the university in the first half of the 20th century. *Chapter 13*, by Maurine Beasley and Joseph Mirando, examines the growth of the scientific method as it pertains to journalistic objectivity primarily through the vehicle of university journalism programs and college textbooks. Although nearly 100 years old now, admonitions by these textbook authors to report facts, not opinions, are as timely as ever. The major players in this period include Joseph Pulitzer, who demanded objectivity as an essential ingredient in his new School of Journalism at Columbia University (as well as in the Pulitzer Prizes), and the last editor of Pulitzer's *World*, Walter Lippmann.

In *Chapter 14*, Lynn Boyd Hinds examines the early decades of broadcast journalism. It was credibility, not objectivity per se, he argues, that was the goal of broadcast journalism in its formative decades. This credibility was built upon three pillars, all evocative of the dimensions of the proto-objectivity initially made in Chapter 1: firsthand accounts, factual reporting and the earned reputation of the reporter. Objectivity played a dual role, Professor Hinds argues. First, it served to assure radio reporters that they were, indeed, journalists, just like their counterparts in print, because the journalistic objectivity preached by Lippmann, Pulitzer and others had become a core value by the late 1920s and early 1930s. Second, appeals to objectivity also functioned to keep news free from external constraints from both the federal government and commercial advertisers. Objectivity was a defense against the federal government, as each radio station cited objective news as proof to the Federal Communications Commission that its broadcasts were in the "public interest, convenience and necessity" when each six-month-license renewal time rolled around. Advertisers, who generally exerted great control over entertainment programming, were less able to control news programs' content by appeals to the neutrality of fact-based, objective reporting. With the advent of television just after World War II, radio news reporters moved into television, bringing that tradition to the new medium. The eyewitness of moving pictures was added to the actuality of sound, and who could argue with objectivity when the eye could plainly see?

The idea that Senator Joseph McCarthy effectively showed the fatal flaws of journalistic objectivity during the "red scare" of the 1950s has become widely accepted. In *Chapter 15*, David Davies explains that, indeed, the simplest forms of just-the-facts journalism were wholly inadequate to deal with a master manipulator like Tailgunner Joe (as McCarthy was commonly known, in reference to his — almost wholly

Part III: The 20th and 21st Centuries • 135

specious, as it turns out — military service during World War II). Both from within the profession and from the outside, interpretation and analysis were seen as essential replacements for he-said-she-said-go-figure reporting. But responding to McCarthy — at least as we see it now — was the easy adjustment for the practice of journalistic objectivity to make in the 1950s. The really hard job, Professor Davies argues, was to figure out how to cover the civil rights movement.

The momentum building against objectivity gained speed in the tumultuous years of the 1960s, all but killing off the venerable goal. In *Chapter 16*, Steven R. Knowlton explores several major social and political changes — the escalation of the civil rights movement, the morass of government lies during the cold war and Vietnam War, and the calamitous end of the Nixon administration in Watergate — and finds that interpretative reporting made major inroads into quality journalism, even into the journalism that still called itself objective. Then the postmodernists in the universities all but ridiculed out of existence what was left of the concept of objectivity. Journalism based exclusively on the official record is gone for the foreseeable future, but the basics of factual and contextual accuracy, appropriate sourcing and the elimination of personal opinion remain central to many, and perhaps most, working professionals.

NOTES

[1] Walter Lippmann, *Public Opinion* (New York: Harcourt, Brace, 1922) and *The Phantom Public* (New York: Harcourt, Brace, 1925).

[2] Nelson Flint, *The Conscience of the Newspaper: A Case Book in the Principles and Problems of Journalism* (New York: D. Appleton, 1925).

[3] Curtis MacDougall, *Interpretative Reporting* (New York: Macmillan, 1963).

CHAPTER 10

Progressivism, Muckraking and Objectivity

By Bruce J. Evensen

Muckrakers would not have shared the certainty of postmodernists that truth is a delusion. Their determination to impose morality on the political and social landscape was grounded in the conviction that the truth was their weapon in uncovering wrongdoing and that the public, when made aware of what was wrong, would do the right thing. To be sure, muckrakers had their opinions about what the right thing was. To read Ida Tarbell's *History of the Standard Oil Company* or Lincoln Steffens' *The Shame of the Cities*, for example, a century after they first appeared as a series of articles in *McClure's* magazine, the leading muckraking magazine of its day, is to encounter finely crafted arguments for corporate and municipal reform. But what really commands the reader's attention is the writers' faith in the power of facts to move audiences to action when those facts were told in a compelling way.

Ida Tarbell saw herself as an historian. From the start of her pathbreaking work on John D. Rockefeller and the Standard Oil Trust, she sought to "make sure of the documents in the case."[1] Rockefeller was worth nearly 1/35th of the U.S. gross national product, $35 billion, when Tarbell and her research associate, John Siddall, began their work of identifying the "sly tricks and privilege" that he had used to corner the nation's oil supplies. What she had in mind, she told Siddall, was "a narrative history of the Standard Oil Company" that would be drawn "almost entirely from original sources." She did not intend for her investigation to be controversial, she said, but she did want her articles on the oil trust to be as "picturesque and dramatic" as the facts allowed.[2]

Tarbell had grown up in the Western Pennsylvania oil fields and knew firsthand the "force and fraud" Standard had used in gaining unfair advantage over competitors.[3] Siddall was a well-connected associate editor of the *Chautauquan*, based in Cleveland; his brother was an attorney for the Rockefeller family. Tarbell and Siddall built their case slowly, beginning with the November 1902 issue of *McClure's*. It began with the story of Tarbell's father, Franklin, a God-fearing farmer and teacher turned river pilot and joiner in the Erie County, Pa., oil boom of

Progressivism, Muckraking and Objectivity • 137

the 1870s. He made his money by making and selling huge wooden tanks that could hold a hundred barrels of oil or more. But in early 1872, Tarbell and other independent oilmen of Titusville met their match in the South Improvement Company. Articles in the December 1903 and February 1904 issues of *McClure's* outlined the secret complicity of the railroads in a rebate scheme hatched by Rockefeller's South Improvement to eliminate the competition of independents. When rail rates to ship oil doubled, Franklin Tarbell took to torching Rockefeller's oil cars. Ida Tarbell's work proved no less incendiary. In May 1911, the Supreme Court ordered the breakup of the Standard Oil Company. That ruling followed the publication of Tarbell's *History of the Standard Oil Company*, which had a 232-page appendix, laying out Rockefeller's criminal practices. Tarbell had hoped that Rockefeller himself would be imprisoned, but he was not, although his reputation was damaged enough that Rockefeller hired Ivy Lee, a former reporter, to patch up his image through the new profession of public relations. For her part, Tarbell had demonstrated that America's democratic institutions would not permit the "contamination of commerce." Rockefeller's public chastening, in her mind, was a triumph of dogged detective work. It would set a standard for the many muckrakers who would follow.[4]

Tarbell's co-worker and close friend at *McClure's*, Lincoln Steffens, began his introduction to *The Shame of the Cities* by reminding readers that he had not written a book but had simply collected six magazine articles he had published on municipal corruption. "Done as journalism, they are journalism still," he insisted.[5] The admonition, he was convinced, had the moral force of facts behind it. "Look out for editorializing," Steffens, a veteran newspaperman, had warned his colleagues at *McClure's*. Taking a position was easy, he said, but it "doesn't count without the facts."[6] His review of bribes, privilege and condoned criminality in St. Louis, Minneapolis, Pittsburgh, Philadelphia, Chicago and New York is a dramatic telling of how "shameless citizens" had engaged in corruption that the civic-minded had an obligation to stop. "The misgovernment of the American people," Steffens argued, "is misgovernment by the American people."[7]

"Tweed Days in St. Louis," published in the October 1902 *McClure's*, and "The Shame of Minneapolis," published three months later, were meticulously researched articles that underscored the necessity, as well as the precariousness, of self-government. "I never exaggerated," Steffens observed. "Every one of those articles was an understatement." He noted that "each article seemed to astonish other cities," but readers living in the cities he reported on, people "who knew what there was to know expressed surprise that I reported so little."[8] Steffens' exhaustive analysis of urban America led him to conclude reluctantly that "the law-abiding backbones of our society, in city after city, start out for moral reform, but turn back" when they see it will cost them something. His analysis of city management led to his early advocacy of civil service reform, vice-law enforcement, nonpartisan local elections and businesslike local government.[9]

Steffens' work convinced him that the task was not to replace "bad men" with "good men," but to work for economic and electoral reform that would prevent the perpetuation of a government of privilege.[10] The bribery that fueled big city machines, he found, "was not an occasional offense, but a common practice" and one that risked transforming the democratic marketplace to "an oligarchy of special interests." He made no pretensions about the science of his inquiry. "I am not a scientist," he told readers. "I am a journalist." Scientists might "gather with indifference all the facts and arrange them patiently for permanent preservation and laboratory analysis." While scientists might be neutral in their findings, Steffens and other muckraking journalists harnessed evidence — facts — to agitate for reform. For Steffens, that meant documenting "how easily the people are fooled, how cheaply they are bought, how dearly sold, and how easily intimidated."[11]

Steffens had been brought to *McClure's* as an editor after 14 years in the newsrooms of New York's *Evening Post* and *Commercial-Advertiser*, where he had served as city editor. But S.S. McClure, the Ulster-born entrepreneur who launched his magazine in 1893, quickly saw that his editor needed an editor. He thought that Steffens would do better to report more and admonish less. He urged him to "write up things as they are" and avoid "bending facts." Blaming municipal corruption "on public cowardice didn't get to the real cause of the trouble," McClure told Steffens. Moving multitudes to change the law and to insist that it be enforced, McClure said, required facts and lots of them. So he sent Steffens back to St. Louis and on to Minneapolis to write more balanced sequels to his earlier work. Steffens later admitted, "We had a pretty hot fight and McClure won." He was prepared to write that "democracy had failed and what we needed was a good dictator." Instead, his fact-filled article, appearing under the title "The Shamelessness of St. Louis" in the March 1903 *McClure's*, received the backing of the local press and led to a citizens movement that created the momentum for municipal reform. "Following the facts bore fruit," McClure asserted. "Faith in the honesty of the majority is justified."[12]

The January 1903 edition of *McClure's* contained an installment of Tarbell's attack on the Standard Oil Trust, Steffens' analysis of municipal graft in Minneapolis and Ray Stannard Baker's examination of unfair labor practices and the right to work. It represented well McClure's self-conscious assault on "the American contempt of law." It cost the magazine $4,000 to reveal the secret history of Standard Oil and $2,000 to uncover the shame of Minneapolis. The cash-starved magazine, despite a circulation of nearly half a million, could have done other articles for less. But few stories, in McClure's mind, were as satisfying. The final

Progressivism, Muckraking and Objectivity • 139

generation of the 19th century had seen a doubling of the U.S. population, a tripling of the number of urban residents and the rise of the billion-dollar corporation and the big-city political machine. "The protection of those who cannot protect themselves," McClure believed, was "the whole function of government." But when government failed to do its job, the muckrakers would do theirs. That was the "overwhelming passion" McClure felt "to fight for those unable to fight for themselves" so each individual could achieve "moral self-respect."[13]

McClure's concept of the just society and journalism's unique role in bringing it into being has been described by Vincent Blasi as the "checking value" in First Amendment theory. As government power increased, Blasi argued, so must the power of the press to affirm "fair play for the dispossessed." In Blasi's view, "the countervailing power of the press in a modern democratic state" challenged the government's control over information and, in so doing, made informed consent and self-government possible.[14] The model emphasizes the value of news over views in the battle of "competing social and individual interests" and posits the press, not government, as having the central role in communicating the information one needs to know in living a public and private life.[15] McClure's assertion that an aggressive press was needed to combat government power "that operated to benefit some at the expense of others" is echoed in Blasi's point that absent the watchdog role of the press, "there is no concentrated force to check government misconduct" and the harm it may cause to private parties.[16]

The formula muckrakers found to awaken readers to their communal responsibilities often involved identifying a problem by humanizing its consequences. Those responsible were cited, a call to action was demanded and a just society was invoked as a standard of amelioration.[17] When embraced by *Collier's, Leslie's, Everybody's, Pearson's, Cosmopolitan, Hampton's, Success* and even *Ladies' Home Journal* in the first years of the 20th century, the strategy became a way to attack trusts and high finance, fight for municipal and electoral reform, curb the corruption of special interests, end many abuses of children, feed the poor and desperate, protect the nation's food and drug supply, and wage war against the sweatshop, the slum, vice and overcrowded prisons.

McClure's decision to document racial intolerance, first by Carl Schurz in January 1904, and then by Ray Stannard Baker a year after that, may not have gone as far as later critics would have liked in critiquing the spread and stain of disfranchisement laws,[18] but contemporaries saw their efforts as important. Booker T. Washington thought Schurz's summary "the strongest and most statesmanlike word that has been said on the subject of the South and the Negro for a long number of years,"[19] and President Theodore Roosevelt thought Baker's reporting of two Southern lynchings "far and away the best discussion of lynching that I have seen anywhere."[20] Schurz was recruited by Mc-

Clure to write "Can the South Solve the Negro Problem?" following his four decades of commitment to the African-American cause, a commitment that had begun during Reconstruction, when Schurz was a commissioner for the Freedmen's Bureau.[21] Baker's study was guided by an abiding commitment "to let light and air in" so "the people will understand and work toward reform."[22]

Baker's spirit of public service had first been evoked by his father and then by the evangelist William T. Stead. Baker was convinced that a career in journalism would be a way to fight the powers of "bossism" and "venality" that had encouraged "the wretched conditions which have become the American way of life."[23] In a series of articles appearing first in *McClure's* and *American Magazine* and then as a book, Baker carefully chronicled the fear and rumors that led to the Atlanta race riots of 1906 and the color line that had been erected through Jim Crow laws. Baker's narrative was composed of a series of vignettes that reflected his keen powers of observation.

Baker wrote of a night porter who was bound over to trial in an Atlanta courtroom after defending himself in a fight with two plainclothes policemen who "thought he looked suspicious." Despite witnesses who testified that the porter's version of events was accurate, the judge lectured him nonetheless: "You mustn't attack white men." Baker cited how a white man and a light-skinned African-American woman had been arrested for living as man and wife. Their three children were grown. One was in college. The father made good wages as a telephone operator. The charge was adultery. "You can't marry under Georgia law," the judge told the couple as he set the trial date. In another case, a white complainant said, "This nigger insulted me!" The defendant denied it, but the judge fined the black man anyway and lectured him, "You mustn't insult white people."[24]

Baker traced the incarceration rates of whites and blacks in the South and described how sawmill operators, brickyard owners and large-scale farmers benefited from convict labor. He found that the "good old boy" network connected magistrates to mayors and bankers to businessmen, each profiting from the chain gang. The corrupt courts, a lack of educational and economic opportunities, and degrading housing and living conditions had created hopelessness. Young African-Americans "show the bleary eyes and the unsteady nerves of cocaine or morphine poisoning," he wrote in *Following the Color Line* as he described their descent into crime. The origin of such vice, he wrote, was racism, codified into law. "The Peachtree people know how to treat Negroes. The Negro is inferior and must be made to keep his place," a Southern white explained to Baker. "Give him a chance and he assumes social equality. The Anglo-Saxon will never stand for that."[25]

When Baker's series appeared in *American Magazine*, he pointed out that he was not in the business of offering solutions to social problems

Progressivism, Muckraking and Objectivity • 141

but was trying to present "a picture of conditions as they were" for Southern Negroes. That was because the calling of the muckraker, in his eyes, was not argument but illumination. "My job is to see as straight as it lies in me to do," he wrote. Only by giving everyone a hearing could he hope to understand the people he wrote about. This kind of writing required inordinate patience, sensitivity and attention to detail.[26] Baker shared an optimism present in many muckrakers. In his private notebooks, he wrote that "good, after all, finally wins over evil." He believed that readers would do the right thing when given the facts. The struggles of the marginalized and the powerless would not be resolved in the triumph of the powerful, but in the demand of the enlightened masses to end social inequities. That was why the responsibility of muckrakers was to help readers develop a "social conscience" that would eventually ensure that no individual or group would be left behind in America's spiritual and material progress.[27]

"The power of the fact is the mightiest lever of this or any day," observed Jacob Riis toward the close of a marvelous muckraking career that powerfully brought the misery of the poor to the attention of Americans.[28] The publication of *How the Other Half Lives* in 1890 and *The Children of the Poor* two years later made Riis, a veteran police reporter, the undisputed chronicler of tenement conditions in industrializing America. Riis' immersion in his subject enabled him to document "the fearfully hopeless odds" against the many "sleepless mothers who walk the streets in the gray of the early dawn, trying to stir a cooling breeze to fan the brow of a sick baby," or the many men and women "who roll off roofs and window sills while asleep" rather than burn in the "fiery furnace" of a hundred thousand suffocating homes.[29]

New York City had more than a million immigrants at the turn of the 20th century, and "spending time on the job" was Riis' way of communicating their cause.[30] Riis considered journalism to be "the highest and noblest of all callings" because of its capacity to publicize patterns of injustice and motivate readers to do something. Informed public opinion, he became convinced, was the only way of defeating those who preyed upon society's most vulnerable.[31] His years of poverty in the Mulberry Street slums, combined with 14 years as a police reporter for the *New York Tribune*, made him a witness to life in the back alleys of big city "dumping grounds," where the well-to-do gawked with "their mouths opening wide with wonder" at the spectacle of it all.[32]

"The reporter who is behind the scenes," Riis observed, "speaks more eloquently to the minds of thousands than the sermon preached in church on Sunday." He saw as his task to go beyond "the foulness and the reek of blood" and catch "the human drift of it." The rare journalist who could do that "performs a signal service" by requiring each reader to take responsibility for the social conditions of ghetto life.[33] "A false prophet in our day could do less harm than a careless reporter," Riis claimed in his introduction to *The Children of the Poor*. That was because Americans demanded "facts, not theories" in their newspapers.[34] That was why he supplemented his narrative with halftone photographs. The first one was published in the *New York Sun* on Feb. 12, 1888, and still others in December 1889 in *Scribner's Magazine*. Thirty-nine halftones and line engravings were included in *How the Other Half Lives*, including the unforgettable claustrophobia of Gotham Court, the shanties of Hell's Kitchen and Sebastopol, the desolation of Blindman's and Mullin's Alleys, the bleak terror of Bandit's Roost, and the dispiriting sickness along Baxter Street and Bone Alley. Riis described Bohemian cigar makers at work, the "twelve-year-old boys who pull threads" for a meager living, the women at their stations in the Division Street necktie workshop, the gravediggers at Potters Field and the "dock rats" hunted by police under a pier at the foot of Jackson Street.

Even in these wretched surroundings, Riis found hope. His pictures revealed two smiling women sewing in an Elizabeth Street doorway. Newsboys washed after work in their lodging house. Riis wrote of a "slow-going honest English coal-heaver," living in a one-room house above a murder scene at the North River docks, his "pleasant-faced" wife of "cheerful lightheartedness" and "two bright and pretty girls" doing the best they could on $5 a week.[35] Helping these poor, Riis concluded, was not the duty of a few fair-minded philanthropists but of a municipal government spurred to action by a caring populace. The only way to bridge the widening gap between the classes, Riis believed, was "a bridge founded upon justice and built of human hearts."[36]

"I have aimed to tell the truth as I saw it," Riis wrote at the end of *How the Other Half Lives*. Theodore Roosevelt found Riis' work "an enlightenment and an inspiration." Urban historians saw it paving the way for the passage of the New York Tenement House Law of 1901, a model of Newsletter enterprise in behalf of the poor.[37] Riis' intense preoccupation with the real, combined with his statistical and photographic summary of the situation, created a response in readers that even he could not have predicted. "If our theory of government is worth anything," Riis observed, it might make "war correspondents" of those reporters who entered the underside of the city.[38]

A majority of the muckrakers were quite prepared to accept a rehabilitated capitalism as a result of their investigations. They trusted an enraged citizenry to force reform. However, even in the case of the period's best-known Socialist muckrakers, Upton Sinclair and Charles Edward Russell, the appeal for action was rooted in evidence. Sinclair's summary of working conditions in Chicago's stockyards, chronicled in *The Jungle*, followed six weeks of arduous fieldwork. "I would sit in the homes of packing-house workers at night and talk with them," Sinclair said. "I would see them at work. I studied every detail of their lives. I talked to their families and their bosses, with superintendents, night-

Progressivism, Muckraking and Objectivity • 143

watchmen, saloon keepers, and policemen, with doctors and lawyers and merchants and clergymen and settlement-workers." The goal was to make *The Jungle* "as authoritative as a statistical compilation."[39]

Sinclair's detective work, appearing in the weekly Socialist paper *Appeal to Reason*, described in excruciating detail "the meat that tumbled out on the floor, in the dirt and sawdust, where the workers had trampled and spit uncounted billions of consumption germs." Meat was stored "in great piles and the water from leaky roofs would drip over it, and thousands of rats would race about on it." Because the rats were nuisances, the packers "would put out poisoned bread for them," meaning that "rats, bread, and meat would go into the hoppers together."[40]

Sinclair warned that his tale of sausage-making in Chicago was "no fairy tale and no joke." Government investigators agreed. Their probe of the nation's food supply, prompted by Sinclair's study and the furor it generated, substantiated his findings. The result, however, was not precisely what Sinclair had planned. He had hoped to "frighten the country" into improving conditions for industrial workers.[41] Instead, Congress enacted on Jan. 1, 1907, the Pure Food and Drug Act, designed to protect the nation's food supply. Sinclair's Socialism may have separated him from many other muckrakers, but his belief in the common decency of the average American, who would insist on change when presented with the facts, was a vision shared by other reformers of the Progressive Era. For Sinclair, that meant journalism in the service of humanity to create a social order "without poverty and war." The ability of Sinclair's prose to capture the experience of Chicago's packinghouse workers moved many readers to empathy and action, even if they resisted his Socialist solutions.[42]

Charles Edward Russell turned to muckraking and Socialism after a long career as reporter, editor and publisher at newspapers in Minneapolis, St. Paul, Chicago and New York.[43] His pitiless description of the Georgia prison system in *Everybody's Magazine* in June 1908 provoked a special session of the State Legislature and eventually an end to the practice of leasing convicts. Russell made headlines with his muckraking reports on tenement landlords, the wealthy and the trusts; but his interest in Georgia's jails was aroused by an ex-convict's letter to the editor of *Everybody's*. A youth's four-year sentence for stealing $300 of his employer's money sent the young man, a first-time offender, to a farm near Milledgeville. Here, shaved and shorn, he stood in a long line before private contractors who would bid for his services, chillingly like the slave auctions of the antebellum South.[44]

Russell's narrative of what happened to a man who is "neither hardened nor sullen" after the chain gang has finished with him was a journey into "Gehenna," a "wild and desolate" place. The maggots that crawled along the prisoner's salt pork, the "filthy huts in which men were doomed to sleep and eat," the high stockades where guards stood

with aimed rifles, the backbreaking work, the beatings and "the manifest terror" made the prisoner feel he didn't have "a chance in the
world."[45] "Bruised and bloody backs" were a common sight under "the
soft Georgia sun," Russell wrote. So was the hardening of a first-time of-
fender into an enemy of the state. Georgia received $353,455.55 in 1907
for 1,890 prisoners sold to private contractors. Russell exclaimed that if
Georgians knew what became of their fellow citizens once they disappeared behind bars, they would repeal the leasing of convicts by a five
to one margin.[46] His prediction was borne out when on March 9, 1909,
Georgia's governor signed into law a bill curbing the practice of leasing
convict labor to private companies.[47]

Russell's series "Beating Men to Make Them Good" for *Hampton's*
in 1909 and "What Are You Going to Do About It?" for *Cosmopolitan* in
1910 and 1911 continued to attack an invisible caste system, arguing
that the weak, the vulnerable and the victimized had fewer rights than
the handful who held power. In "Confessions of a Muck-Raker," Russell
wrote that he might have gone on to a career writing books, "which I
knew no one would ever read," believing injustice was "no special concern of mine," if the testimony of a brave few had not "plunged me into
the fight."[48] Russell believed that the work of the muckraker was the
gathering of evidence, the marshaling of facts and the "discovery of in-
numerable and indispensable details" that proved one's case.[49]

Russell's advice to other muckrakers that they "never give credence
to any claim without complete investigation"[50] describes Thomas Law-
son's work on the stock market and insurance industries; William Hard,
Edwin Markham and John Spargo's investigation of child labor; George
Kibbe Turner's crusade against vice; Samuel Hopkins Adams' attacks
on patent medicine; John Mathews' criticism of bureaucracy; William
English Walling's muckraking reports on racial prejudice; and C.P.
Connolly's warning against those who put private interest before the
public good. When Frank Norris wrote of life in the mines and Marie
Van Vorst chronicled the lives of women at work, they were following
the muckraking article of faith that an enlightened understanding of social injustice would lead to a just society. And when Mary Alden Hopkins described the aftermath of the Newark factory fire and Rheta
Childe Dorr published her essay on what eight million women want, it
followed a muckraking pattern to capture the crucial detail to expose the
hidden situation. The investigations of Louis Brandeis into insurance
fraud and Ernest Crosby into machine politics asked readers to do their
parts in demanding more of municipal officials and the regulatory
agencies those officials had created. The exposure by Georgine Milmine
and Judson Welliver of the creeping materialism of religious institutions, along with Louise Eberle and Henry Beach Needham's depictions
of special interests, helped civic reformers press their cases and win
changes in the law. As William Kittle put it, no one, least of all the na-

Progressivism, Muckraking and Objectivity • 145

tion's leading newspapers and the powerful wire services "with their commercial ties to industrial corporations and trusts," was immune from the requirement to "serve the public good."[51]

It was their faith in facts as well as in their fellow citizens that made muckrakers no enemy of objectivity. Their detective work and literary passion often communicated a general evil by focusing on a particular experience. That often made their work more descriptive than analytical. Some muckrakers offered solutions, but a great many trusted an enlightened citizenry and their elected officials to do the right thing when the truth became known. The reporters writing at the beginning of the century considered the best bet for preserving and improving democracy was to trust in the rationality of readers. They observed well, wrote passionately and persuaded a great many of their countrymen to participate in public life as a means of creating a just society. Their achievements rested on their faith that finding and reporting facts would ultimately reveal the truth.

NOTES

[1] Ida Tarbell, *All in the Day's Work: An Autobiography* (New York: Macmillan, 1939), 204-6.

[2] Ida Tarbell's Sept. 11, 1901, instructions to Siddall are cited in Kathleen Brady, *Ida Tarbell: Portrait of a Muckraker* (New York: Seaview/Putnam, 1984), 125-6.

[3] Ida M. Tarbell, *History of the Standard Oil Company* (New York: McClure, Phillips, 1904), 268-9, and Tarbell, *All in the Day's Work*, 16 and 27-9.

[4] Tarbell's sense of accomplishment and faith in facts is clearly established in her correspondence with S.S. McClure, the founder of *McClure's Magazine*, in a series of letters they exchanged in the fall of 1937. See McClure mss. Correspondence. Box 8. Folder 54. Lilly Library. Manuscript Department. Indiana University. Bloomington, Ind. Tarbell's commitment to the careful cultivation of sources and the authority of information in helping to create a moral order, is seen in "My Religion," a summary of her spiritual and professional convictions, that can be found in the Lawrence Lee Pelletier Library of Allegheny College in Meadville, Pa., particularly pp. 7-8.

[5] Lincoln Steffens, *The Shame of the Cities* (1904; new ed., New York: Sangamore Press, 1957), 1-2.

[6] Steffens' admonition against editorializing appears in his letter, dated March 3, 1904, to co-worker Ray Stannard Baker and is quoted in Robert C. Bannister, Jr., *Ray Stannard Baker: The Mind and Thought of a Progressive* (New Haven: Yale University Press, 1966), 106.

[7] Lincoln Steffens, *The Autobiography of Lincoln Steffens* (New York: Harcourt, Brace, 1931), 433-4.

[8] Steffens, *The Shame of the Cities*, 11-12.

[9] The development of Steffens' attitude toward municipal government and his determination to "find the facts" is expressed in the pages of the *New York Commercial-Advertiser*, where he served as editor. See, particularly, issues of the pa-

per that appeared during the electoral campaign of October and November 1898. The importance of research and interviews in Steffens' work is analyzed in Harry Stein, "Lincoln Steffens: Interviewer," *Journalism Quarterly* 46 (1969): 727-9. Steffens' growing dismay over the pace of municipal reform is found in his *Autobiography*, 208-38.

[10] See his preface to *Lincoln Steffens Speaking* (New York: Harcourt, Brace, 1936), ix-xi; and Lincoln Steffens, *The Struggle for Self-Government* (New York: McClure, Phillips, 1906), 16-31.

[11] Steffens, *The Shame of the Cities*, 12-3.

[12] An account of the interplay between McClure and Steffens on the municipal reform series appears in Justin Kaplan, *Lincoln Steffens: A Biography* (New York: Simon and Schuster, 1974), 108-12. McClure's commitment to furthering the work of democracy through his magazine is described in several letters to his wife. See, particularly, letters dated Sept. 2, 1895, and March 22, 1903. The first appears in McClure mss. Correspondence. Box 3. Folder 10. The second appears in McClure mss. Correspondence. Box 4. Folder 8. Lilly Library. Manuscript Division. Indiana University. Bloomington, Ind. McClure's confidence in achieving municipal reform by trusting readers with information is captured in S.S. McClure, *My Autobiography* (New York: Frederick Ungar, 1963), 265-6.

[13] Statements by McClure on the social responsibility of the press appear in his Jan. 30, 1904, address to the Twentieth Century Club of Brooklyn and his April 10, 1911, remarks to members of the 57th Street branch of the Y.M.C.A. The comments appear in McClure mss. Box 4. Folder 12; and, Box 6. Folder 6.

[14] Vincent Blasi, "The Checking Value in First Amendment Theory," *American Bar Foundation Research Journal* 85 (1977): 523-5.

[15] For the relationship of Blasi's theory to other 20th century models of a free and responsible press, see Theodore L. Glasser, "Press Responsibility and First Amendment Values," in Deni Elliott, ed., *Responsible Journalism* (Beverly Hills: Sage, 1986), 81-95; Edwin Baker, "The Process of Change and the Liberty Theory of the First Amendment," *Southern California Law Review* 55 (1982): 302-12; Edwin Baker, "Press Rights and Government Power to Structure the Press," *University of Miami Law Review* 34 (1980): 834-41; T. Barton Carter, Marc A. Franklin, and Jay B. Wright, *The First Amendment and the Fourth Estate*, 4th ed. (Westbury, Conn.: Foundation Press, 1988), 17-36; and Elizabeth Blanks Hindman, "First Amendment Theories and Press Responsibility," paper presented at the Association for Education in Journalism and Mass Communication national convention, August 1991, Boston, Mass.

[16] McClure's remarks were made at Brooklyn's Twentieth Century Club on Jan. 30, 1904. Blasi, "The Checking Value in First Amendment Theory," 539-41. See also, Vincent Blasi, "The Newsman's Privilege: An Empirical Study," 70 *Michigan Law Review* (1971): 229 and 253-4.

[17] Aspects of this method can be found in Harry H. Stein, "American Muckraking of Technology since 1900," *Journalism Quarterly* 67 (1990): 401-9.

[18] Robert C. Bannister, "Race Relations and the Muckrakers," in John M. Harrison and Harry H. Stein, eds., *Muckraking: Past, Present, and Future* (University Park, Pa.: Pennsylvania State University Press, 1973), 45-64; John Hope Franklin, *From Slavery to Freedom*, 2nd ed. (New York: Knopf, 1956), 428-32; and Gunnar

Myrdal, *An American Dilemma*, vol. 2 (New York: 1944), 1017-22.

[19] Letter from Booker T. Washington to Carl Schurz, dated Dec. 28, 1903. Booker T. Washington Papers. Manuscript Division. Correspondence. Library of Congress. Washington, D.C. Quoted in Harold S. Wilson, *McClure's Magazine and the Muckrakers* (Princeton: Princeton University Press, 1970), 162-3.

[20] Ray Stannard Baker, *American Chronicle: The Autobiography of Ray Stannard Baker* (New York: Charles Scribner's Sons, 1945), 192-3.

[21] Peter Lyon, *Success Story: The Life and Times of S.S. McClure* (New York: Charles Scribner's Sons, 1963), 252-3.

[22] Baker's comments appear in his general discussion of the making and mobilizing of public opinion and in *McClure's Magazine* 26 (March 1906), 548-9.

[23] Baker's description of the life experiences and personal influences that affected his muckraking appears in Baker, *American Chronicle*, 2-5, 17-9, 57-60, 92-3 and, 176-8; and Ray Stannard Baker, *Woodrow Wilson and World Settlement*, vol. 1 (Gloucester, Mass.: Peter Smith, 1960), 13-4 and 21. Stead's efforts to establish the United States as the moral compass of the world are described in William T. Stead, *If Christ Came to Chicago: A Plea for the Union of All Who Love in the Service of All Who Suffer* (Chicago: Laird and Lee, 1894) and William T. Stead, *The Americanization of the World or the Trend of the Twentieth Century* (New York: H. Markey, 1902).

[24] See Baker's "What Is Lynching?" series in *McClure's Magazine* 24 (1905), 299-314 and 422-30, and "The Clash of the Races" in the May 1907 number of *American Magazine*. Also, Ray Stannard Baker, *Following the Color Line: An Account of Negro Citizenship in the American Democracy* (1908; new ed., Williamstown, Mass.: Corner House Publishers, 1973), 31-5 and, 45-50.

[25] Baker, *Following the Color Line*, 46-7 and 88-9.

[26] Letter from Baker to M.F. Woodlock, dated July 2, 1912, and quoted in Wilson, *McClure's Magazine and the Muckrakers*, 203-4.

[27] For a summary of Baker's belief in spiritual and material progress and his muckraking, see his Notebooks C, J and K, written between 1903 and 1908, and available in the Baker Papers of the Library of Congress. In Notebook C, examine 23-4, 36-8 and, 142-5. In Notebook J, see 116-8. In Notebook K, see 131-5.

[28] Jacob A. Riis, *The Making of an American* (New York: Macmillan, 1901), 99-100.

[29] Ibid., 126-8.

[30] For an appreciation of Riis' contribution to the work of muckraking reporting on living conditions of the urban poor, see Norman Sims, ed., *The Literary Journalists* (New York: Ballantine, 1984), 7-10; Louise Ware, *Jacob A. Riis: Police Reporter, Reformer, Useful Citizen* (New York: Appleton-Century-Crofts, 1938), 16-31; Lincoln Steffens, "Jacob A. Riis: Reporter, Reformer, American Citizen," *McClure's*, August 1903, 419-25; and Roy Lubove, *The Progressives and the Slum: Tenement House Reform in New York City, 1890-1917* (Pittsburgh: University of Pittsburgh Press, 1974), 3-13.

[31] Jacob I. Riis, *The Battle with the Slum* (Montclair, N.J.: Patterson Smith, 1902), 17-21; Jacob A. Riis, *The Children of the Poor* (1892; new ed., New York: Arno Press, 1971), 277-85; and Howard A. Good, "Jacob A. Riis," in Thomas B. Connery, ed., *Sourcebook of Literary Journalism: Representative Writers in an*

Emerging Genre (Westport, Conn.: Greenwood Press), 81-9.

[32] Riis, *The Children of the Poor*, 2-3; Alexander Alland, *Jacob A. Riis: Photographer and Citizen* (New York: Aperture, 1974), 24-7; and Jacob A. Riis, *Out of Mulberry Street* (New York: Macmillan, 1898), 56-9.

[33] Riis, *The Making of an American*, 198-204.

[34] Riis, *The Children of the Poor*, v-vi.

[35] Jacob Riis, *How the Other Half Lives: Studies Among the Tenements of New York* (1890; reprint, Cambridge: Belknap Press, 1970), 209-41.

[36] Ibid., 198-9.

[37] Ibid., 197-8; Theodore Roosevelt, *An Autobiography* (New York: Macmillan, 1916), 173-4; Francesco Cordasco, *Jacob Riis Revisited* (Garden City: Doubleday, 1968), xx-xxi; and Robert H. Bremner, *From the Depths: The Discovery of Poverty in the United States* (New York: New York University Press, 1956), 32-6.

[38] Riis, *How the Other Half Lives*, 50-5.

[39] Sinclair discussed his early muckraking work in a 1958 interview that appears in Arthur and Lila Weinberg, eds., *The Muckrakers: The Era in Journalism That Moved America to Reform* (New York: Capricorn Books, 1964), 205-6.

[40] Upton Sinclair, *The Jungle* (New York: Doubleday, Page & Co., 1906), 161-2.

[41] Sinclair's purposes in writing *The Jungle* are probed during a 1961 interview that became part of a 1993 documentary on "The Great Depression" that was jointly produced by the Corporation for Public Broadcasting and the British Broadcasting Company. Sinclair's segment is called "We Have a Plan."

[42] The evolution of Sinclair's passionate concern for the dispossessed is described in his private papers at Indiana University's Lilly Library in Bloomington. See particularly his early letters to his mother, Priscilla, in Sinclair mss. Box 1. Folder 5. Related autobiographic observations can be found in Upton Sinclair, *The Autobiogaphy of Upton Sinclair* (New York: Harcourt, Brace & World, 1962), 27-32, 55-6, and 111-2. Also, Upton Sinclair, *Cry for Justice: An Anthology of Social Protest* (New York: John C. Winston, 1915), 18-9; Upton Sinclair, *Cup of Fury* (Manhasset, N.Y.: Channel Press, 1956), 12-5 and 20-1; and Leon Harris, *Upton Sinclair: American Rebel* (New York: Thomas Y. Crowell, 1975), 11-4 and 168-71.

[43] Russell's conversion to socialism and later decision to run for office as a Socialist Party candidate are described in Charles Edward Russell, *Why I Am a Socialist* (New York: Hodder & Stoughton, 1910) and *Bare Hands and Stone Walls: Some Recollections of a Side-line Reformer* (New York: Charles Scribner's Sons, 1933).

[44] Charles Edward Russell, "A Burglar in the Making," *Everybody's Magazine*, June 1908, 753-4.

[45] Ibid., 755-6.

[46] Ibid., 757-8.

[47] *Atlanta Constitution*, 20 September 1908, p. 1, and 3 March 1909, p. 1.

[48] Charles Edward Russell, *Lawless Wealth* (New York: B.W. Dodge & Co., 1912), 281-3.

[49] Ibid., 285-7.

[50] Charles Edward Russell, *The Uprising of the Many* (New York: Doubleday, Page & Co., 1907), 346-58; Russell, *Lawless Wealth*, 286.

[51] William Kittle, "The Making of Public Opinion," *Arena*, July 1909, 33-5.

CHAPTER 11

Objectivity and the Trappings of Professionalism, 1900-1950

By Barbara M. Kelly

The modern principle of objectivity in journalism was an aspect of a wider movement known as *modernism*, a response to the major shifts in technology, economics and beliefs that had accompanied the Industrial Revolution. It was marked by the spread of reforms and social change. Although scholars of modernism debate the exact moment of its birth, all agree that it was in its primacy during the years following World War I, particularly in America.[1]

Modernism affected different fields at different times over the course of the 19th and early 20th centuries but was typified by industrialization, urbanization and the rise of a white-collar middle class of urban workers. The new middle class was better educated, more affluent and more professional than their 19th century counterparts. Their occupations were the result of industrial capitalism and included middle-management office workers, social welfare professionals and educators. Among those who would eventually join their ranks were the journalists in the major cities.

This shift marked the climax of a movement that had its roots in the late 19th century but which culminated in a new view of news and the newsman that followed World War I. It was the climax of the transition of the newsman from printer to journalist and reflects a number of contextual changes that were taking place in America in the inter-war years. As the first codes of conduct were adopted, objectivity became the cornerstone of the established press in the period between World Wars I and II.[2] For journalists, objectivity represented both a reform in the nature of news coverage and evidence of their rise to professional status. It also represented a clear break with the policies that had blurred the distinction between the fourth estate and its official adversaries in government during World War I.

The concept of objectivity was both a literary style and an ethical ideal; for many, it was both. However, for the purposes of this chapter, those ideas will be treated separately. As a style that incorporates the removal of nuanced words, the limiting of the content to the factual data and the use of attribution, objectivity serves as a framework structured mechanically into the article, enhanced by the use of a formulaic model known as the inverted pyramid. As an ideal, it may be defined as a system of treating the news as a product, separate from the reporter of the article. The reporter remains a passive observer, rather than a participant in, or an interpreter of, the events being covered.

Emerging out of the Enlightenment's emphasis on rationalization, classification and categories, the scientific revolution of the second half of the 19th century had introduced a set of standards for empirical research, attribution and objectivity into the laboratory. The ensuing rise of the logical positivism schools in Austria and Germany in the 1920s emphasized the logical analysis of the new scientific knowledge. These standards would now be extended to include the quest for objective, impartial news coverage.

As the debate intensifies on whether or not objectivity was — or could ever be — fully realized, the definition of the concept has shifted back and forth between these two meanings, making it, like a moving target, difficult to analyze.[3]

Journalistic objectivity was honored as much in the breach as it was in practice. Nevertheless, by 1920 it had become axiomatic that objectivity was an ideal to be sought by the professional journalist. Even when the content was highly emotional by today's standards, the writing followed the format of objectivity, opening with the five fact-related questions: the Who, What, When, Where and Why of the story. The structure was believed to ensure objectivity by standardizing the narrative. The answers to these questions could only be factual: "The Lindbergh baby [who] was kidnapped [what] on March 1 of 1932 [when] from the Lindbergh home in Englewood, New Jersey [where]. A ransom request for $50,000 [why] was found by Charles Lindbergh." The story began with these facts, and the facts shaped both the narrative and the subsequent interpretation of the event.

In the early 1900s, objectivity was an ideal to which the press aspired. It represented not only the journalists' desire to present the truth in as accurate and unbiased a manner as possible, but also an attempt to recover their status as independent gatherers of news. Their image had been tarnished by the sensationalism of yellow journalism at the turn of the century. Even though the muckrakers of the Progressive Era believed in the power of facts, the excesses of some of their reporting had raised suspicions about journalists' motives. Some historians claim that journalists' reputation suffered also from accusations that they had been instrumental in the government's propaganda machine during World War I.[4]

During that war, the press had been cooperative in presenting dispatches from George Creel's Committee on Public Information as if the information they contained were news. The committee was composed of "as brilliant and talented a group of journalists, scholars, press agents, editors, artists, and other manipulators of the symbols of public opinion as America had ever seen united for a single purpose." Thus, the press found itself in the position of drumming up support for America's involvement in what was generally viewed as a European war. Combined with the publication of misinformation distributed by the committee and the avoidance of the various legal sanctions on expressing dissent, the press might well be viewed as having ceded its primary role of fourth estate, serving instead as a tool of the very government forces that tradition had charged it with monitoring. Likening the committee to "a gargantuan advertising agency" whose "associates were literally public relations counselors to the United States government,"[5] the historians James R. Mock and Cedric Larson chastised the press for its abdication of duty even while expressing admiration for the effectiveness of the process.

This episode may well explain the inclusion of "independence" as a major section of its Code of Ethics when the American Society of Newspaper Editors produced its Canons of Journalism in 1922. Indeed the preamble to the Canons made clear what the society viewed as its goals:

> The primary function of newspapers is to communicate to the human race what its members do, feel and think. Journalism therefore demands of its practitioners the widest range of intelligence, or knowledge, and of experience, as well as natural and trained powers of observation and reasoning. To its opportunities as a chronicle are indissolubly linked its obligations as teacher and interpreter.
>
> To the end of finding some means of deifying sound practice and just aspirations of American journalism, these canons are set forth:

With this as background, it is tempting to view the first of the canons as a subtle warning against future co-optation of the newspaper in the service of power.

> RESPONSIBILITY — The right of a newspaper to attract and hold readers is restricted by nothing but considerations of public welfare. The use a newspaper makes of the share of public attention it gains serves to determine its sense of responsibility, which it shares with every member of its staff. A journalist who uses his power for any selfish or otherwise unworthy purpose is faithless to a high trust.

As an ideal, journalistic objectivity would come to mean more than simply the absence of bias, although clearly that was a major element. Whereas in 1860 it was considered not only appropriate but also desirable to write with rhetorical flourish, enhancing the article with colorful

FAIR AND BALANCED • *152*

description and terms, and inventing and expanding the facts in order to convey a larger truth, by 1920 the principle of objectivity had become the standard, an ideal to be sought after even if never attained. As a result, the *formula* for objective writing dominated the pages of the established urban dailies, even where the facts of the stories may have been selected with bias. The formula quickly spread to smaller, local publications and became the standard by which professional journalists were judged by their peers.

As a style, objectivity is typified by the inverted pyramid, in which the bulk of the story — the critical information — is outlined at the beginning through the answers to the five questions — Who? What? Where? When? and Why? — known to the industry as the "five Ws." In addition, the physical shape of the printed column — with its concentration of data in the opening paragraph — replicates the inversion: the primary headline, in large font, is followed in descending order by subheadings in increasingly smaller fonts.

The article must include attributions to primary sources, either participants or expert analysts, and each attribution should be confirmed by at least one additional source. The inclusion of attributions to authoritative sources is intended to support the information in the story and to permit verification of the facts. Finally, the text is marked by neutrality in vocabulary — the absence of modifiers, both adjectives and adverbs, and the avoidance of connotative nouns and verbs.

By the turn of the 20th century most people expected that the news coverage would be factual in both content and format. Few readers expected their newspapers to be without some position on events and issues, however; most expected that the slant or opinion, whether in editorials or in news articles, would be in harmony with the position taken by the editor or the publisher, and many newspapers proudly proclaimed their allegiance to one or the other of the major political parties.[6] Each of the newspapers, particularly in the major cities, held a philosophical position that its readers had come to know and appreciate. Readers of the *World Telegram* expected, and found, an interpretation with which they could agree, while readers of the *Herald Tribune* or the *New York Times* could be comfortable with what they found not only on the opinion pages of these papers, but also in their interpretation and coverage of the news.

In 1922, when Walter Lippmann analyzed the role of the journalist in forming and maintaining public opinion, he was reflecting on almost a century, a time when the concept of information and news was being reshaped from a craft into an industry.[7]

Although objectivity as a model for reporting the news peaked in the decade between 1920 and 1930, its evolution began in the 17th century, and it was strongly influenced by the Industrial Revolution of the 19th century.[8] In its later development, it was part of an evolving con-

Professionalism, 1900-1950 • *153*

text in which American society as a whole shifted from rural to urban, from agricultural to industrial, from practitioners to professionals. It held sway as an ideal from about the end of World War I until the onset of the civil rights era.[9] The shift was influenced by changes in technology, in business and in culture. Changes in the concept of news and the standards for reporting it were additional manifestations of the change.

The factory system of the 1830s had standardized both products and production, brought the workplace to a central area and replaced the all-purpose craftsman with specialists in the various subsets of production who were required to know only one aspect of the job. From the technological advances that enabled the successful rise of the penny press to the socioeconomic shifts that created its readership, the newspaper industry would follow this same pattern.[10]

In part the transition to the more balanced narrative of the 20th century was the result of the new schools of journalism, which added theory to practice and transformed news coverage into a set of standards that could be transmitted from teacher to student. Beginning in 1908, the newly established schools of journalism did much to promote journalism as a profession, rather than a trade.[11] The generation that graduated from these schools would be the ones to codify objectivity as both a style and an ideal. By 1920, the first graduates of journalism schools were becoming a seasoned crew of journalists, not only trained but also educated in their field, a field that had changed from a trade to a profession. The process created new career paths and enhanced status for journalists as participants in America's social and political discourse.

The imposition of academic and professional standards on journalism permitted the shift to a new autonomy as the newspapers emancipated themselves from the mercantile establishment on which they had come to depend.[12] They established a new identity for the press as agencies charged with presenting facts and truth as the raw material of democracy.

Gone was the florid writing of J. Gordon Bennett's *Herald*; and, to some degree, the sensationalism of Hearst's yellow press. The journalists of the 20th century would be professionals: educated rather than trained, objective rather than involved, taking their cue from the work of the doctors and scientists who remained detached from the outcome of their work.

Despite these claims, journalists' understanding of objectivity did not preclude their writing emotional, indeed often lurid, accounts of events that were in themselves sensational, like the kidnapping and murder of the Lindbergh baby, the finding of the body of Starr Faithful, the first execution of a woman by electrocution or the coverage of the Sacco-Vanzetti and Scopes monkey trials.

Between the Civil War and World War I, science had invaded the workplace, the schools and the home. In 1896 Lord Acton stated with great confidence that, "an objective account of the past was now possible, since its sources were at last free to be scrutinized."[13] Within 20 years of Acton's remark, the quest for — and belief in — pure truth and objectivity in recounting the past had been adopted by journalists, who would also come to believe that it was not only possible, but essential, to identify and report an objective account of the present.

Added to these cultural influences was the scientific rationalism that emanated from the German universities. Its emphasis on empirical observation, quantification, verification, replication and publication extended beyond the universities to other forms of information, with an implicit promise of rationality and objectivity achievable through the use of hard scientific data.

The kindred fields of the social chronicler — history and journalism — abandoned their expansive narrative style to follow the model of the social sciences. In history the custody of the past was transferred from the troubadours and the gentleman scholars to the academic analysts. Journalists abandoned their literary style in favor of the concise model of the social sciences. Both approaches were based on a quest for a balanced truth, delivered without political opinion or ideological rhetoric.

Underlying these changes was the rise of a new faith in the existence of a pure truth unaffected by the trappings of power or belief, which reflected a new faith in progress and science. Objectivity would become the ideal for newsmen of every level, for, as chroniclers of the present they could be no less scientific than those who chronicled the past. And, as with all professions in the 1920s, standards were needed and established. Among the standards established were the Canons of Journalism established by the American Society of Newspaper Editors, which laid out an ethical basis for their work, and the inverted pyramid, which laid out the structural basis for their writing.

The definition of the term *journalist* was being reshaped at the turn of the century with the creation of a new class of middle managers and the professionalization of what had formerly been artisans and tradesmen. The traditional professions expanded into a variety of specialists, and among them could be found the new breed of journalists, who were professionals with academic standing, a published set of standards, professional associations and middle-class status. These professionals would drive the rise of objectivity.[14] By 1920 they had established professional associations to set standards for the education and ethics that would support their field.[15] In the process, the news gatherer changed from a freelance correspondent to a salaried journalist, from an on-site diarist to a professional chronicler of events, and, in the case of war correspondents, from an adventurer to an educated professional.[16]

In addition to the rise of class, status and education among its practitioners, the journalism of the 1920s was a product of a number of other influences from the late 19th century. Among these were new ideas about labor management: the centralized use of space, the value of a specialized work force and the study of time and motion. These concepts had invaded all aspects of urban life by the end of World War I. From the centralization of activities into districts within the city — Printers Row, Ladies' Mile, the theatre district — as well as the creation of residential suburbs, the forces of centralization marked the physical layout of the modern city. Within the factory, the specialization of tasks was reflected in the rise of specialized spaces and a rationalized flow of work from one dedicated area to another.[17]

The specialization is evident in the division of newspaper content into departments with dedicated writers and editors, departments that developed along with the new journalism of Hearst and Pulitzer. In the new format, news was located on the first pages, and opinion was located at the back of the news section, while other topics, such as sports, were segregated into special pages of their own. Readers could get the truth or its interpretation by merely turning from one end of the paper to the other. Headlines guided the reader through the many subtopics of the articles, further dividing the content into categories: a brief overview for the hurried reader followed by details for those with more leisure time.

By 1900 the terms *journalist* and *journalism* had become synonymous with news-gathering and reporting, rather than with diarists and diaries, daybooks and record keepers, as in the 19th century. Derived from the Latin word for "daily" — *diurna* (modified by the French to '*jour*') the term had originally defined the individual who gathered, organized and printed the news of the day. By 1920, this was no longer the work of any one individual, having been broken down into its component parts. The owner/printer became the owner/editor, then the owner/publisher as the news became an industry.

In the 20th century the industry involved layers of management, branches of labor and castes of power. It is the editor, the columnist and the bylined reporter who most come to mind when one thinks of journalists. The publisher hired the editor, who hired the reporter, who used the services of the stringer. The publisher also hired the compositor and the pressmen, the distributors, the kiosk owners and the street newsboys. As the century progressed even the individual publisher would give way to a board of directors.

Who then was the "journalist" for whom the guidelines were developed? Clearly, the editors were key to the process.[18] The editors were generally seasoned journalists, who had either served considerable time with a single publisher — or had made their reputation with his competitor. It was these writers who were most likely to be trusted to articulate the position of the newspaper. In this, the industry was reflecting the new class consciousness that had emerged from American industrialization.

Meanwhile, as the rationalization of production separated labor from capital, installing a new tier of worker — the middle manager — as a buffer between the two classes, the condition of the American working class deteriorated. Thus distanced from the results of their own practices, capitalists like George Pullman, Andrew Carnegie and Henry Clay Frick were able to ignore the condition of the workers until the final decades of the 19th century, when strikes and boycotts became deadly and paralyzed American business.

Reformers offered theories to ameliorate the social disparities as well as the strikes and boycotts that accompanied them. From the Social Darwinists, who argued that poverty was nature's means of eliminating the least fit, to the advocates of the Social Gospel, which held that the poor needed only education, shelter and nutrition, the American public attempted to resolve the situation of its poorest citizens.

Andrew Carnegie's Gospel of Wealth presented the idea that the new millionaires of industrial capitalism had a moral duty to the rest of society to be the stewards of America's new wealth, using it to leave the world a better place. Joseph Pulitzer's endowment of the School of Journalism at Columbia University, which opened in 1912, was just another step in this process. Having himself risen from relative obscurity as an immigrant worker to great wealth and international renown, Pulitzer's legacy was to establish the university as the guardian of his field, conveying standards for journalists that he himself had been too busy to employ.

Moreover, in an age in which the middle class was coming into its own by means of education and professionalism, reporters had recognized that they could either join the middle class or remain at the bottom of the heap.[19] The combination of education, professional association and steady employment needed only one further element, an industry-wide standard or code of conduct.

The United States census of 1920 revealed officially what many observers had already sensed — the population of the United States was no longer rural. More Americans lived in cities than on the farms and small towns. A new America — urban, modern and rational — was replacing the traditional America of Jefferson's "yeoman myth." Both the yeoman and the landed aristocracy of Anglo-Americans were losing ground, not only in real numbers but also in influence. They were being replaced by a new combination of immigrant labor and white-collar professionals, among whom were a new breed of journalists, college-educated, professional and in most cases salaried members of a news staff. They lived and worked in ever-larger cities and towns where sheer numbers of residents made behavior more impersonal, and people looked to the newspapers to make sense of their world.

The first code of ethics for the field was produced by and for editors and publishers, rather than printers and reporters, suggesting that by

1910, the industrialization process had produced in the publishers a sense of loss of control over their business. The owner could not continually observe his workers, as Scrooge could observe Bob Cratchit. To collect the news, produce the paper, sell the ad space and distribute the finished product, he had to depend on the work ethic of others in a widening chain of command.

As with the railroads, the business of the newsman was far-flung. Reporters, artist/photographers and correspondents had to be at the site of the action, and that site moved from place to place, as did the action. Editors, printers and compositors, along with distributors and salesmen, had to be in a fixed place with the tools of their trade at hand. Although the telephone, telegraph, railroads and trucks would make the managing of such an empire possible, it also led to a form of what Marx identified as alienation of the worker — in this case from the employer.

Industrialization alienated or distanced capital (the publisher) from labor (the reporter) and led to the hierarchical distribution of power within the industry.[20] This distance was both physical and social. The high-rises built both as buildings to house the newspapers and as monuments to their publishers reduced both the opportunity and the inclination of capital to encounter or include the opinions of labor.

By 1890 and the advent of the new journalism, the power had shifted to the head office, to people who made business decisions, rather than news decisions. When policy-making shifted to publishers and editors, the news became a filtered process. Reporters could cover an event and file an article, but it was the editors who decided what would or would not be printed and where any particular article would appear in the paper.

The new social order of publishing made opinion the prerogative of editors and publishers; objectivity left reporters and news gatherers with fewer venues for expressing their opinions. This *de facto* reinterpretation of the First Amendment reinforced the reality that it was the press — in the person of the owner/publisher — whose freedom of expression had been guaranteed. Lacking a press of his own, the reporter had no such rights. His responsibility was to convey the facts, not to interpret them.

For all their dedication to the ideal of objectivity, it is sometimes difficult to determine just what the journalists of this period meant by the term, particularly since so many news articles of the period appear to be less than objective in any modern sense of the word.[21] Nevertheless the practice and form spread across the industry, fueled by the publication of numerous professional guidelines and codes of ethics.

The first formal code to emerge from the new associations was the code of ethics for publishers written by William E. Miller and officially adopted by the Kansas Editorial Association in 1910. It was followed over time by several other codes of journalistic ethics in several states —

notably, in Missouri and Texas in 1921. These were followed by codes in South Dakota and Oregon in 1922 and, in the same year, by the first national version, the Canons of Journalism adopted by the American Society of Newspaper Editors.[22] It is instructive to note the overlap here between editor and publisher. Whereas in today's world of journalism, the editor is an employee of the publisher, albeit a critical one, in the early 20th century, the terms as well as the responsibilities often overlapped.

An examination of the issues addressed by these documents suggests that objectivity as an ideal was not their only, or their primary, driving force. When any institution takes the time and energy to produce and agree to a set of rules and regulations, it usually signifies the recognition of problems that can no longer by addressed by the traditional patterns of behavior.

The Kansas Code of Ethics for Publishers predates the Canons of Journalism by only 12 years. The differences between the two documents illustrate how the industry was not only changing, but also reevaluating its position in those years. In the terseness and brevity of its language, the Canons of Journalism also reveals the impact of the style of objectivity on its creators.[23]

Following from David J. Rothman's insight that rules and regulations are a clue to the problems of an institution, we can examine the directives in both documents to see what the issues were that gave rise to them.[24] With a slight shift in perspective, the Codes and Canons can serve as a guide to what publishers and editors themselves perceived to be the problems within their industry, as well as to the solutions they advocated.[25]

The Code is divided into three sections: Advertising, News and Views; the last section is labeled "For the Editor." It is written in outline form and comprises some 2,200 words, of which the section on advertising contains a total of 1,676 words. The balance of the code — fewer than 600 words — addresses issues of news and editorial policy. The language suggests an internal agreement, rather than a statement of policy to an external audience, and reflects the fact that in 1910 the gap between editor and publisher was less rigid than it would become a decade later.

It is apparent that the Code was a defense against the rising influence of advertisers, government officials and others who had begun to see the value of the media as a tool of persuasion. Given that both advertising agencies and public relations firms were relatively new fields in 1910, this emphasis suggests that the codes may have been a reaction to the growing power of those who wielded the checkbook. How were the editors and publishers to handle this new genie that was not only out of the bottle, but buying space and supporting their industry? The delicate balance between journalistic freedom and the need to provide a comfortable environment for advertisers was a logical rationale for the publishers to overcome their differences, join forces and establish their collective autonomy. It was far too late to return to the pre-penny press method of supporting publication through prepaid subscriptions from an elite, partisan readership. The method they chose and the language they used suggest that they were attempting to establish a moral high ground in carving out their niche.[26]

Advertising is defined, and its boundaries are carefully drawn. There is a concern that newspaper publishers are engaging in "sweetheart deals" with advertisers and/or their agents. Fine lines are drawn between what today's journalist would recognize as Daniel Boorstin's "pseudo-events" and paid advertisements.[27] Advertising is defined as "news or views of a business or professional enterprise which leads directly to its profits or increased business."

Anonymity in advertising is also a concern as a deceptive practice. Here is the basis of the later demand for attribution, to protect against anonymous libel. The Code calls for clear identification of the author of an advertisement, located close enough to alert the reader that it is an ad and that it was placed by a particular agent or other responsible individual. "The authorship of an advertisement should be so plainly stated ... that it could not avoid catching the attention of the reader."

Thus the first article of the Code, which privileges the relationships between publishers and their advertisers, was a sign that the relatively new field of the advertising agency was beginning to stress the publishers and that the publishers believed they needed to generate a unified front to restrain the power of the checkbook. But the advertisers were not the only enemy. If the publisher (and, a decade later, the editors) were going to be able to retain their control over their product, they would have to establish a cordon around their most sensitive area: content.

Another issue that suggests a concern for the autonomy of the publisher is that termed "freedom of space." Although no peril is identified, it would appear that the advertising agent/space broker had begun to wield considerable power over the publisher.

There is an attempt to standardize the rates and make all transactions aboveboard, suggesting that the game is being played on an uneven field. Issues of trading free reading matter or other benefits in lieu of cash payments, as well as the "giving of secret rebates," are condemned, again suggesting that they were not mere abstractions in the mind of the reformers. Thus the codes were intended as a means of reining in the publishers' less ethical colleagues as well as the advertisers and their agencies.

Drawing on the 1910 Code's statements on news, we can infer that the members of the Kansas Editorial Association saw a number of reporting practices that needed reform. Among these practices are listed the misleading presentation of events or the inclusion of dubious facts, such as the publication of false dispatches, illustrations and interviews, particularly those that may affect the outcome of political and/or economic issues.

They are also concerned with the inclusion of interpretations and conclusions without signature or attribution. The use of quotation marks around the reporter's own opinions or paraphrases, in order to suggest attribution to an expert or authority, is condemned. Muckraking is attacked in the injunction against the destruction of reputations, particularly those of the elites, through the premature display of individuals' names and photographs, particularly in criminal cases.

The interest in objective journalism appears in the codes' distinction between truth and fact. Where earlier it had been considered appropriate to print considered opinions or theoretical conclusions because they appeared to have all the elements of truth, the code now called for substantiation and factual data. Opinions, conclusions and presumptions were to take the form of attributed interviews.

Where editors felt the need to draw a conclusion, it was to be in a signed article, rather than the impersonal forum of the news because "the reader is entitled and has the right to know the personal identity of the author." Reporters were to be dismissed for accepting courtesies, favors or other opportunities for self-gain from anyone who might benefit from the way in which a report was presented.

The Code's statements opposed sensationalism for its own sake and called for editors to delay the printing of articles about "offenses against private morality" until after an arrest, and to bury such articles in the interior pages, if not to ignore them entirely.

The definition they provided of news incorporates the beginning of a definition of objectivity: "You will note by our definition of news that it is the impartial portrayal of the decent activities of mind, men and matter."

They called for independence in editorial policy as well as in reporting. As newspapers became publicly held businesses, the influence of stockholders or lenders was to be avoided. The Code defined the newspaper as an entity apart from a "class publication" in that the newspaper should be expected to present a variety of viewpoints on an issue, rather than echoing a party line.

In the section pertaining to the views or editorial policy of a paper, the Kansas Editorial Association argued, "Whereas a view or conclusion is the product of some mind or minds, and whereas the value and significance of a view is dependent upon the known merit of its author or authors, whether by the signature in a communication, the statement of the reporter in an interview, or the caption in a special article, and the paper as such should in no wise become an advocate."

Thus, without using the term, the association was beginning to shape its understanding of the new objectivity in journalism as meaning impartiality and detachment.

Taken together, these guidelines suggest a series of existing abuses, which the editors were trying to overcome. Their concern with influence, impartiality, evidence and data presage the objectivity that would become more explicit in the ASNE's Canons of Journalism of 1922. The 1910 guidelines are called simply a "Code," whereas the ASNE authors imparted a religious connotation to their guidelines. They are "Canons," a term that derives from the Greek word for rule or law and is used in ecclesiastical law to indicate both those individuals who choose to live according to a common rule or law and the rule or law itself.[28] The Canons is a more public document than its predecessor. It opens with a preamble stating the organization's basic principles, which are rooted in the freedom of expression guaranteed by the Constitution:[29] "The First Amendment, protecting freedom of expression from abridgment by any law, guarantees to the people through their press a constitutional right, and thereby places on newspaper people a particular responsibility. Thus journalism demands of its practitioners not only industry and knowledge but also the pursuit of a standard of integrity proportionate to the journalist's singular obligation."[30] The Canon has six sections, which begin with a discussion of the association's position on the principles of Responsibility, Freedom of the Press and Independence. This is followed by three sections on news, which are subdivided this way: Sincerity, truthfulness, accuracy; Impartiality; Fair Play; and Decency.

Although even in the Canons "objectivity" is not used with the same force or meaning that it would come to hold, the concept is clearly implicit in the categories and principles that the document does address: truthfulness, impartiality, freedom from influence and obligations. This reading suggests that the Canons of Journalism were a more polished method of resolving earlier problems in a more professional and less overt manner. In the earlier document, objectivity may more accurately have been interpreted as autonomy. That is, rather than defending the author's right to print what he thinks, the emphasis is on the publisher's right to set news policy. The power of the press is arrogated to the editors and publishers rather than the advertisers, their brokers or their agents.

The Code protects and defines a business; the Canons, a profession. The target in 1910 is the publisher — the industrial capitalist of journalism; in 1922 it is the journalist. The Code appears to be one of ethics as they affect the industry, whereas the Canons (1922) targets a wider group of practitioners within the industry and spends a larger proportion of its language on the quality and nature of the news that will be printed.

Not only advertisers, but also officials would have to be held in check if the papers were to retain their autonomy, and only by creating a unified front could the publishers prevent a sellout by competitors.

The form, if not the function, of objectivity persisted through the 1930s, despite increasing concern that it was failing to achieve its objectives. It was becoming apparent that in their efforts to remain detached from the news they delivered, journalists were providing a vehicle for others to insert the very distortions that objectivity was designed to avoid. The use of attribution, intended to bolster the factuality of the news by quoting those directly involved in an article, had become a tool for the more sophisticated to use in furthering their own agendas. Those who, by virtue of their position and accessibility, were the most frequently quoted were able to control the direction or tone of the reports, despite — or because of — the neutral scheme of objectivity.

The Great Depression of the decade as well as the buildup for World War II hampered those who would change the role of the press from vehicle to interpreter. As in time of war, there is in times of financial crisis a tendency to rally around the flag and whichever political leader happens to be carrying it at the moment. The man of the moment was Franklin Delano Roosevelt.

Using such mechanisms as his radio "fireside chats" and his unspoken agreement with the press to ignore his handicap, Roosevelt was adept at manipulating public opinion. The media of the 1930s and 1940s, from movies to radio to print, played a role in presenting a feel-good mentality as the nation struggled to ride out or overcome the Depression and World War II. These were not the times to introduce interpretive, much less adversarial, journalism.

As the nation mobilized for World War II, Roosevelt established the Office of War Information in 1942. Modeled after George Creel's Committee on Public Information during World War I, the OWI was charged with controlling the flow and spin of the information that would emerge from Washington.

In pursuit of higher national aims, the press was reluctant to change the model of objectivity during a time of war. Nevertheless, there was a growing awareness among journalists that the *function* of objectivity was being lost through their adherence to its *form*. The pursuit of pure, objective truth was beginning to founder.

As early as 1933, Charles A. Beard had begun to challenge the faith in a purely factual approach to history modeled on the scientific approach to laboratory research and rooted in the logical positivism of the Berlin Circle.[31] In his address to the American Historical Society, he announced, "Contemporary thought about history, therefore, repudiates the conception ... that it is possible to describe the past as it actually was, somewhat as the engineer describes a single machine."[32] Journalists were beginning to agree.

As the Depression at home deepened and the political climate in

Europe worsened, the American Society of Newspaper Editors also modified its stance on objectivity. It called for more interpretive reporting in its 1933 resolution, which resolved that "editors should devote a larger amount of attention and space to explanatory and interpretive news and to presenting a background of information which will enable the average reader more adequately to understand the movement and the significance of events."[33]

It would take another two decades and the rise of a demagogue for journalists to recognize that in practice, the ideal of objectivity as they conceived it could be compromised by the very mechanisms that had made it possible: the absence of nuanced words, the limiting of the content to factual data and the use of attribution. In practice these structures combined to set up a situation in which the words of a Hitler, a Stalin or. later, a Joseph McCarthy, would be printed verbatim without any interpretive analysis. By 1953 the Associated Press Managing Editors Association would recognize the flaw in the system: the fact that in printing such accusations — however "objectively" — they could not remain uninvolved in the outcome. The APMEA raked the coverage of McCarthy over the coals in one of its most rancorous debates. McCarthy was the subject, but "objectivity" was the issue.[34]

It was becoming apparent to those who held high ideals of journalism that in their quest for objectivity they had lost sight of the primary role of the fourth estate — to speak truth to power. As that form of objectivity had become the standard of journalism, with its formulaic use of who, what, where, when and why, journalists had compromised the deeper ideals that had made that standard valuable. If they were to live up to their ideals, they would have to add another set of questions: "at what cost?" and "to whose benefit?" They would, in short, have to become interpreters of the facts to convey the news.

It has been argued that objectivity was a myth, an unattainable goal and, by extension, a fiction.[35] But myths are not fictions; rather, they are the elements that hold societies together. They serve as a means of encapsulating a set of beliefs, structuring the cultures that create them. Even when individuals vary from the precepts of the myth, they know what it is that they are violating and how far they can stray with impunity. In this way, the ideal of objectivity served as a structuring myth for the newly developing culture of journalism that developed in the larger cities between the two world wars.

That some have fallen short of its ideals does not negate the fact that the industry used the framework of objectivity — the five w's, the inverted pyramid, the official quotations and the lack of embellishment — as its blueprint for better coverage. It defined better coverage as a form of scientific endeavor, seeking out and reporting the news as dispassionately, evenhandedly and fairly as is humanly possible.

Whether or not they lived up to their ideals, that is, whether or not

FAIR AND BALANCED • *164*

it is possible to remain objective in covering an article, will continue to be debated. But the form of objectivity was adopted as promoted throughout the period, perhaps in the assumption that function would follow form.[36]

Viewed from the distance of half a century it is easier to see the quest for objectivity as a stage in the evolution of journalism, rather than a singular movement. As the penny press was a transition from the elitism of the earlier party and mercantile press, as the mass-market newspapers of Pulitzer and Hearst were a transition to an industrial press, so the objectivity of the inter-war years can be seen as a transition away from both the sensationalism of Pulitzer and Hearst and the complicity of the press in the government's efforts to shape and control the flow of information during World War I. Objectivity served as both a search for greater accuracy and a corrective to earlier abuses. That its advocates were not always successful in achieving their ends should not obscure the validity of their intentions.

NOTES

[1] For a précis of the various interpretations of modernism see Arthur Asa Berger, *Postmortem for a Postmodernist* (Lanham, Md.: Rowman & Littlefield, 1997), 35.

[2] See also J. Douglas Tarpley, "The Canons of American Journalism: The ASNE and SPJ Codes and Statement." Paper presented at the conference "Journalism: Truth and the 21st Century," 11 August 1998. Reprinted at www. gegrapha.org/resources/tarpley1.htm.

[3] See, for example, the work of John C. Merrill, notably, *Journalism Ethics; Philosophical Foundations for News Media* (New York: St. Martin's Press, 1997) and his debate with Everette Dennis in Everette E. Dennis and John C. Merrill, *Media Debates; Issues in Mass Communication* (White Plains, N.Y.: Longman, U.S.A., 1996). See specifically the debate on objectivity in Chapter 9, pp. 106-19.

[4] See, for example, James R. Mock and Cedric Larson, *Words that Won the War; the Story of the Committee on Public Information 1917-1919* (Princeton, N.J.: Princeton University Press, 1939), and John Morton Blum, *V was for Victory* (New York: Harcourt, Brace, Jovanovich, 1976). The press had been cooperative in presenting the information from George Creel's Committee on Public Information during the early years of the war. The committee itself was instrumental in drumming up support for America's involvement in what was generally viewed as a European war.

[5] George Creel, "Wartime Censorship," 421-5 in Walter M. Brasch and Dana R. Ulloth, *The Press and the State; Sociohistorical and Contemporary Interpretations* (Lanham, Md.: University Press of America, 1986). Creel's piece was originally published in his *How We Advertised the War* (New York: Harper Brothers, 1922).

[6] The idea of a byline, by now a mark of a reporter's status within the paper's ranks, had its start during the Civil War as a means of determining authorship so the military could keep track of the distribution of secret or sensitive information. Maury M. Breecher, "Meet Only Reporter Court-Martialed in U.S. History,"

Media History Digest 13:1 (Spring-Summer 1993): 48-58.

[7] Walter Lippmann, *Public Opinion* (1922; reprint ed., New York: Free Press Paperbacks, 1997).

[8] As chapters in this book have shown, this concept of objectivity as an ideal is more than the casual result of the evolution of the newspaper.

[9] See David Davies' chapter 15 on "The Challenges of Civil Rights and Joseph McCarthy" later in this book.

[10] Michael Schudson: *The Power of News* (Cambridge: Harvard University Press, 1995).

[11] See Maurine Beasley and Joe Mirando's chapter 13 on "Objectivity and Journalism Education" later in this book.

[12] This replicated their earlier shift away from dependence on the social elites and the political party system, during the early years of the nation.

[13] Quoted in Garry Wills, *Papal Sin; Structures of Deceit* (New York: Doubleday, 2000), 233. See also Edward Hallett Carr, *What is History? The George Macaulay Trevelyan Lectures Delivered at the University of Cambridge, January-March 1961* (New York: Vintage Books, 1961), 3. Carr cites *The Cambridge Modern History: Its Origin, Authorship, and Production*, (Cambridge, Eng.: Cambridge University Press, 1907). See also David Hackett Fischer, *Historians' Fallacies; Toward a Logic of Historical Thought* (New York: Harper Colophon Books, Harper & Row, Publishers, 1970).

[14] Robert H. Wiebe., *The Search for Order 1877 to 1920* (New York: Hill and Wang, 1967).

[15] Among these associations were the National Newspaper Association (founded as the national Editorial Association in 1885), the American Newspaper Publishers Association (founded in 1887) and the American Society of Newspaper Editors, which organized in 1922, after a halting beginning in 1912.

[16] During the Civil War, for example, the editors of the penny press sent freelance writers to the battle scene. Their work was dangerous, difficult and badly paid. Wm. David Sloan, *The Media in America; A History*, 5th ed. (Northport, Ala.: Vision Press, 2002), 160.

[17] Within the home, specialization was carried to an extreme with the proliferation of dedicated rooms – billiards rooms, morning rooms, nurseries and dens – as well as specialized implements ranging from pickle forks to ice-cream spoons, as urbanization and its accommodations marked the turn of the century.

[18] At this point the line between editor and publisher was still quite vague, particularly in the smaller and local press, where the generalist still prevailed.

[19] As early as 1880, Charles Dana had begun to favor college graduates for his reporting staff, and by 1900 the trade publication *The Journalist* announced that college-educated reporters were "the rule."

[20] See, for example, Herbert G. Gutman, *Work, Culture and Society in Industrializing America: Essays in Working Class and Social History* (New York: Knopf, 1976).

[21] This was particularly so in the tabloids, where headlines and photos continued the sensationalism of the "new journalism" of the 1890s. The picture of the murderess Ruth Snyder strapped into an electric chair under the headline "DEAD!" in the *New York Daily News*, 13 January 1924, was only one such ex-

ample, albeit perhaps one of the most lurid.

[22] "Code of Ethics or Canons of Journalism" published in *Problems of Journalism*, American Society of Newspaper Editors, 1932.

[23] These codes are reproduced in their entirety in Appendix A to Tarpley, "The Canons of American Journalism."

[24] It is possible to trace the history of social problems by noting the issues against which a society legislates. So, for example, the absence of legislation against cellphones in the classroom during the 1950s does not support the assumption that cellphones were rampant, but rather that there was no perceived need to legislate against them. Similarly, the inclusion of such an injunction on course outlines/syllabi in the 2000s suggests that a cellphone problem exists.

[25] David J. Rothman, *Conscience and Convenience; the Asylum and its Alternatives in Progressive America* (Boston: Little Brown, 1980). See also Rothman, *The Discovery of the Asylum* (Boston: Little Brown, 1971).

[26] "Canon" has long been associated with religious law and regulation.

[27] Daniel Boorstin, "From Newsgathering to News Making: a Flood of Pseudo-Events," in *The Image: A Guide to Pseudo-Events in America* (New York: Atheneum, 1972).

[28] "Canons Regular of Prémontré" from its Web-page FAQ at Prémontré.org.

[29] It is suggestive that the use of preamble followed by the list of principles serves to associate the Canons with the American Constitution.

[30] Tarpley, "The Canons of American Journalism."

[31] The Berlin Circle, like the Vienna Circle, was composed of a number of German and Austrian philosophers. Seeking rationality, logic, and verifiability, their work was instrumental in shaping a new philosophy of science from the 1920s until the 1950s.

[32] Charles A. Beard, Annual Address of the President of the American Historical Association, 28 December 1933, Urbana, Ill. Published as "Charles A. Beard, 'Written History as an Act of Faith,'" *American Historical Review* 39:2 (1934): 219-31.

[33] Quoted in Michael Schudson, *Discovering the News* (New York: Basic Books, 1978)., 148.

[34] See David Davies' chapter 15 on "The Challenges of Civil Rights and Joseph McCarthy" later in this book

[35] See for example "Journalistic Objectivity" in Dennis and Merrill, *Media Debates*, 106-18.

[36] For example, in his study of both local and wire reports, Harlan Stensaas found a steady increase in the number of "objective" stories from 1865 to 1934. From a low of approximately one-third in 1865 to a high of 80 per cent in 1934, the stories increasingly used the form of objectivity. Stensaas found a strong relationship between the use of the "inverted pyramid" and authoritative sources, but little difference between the objectivity found in local stories and those in the wire reports. He saw no evidence that the press associations had influenced the development of objectivity. Harlan S. Stensaas, "The Rise of Objectivity in U.S. Daily Newspapers, 1865-1934," Ph.D. dissertation, University of Southern Mississippi, 1986.

CHAPTER 12

Readers, Research and Objectivity
By Douglas B. Ward

The modern concept of mass media came of age as consumption moved to the center of American life at the turn of the 20th century. Magazines such as the *Saturday Evening Post* and the *Ladies' Home Journal*, plus daily newspapers in New York, Philadelphia, Chicago and other cities, grew fat on the advertising of automobiles, soap, ready-to-wear clothing, musical instruments, department stores and hundreds of other consumer products and retail stores. Advertising quickly replaced subscriptions and single-copy sales as the chief source of income for magazines and newspapers, and as it did, it shifted the priorities of American journalism. Publications needed advertisers to survive, and advertisers needed the attention and the trust of a consuming public. Readers, long the lifeblood of all publications, took on new importance in an era of intensified competition and an increasing emphasis on publishing as a business proposition.

As publications and advertising agencies sought to get a better idea of who readers were, they turned to science and its promise of a more reliable, objective truth. Although the term *objectivity* was not commonly used until the 1920s, the ideals of modern objectivity were clearly apparent years earlier as the worlds of advertising and publishing used social science to guide the sales of consumer products and to better understand readers. Through such means as surveys, categorization, statistical averaging, questionnaires, interviews and observation, advertising agents and the advertising departments of magazines and newspapers strove to achieve objectivity. That is, they sought to move beyond the perspective of the individual to a broader view that could be reached only by investigation grounded in the methods of science, by the accumulation and analysis of facts.

Even though science was seen as a means of filtering out individual biases and providing an objective means of evaluation, market researchers approached each problem with the preconceptions of capitalism. That is, profit and growth were the ultimate goals, and the public was seen as little more than a means to an end. Advertisers did not want to reach everyone. Rather, they wanted to reach only those people who had the means and inclination to *buy* the new products that were flooding into the marketplace, and they were quick to cast aside anyone deemed an unlikely purchaser. So as the journalism profession came to rely on more objective methods of market research, the results of that research put more pressure on journalists as they tried to adhere to the value that had only recently been given the name *objectivity*. The long-held ideal of a publication created on the instinct of its editor began to compete with a new ideal of a publication whose content and readership could — and should — be analyzed and adjusted scientifically. This chapter argues that the promises of objectivity, in the form of readership research, allowed the values of advertising to seep unwittingly into journalistic thinking at a time when publications were trying to erect walls between business and news operations. It tracks two concepts of readers and looks at how those concepts began to conflict as the influence and importance of advertising grew in the early 20th century. As market research worked its way into newsrooms, it took with it the values of the business world and an underlying goal of gathering information to increase consumption. Still today, the goal of informing the public constantly struggles with the goal of profit. The news is a product, and the reader is a consumer and a commodity — these were concepts that began to crystallize at the turn of the 20th century.[1]

Since the early republic, newspapers have helped give shape to democracy and community. The reader was a customer in some sense, but the reader was foremost a citizen. Thomas Jefferson, who saw newspapers as vital to democracy, proposed their free distribution in 1801. To promote democracy, early administrations granted newspapers enormous subsidies and other benefits, including the cheap second-class mailing permits publications still enjoy today. In 1846, when he took over the *Daily Eagle*, Walt Whitman announced: "We really feel a desire to talk on many subjects to *all* the people of Brooklyn." James Gordon Bennett Sr. saw a need to edit his *New York Herald* for "the great masses of the community," from the merchant to the mechanic, the private family and the public hotel. And Edward W. Scripps, who assembled the first modern newspaper chain in the late 19th century, minced no words about his mission: "God damn the rich and God help the poor."[2]

Although the claims contain a great amount of hyperbole, they speak to the goal of the press as a tool of democracy, a voice bolstered by the First Amendment, a means of disseminating information to a vital citizenry. This model of reader as citizen persisted into the 20th century, but it was gradually forced to compete with a new model of the reader as circulation, and — more important — advertising began to grow in newspapers and magazines. The values of business filtered through publications, and the citizen reader began to be considered also as a consumer and a customer, something easily seen in the thinking of Curtis Publishing Company, publisher of the widest circulating magazines of the era.

Readers, Research and Objectivity • *169*

In the early 1880s, when he established the *Tribune and Farmer*, a weekly paper whose women's department eventually became the *Ladies' Home Journal*, Cyrus H.K. Curtis offered his paper for 25 cents a year, instead of the usual $1, if subscribers signed a pledge to pay attention to advertising. He was able to boast that "all our readers are peculiarly the very class who read and answer advertisements." Throughout the late 19th century and early 20th century, Curtis and his staff tried to make the case that Curtis publications reached the elite of American society: people with culture, taste and refinement, and, most important, people with money.[3] The company told advertisers that Curtis publications appealed only to "the intelligent, the earnest and the progressive." The *Ladies' Home Journal* was "designed for the home loving," and as the magazine's managing editor, William V. Alexander, explained in 1905, "we try to give our readers what in our judgment they seem to care for most.... [W]e have to think of the millions." In the 1920s, George Horace Lorimer, editor of the *Saturday Evening Post*, said that his magazine appealed "to two classes of men: Men with income, and men who are going to have incomes, and the second is quite as important as the first to the advertiser." Similarly, with its farm magazine *Country Gentleman*, Curtis insisted that "the exceptional and constant increase in the wealth" of readers "means that from season to season they will be more and more desirable customers for high-grade merchandise of many sorts."[4]

Curtis was not the only publication to make such claims. *Good Housekeeping*, for instance, portrayed itself as a "magazine whose advertising pages, as well as its editorial pages, keep 'clean company,'" and in doing so it "wins the confidence of its readers — and, therefore, results for its advertisers." In 1902, the *Fourth Estate*, a trade publication of the newspaper industry, said a successful publicity campaign needed to include newspapers because "it is absolutely necessary to attract the attention of the man who has money to invest. He reads the newspaper, for that is just as much a part of his business as anything else." And in 1916, *Collier's* promised that it could tell advertisers "what people read your advertising, who they are, where they live, how they make their money and how much of your product they can buy." *Collier's*, the magazine said, "comprises a larger and more compact market of *readers with buying power* than any other general magazine can show."[5]

That new model of the reader flowed directly from the values of advertising. Advertising is older than American periodicals, but the scale on which it developed around the turn of the 20th century was unprecedented. The Industrial Revolution had given rise to more efficient methods of manufacturing, and improved systems of transportation (from trains to automobiles) and communication (from the telegraph to the telephone and the typewriter) allowed products (including periodicals) to be produced and transported quickly, cheaply and easily on a wide scale. By the late 19th century, these advances in technology had allowed corporate leaders to shift more of their attention from production to marketing and distribution. The United States, and especially its cities, had begun to swell, populated by tens of thousands of literate wage earners who, as purchasing power increased, were a ready market for the multitude of branded goods that were being created.[6]

The chief means of reaching this new consuming public was advertising. It proliferated in magazines, newspapers, billboards, street-car posters, store-window displays, direct mailings, fliers and just about anywhere else a trademark could be displayed. Between 1900 and 1914, the number of national advertisers rose from about 6,000 to about 13,000, and as early as 1907, advertising accounted for half of the pages in most magazines. By one estimate, spending on advertising reached $600 million a year by 1911 and exceeded $1 billion a year by World War I.[7]

The growing use of advertising in the expanding consumer society was intended not only to find customers, but also to find and keep the "best" customers — customers with disposable income, those who would buy again and again, or, for makers of such durable goods as pianos and automobiles, customers who would and could put up the money necessary to make a substantial purchase.

Increasingly, as the world of advertising sought to identify those choice customers, it worked with such an idealized notion of its audience that nearly everything except consumption was discounted. In 1915, a copy writer admonished his colleagues for living in a fantasy world he called "Advertising Land," where people sat at home and waited eagerly for the next issue of *Marvelous Monthly*, clipped coupons, kept their hope chests stuffed with free samples and brochures about buying wedding rings on credit, wrote away for free booklets and walked around in a daze, saying little but "U-m-m-m, it's good!" The writer of the satire, F.R. Feland of the George Batten Agency, wondered whether his profession had not lost touch with the people it was trying to reach. "Is this country of ours really a country or is it the pipe dream of a tired copy writer?" he asked. "Are citizens real people or are they cloud shapes, formed in the drifting smoke of a commercial artist's cigarette?"[8]

Gradually, advertisers did indeed begin to demand real people, not cloud shapes, and the most confident publications responded by offering more objective measures, independent circulation audits, to satisfy their skeptical customers. Individual publishers and advertising agencies also began to devise ways of adding new detail to those raw numbers. Among the most influential was the Chicago agency run by John Mahin. His monthly *Mahin's Magazine* began to show advertisers the value of demographic research and how such factors as population shifts, employment trends and income variations could affect an area's

Readers, Research and Objectivity • *171*

sales potential and could be used in planning an advertising campaign. Others also began experimenting with audience studies. Walter Dill Scott, a professor at Northwestern University and a writer for *Mahin's Magazine*, surveyed Chicago daily newspaper readers for his 1908 book, *Psychology of Advertising*. In 1911, R.O. Eastman of Kellogg's conducted his first study of magazine readers: a postcard survey for about 50 members of the Association of National Advertising Managers. That same year, George Batten, an advertising agent, chose 100 homes in a Wisconsin town of 3,000 people and conducted interviews to find out what periodicals they read.[9]

Between about 1913 and 1919, daily newspapers in Chicago, New York, Philadelphia, Minneapolis, Indianapolis and Seattle, as well as magazines such as *Successful Farming* and *Woman's World* set up research departments, which were sometimes called "merchandise bureaus," focusing on such areas as sales, wholesalers and retailers, audiences and consumers. By 1916, as one manufacturer noted, research was "in the air. Everyone is being investigated."[10]

In 1913, Kellogg's, the breakfast food company, dispatched an army of survey takers to 209 cities across the United States. The surveyors went into more than 16,000 homes in 40 states and quizzed people about the magazines they read. What were their favorites? To which did they subscribe? Which did they read regularly? The results were tallied by both region and city size. Surveyors were also asked to write down their impressions of the people and the communities they visited and to classify residents in one of four categories: upper class, upper middle class, lower middle class ("the common people") and a fourth class that R.O. Eastman of Kellogg's described as a step above "the Slavs and Armenians and the illiterates, but the lowest class of people that have the magazine-reading habit."

Eastman told the Curtis advertising staff that year that the idea of the survey was "to know what we are buying." That is, advertisers wanted to know who read such publications as the *Saturday Evening Post*, the *Ladies' Home Journal*, *Pictorial Review*, *Literary Digest* and other mass-circulation magazines, and how the audiences of those magazines differed. He said advertising needed to be analyzed as thoroughly as coal. American businesses, he said, should work toward "buying and selling advertising by its heat units, by its power units, by what it will do." That could be achieved only by better understanding the reading public, which was quickly becoming a buying public.[11]

Though publications used research in part to appease advertising agencies, the agencies used research, and its promise of objectivity, to address a credibility problem. Long associated with the hucksterism of patent medicine and the humbug of P.T. Barnum, American advertising sought to establish itself as a credible, reliable profession along the lines of law and medicine. As one practitioner wrote in 1912, advertis-

FAIR AND BALANCED • *172*

ing needed to quit relying on "vague Tradition, simple 'Say-so,' Ready-made Beliefs, Hand-me-down Axioms, 'Guff,' 'Con' and Dogma of the dog-gone variety" and to base its work upon *"Investigated Information,* Unbiassed *Evidence,* and Sure Knowledge of *clearly-proven Facts,* boiled down and pre-digested for ready reference into a mass of *Certified Data....*"[12] That is, advertising needed to establish its credibility by immersing itself in science. As Robert H. Wiebe has written, most people at the turn of the century "assumed an automatic connection between accurate data and rational action.... Information would flow upward through the corporate structure, decisions downward."[13]

This emphasis on the collection and analysis of data is easily seen in the work of Curtis Publishing Company, a pioneer in the use of market studies, whose first research director, Charles Coolidge Parlin, became known as the man who "deals in facts and figures."[14] Curtis conducted its first magazine audience study in 1915 and conducted its first extensive newspaper study in 1919 and 1920 as a means for guiding the decisions of its *Public Ledger* in Philadelphia. The *Ledger* survey offers a rare look at the way the values of advertising began to compete with the values of journalism in the early 20th century. The *Ledger* survey did not seek to define the newspaper's readership — Curtis did that itself by choosing to interview people such as businessmen, political figures and teachers — but was used instead "to formulate concrete suggestions for the betterment" of the editorial product. How, in other words, could the newspaper attract more readers? The survey was made at the request of *Ledger* editors and of Cyrus Curtis, who had purchased the newspaper in 1913 in hopes of turning it into a national daily that would help improve the image of Philadelphia.[15]

As staff members from Curtis' Division of Commercial Research formulated a plan for the *Ledger* newsroom, they grounded their opinions in the workings of advertising. The success of the advertising columns depended to a great extent on the success of the news and editorial columns. If a newspaper could not attract readers, it could not attract advertisers, and if it did not have advertisers, it could not afford to pay its journalists. It seemed probable, Curtis researchers wrote, "that serious losses in advertising or circulation whenever they occur are apt to reflect unsound editorial policies; for, what in the long run is best for one department must be best for all."

They advised the *Ledger* staff to concentrate on three things: becoming city boosters, improving the accuracy of local news and avoiding sensationalism. Their advice on accuracy may have encouraged the growing trend toward objectivity among journalists, but their other admonitions tugged in the other direction. They urged the paper's morning and afternoon editions to follow a unified editorial policy and to be less aggressive in taking on public officials and in taking unpopular stands on controversial issues in editorials and news articles. In other words, they urged the paper to abandon the principles that were central to the idea of readers as citizens — a marketplace of ideas — and instead simply focus on the marketplace. Journalism was a commodity that could be shaped and packaged just like any other commodity. The trick was to win enough market share to achieve profitability. Curtis researchers urged going after the "right" market, the readers with money — the type of consumers whom advertisers most desired. A consistent, conservative and thoughtful editorial policy would do just that, they wrote.[16]

Worrying about the effect of movies, radio, automobiles and competing magazines, Curtis began looking more substantively at the readership of its *Saturday Evening Post*, the widest-circulating magazine of the era, in the mid-1920s. In 1925, the company sent staff members to four towns, where they called upon mostly men in offices and homes, drugstores and groceries "to obtain something rather definite as to the intensity with which the *Post* was being read." The first broad study of *Post* readership seems to have been done in 1930, and was followed up in 1936 and 1939.[17]

In the 1930 study, Curtis said that certain basic things were known about all publications: total circulation, advertising volume, the class of advertising published and physical appearance. Several lesser known things were just as important, though, Curtis argued: how long a magazine was kept in a home, how many readers it had per copy, how readership was broken down by sex and occupation, and whether advertising was read. "There is no standard of measurement by which the biggest factor in publishing may be reckoned — the extent to which its columns are valued by the reader," the company wrote. And, as it had done after earlier surveys, the company made its case that the magazine reached a disproportionate percentage of high-income people, from executives and professionals to merchants and shopkeepers.[18]

The next year, Curtis translated its estimates into consumption, saying that the *Post's* nearly 3 million copies were read each week by 11.4 million people who ate 239.4 million meals, had 220,000 birthdays and more than 120,000 anniversaries, marriages or engagements. It prepared for those readers an imaginary meal of oyster stew, rolls, butter, coffee, ice cream and cake, estimating that it would require 60,000,000 oysters, 11,400,000 rolls, 236,000 pounds of butter, 228,000 pounds of coffee, 1,900,000 quarts of ice cream and 570,000 cakes. "Discount this as you will," the company wrote. "It's a market."[19]

The surveys, questionnaires and interviews that Curtis and other publishers used helped them broaden their knowledge of readers by compiling composite statistical profiles that moved beyond the guesswork of previous years. Those studies, though, despite their claims of scientific truth, could be highly subjective. Researchers sought not to get an idea of the population as a whole; rather, they narrowed the market first to people most likely to read and buy, excluding blacks, immigrants from Eastern Europe, anyone considered illiterate and anyone poor — leaving what Curtis Publishing frequently referred to as "worth-while white families." In 1915, an editor for *Country Gentleman*, Curtis' farm magazine, said that to understand the magazine's audience, "we must begin by eliminating the illiterate and peasant type, and the foreign type who do not read English papers." Similarly, when the J. Walter Thompson advertising agency tried to determine the number of magazine-reading families in the United States in 1928, it immediately eliminated two-thirds of foreign-born whites, nine-tenths of Negro literates and "All Indian etc. literates." And in the mid- and late 1920s, Curtis Publishing claimed to have more readers in what it called the "Red Zone" — the most-affluent areas — than any other magazine. That was not a coincidence, it said, but rather the result of a 25-year sales effort that it called "a perfectly selfish enterprise in every phase of its development. We are anxious to build as large a volume of permanent circulation as we can. We are anxious to have it among people who will patronize our advertisers because our revenue comes from them and they must get their profits before we can get ours."[20]

Using this model of readers as consumers, magazines and newspapers of the early 20th century sought to *create* a readership, or at least an image of one that advertisers would buy. Similarly, as market researchers began to use social science to investigate audiences, they made consumption their central consideration. Those biases are easily seen in the work of three researchers in the 1920s. In 1921, two of them, George Burton Hotchkiss, the head of the Department of Marketing and Advertising at New York University, and Richard B. Franken, a lecturer at the university, conducted a survey of newspaper reading by professional men in New York City. The study was a follow-up to one that had been conducted the year before of college students. The intent of their study, Hotchkiss and Franken said, was to get a better sense of readers' interest in various sections of newspapers. Advertisers paid different rates for different locations within newspapers, but they had no real sense of how much interest people had in various types of news and features and, therefore, how much attention advertisements next to those types of articles might get. "Advertisers who desire to use newspaper space have a convenient and sure method of determining the *quantity* of circulation possessed by any paper," the researchers wrote, "but they frequently have no way of measuring its *quality*."

Hotchkiss and Franken went to great lengths to tabulate the interest in various sections of newspapers in New York, providing charts and graphs and statistical summaries about the readership of everything from general news to cartoons, death notices to market news. They compared morning and afternoon papers and calculated the time that men of different professions spent with various newspapers. They carefully

Readers, Research and Objectivity • 175

explained their methods, said that sampling ensured that the responses were representative of a larger group and explained that even though the study had been financed by the *New York Tribune*, it was independent and unbiased.

They were likewise forthright about the people they chose to survey. They had no intention of sampling the city as a whole or even the entire readership of the widest-circulating daily newspapers. Rather, they were interested in only the views of stock exchange members, national advertisers, forwarding and shipping agents, doctors, and lawyers. Those types of people, they said, "are considered to have the characteristics of the 'quality' group of readers." That is, they were the men — and all the respondents were men — who were deemed the best audience by advertisers.[21]

A few years later, in the mid-1920s, George H. Gallup, a journalism teacher at the University of Iowa who later rose to fame as a pollster, began experimenting with ways to judge readers' interest in various components of newspapers. Unlike most previous researchers, Gallup was interested primarily in helping reporters and editors, as opposed to the business side of news organizations. His intent was to apply the methods of social science to a newspaper's readership to give editors a new tool for making decisions. "Other institutions long ago discarded hit and miss methods, but the newspaper still trusts largely in the instinct or 'hunch' method of selecting news and features," he wrote in 1930. How many editors had actually watched someone read a newspaper? he asked. With competition from radio and magazines increasing, could editors really afford to leave their decisions to the tenuous belief in intuition? In responding to those questions, Gallup promoted the use of statistical analysis to elevate editors' understanding of readers. "No editor can hope to know the varied and changing interest of the many groups and classes which he serves without the aid of fact-finding methods," he said. He said his method "brings definite and reliable information, capable of statement in quantitative terms, regarding every feature of the newspaper."[22]

Over six years in the 1920s, Gallup tried more than 50 methods of measuring readers' interests before he found one that satisfied him. That method became the subject of his doctoral dissertation at the University of Iowa, and later a book. Gallup alternately called his method "scientific" and "objective," a means of getting to the truth of what readers wanted. His method was simple in design: taking a representative sample of readers and going through a day's newspaper with them, and marking every news article and feature they read. By 1930, Gallup had conducted his survey for six newspapers, and he suggested that as his work expanded, he would be able to offer editors a "theory of normal interests" for various occupational groups and each type of feature, department and advertisement.[23]

Gallup saw his work as especially useful at a time when newsprint prices were rising and newspapers were trying to save money by reducing the number of pages they printed. And he saw it as a means of evaluating the syndicated features that papers printed, asking, "Are newspapers 'over-featured'?" He said editors had often used different methods for determining readers' opinions: positive and negative letters, contests, conversations with friends, questionnaires and interviews. In nearly every case, he said, "an insurmountable human element" got in the way. In other words, the methods were not objective.

Implicit in Gallup's argument was the understanding that more was better in a market economy. How could the most popular features be distinguished from the least popular? How could editors attract the most readers at the least cost? His arguments resonated at a time of intensifying competition, as editors and publishers found themselves under mounting pressure to increase circulation figures. No longer was *an* audience acceptable; only the *largest* audience was. Anything smaller might allow a competitor to siphon away advertising dollars, thus threatening a publication's survival.

Gallup's work, which attracted considerable interest among editors and was crucial in legitimizing the use of readership studies in newsrooms, clearly achieved the goal of objectivity he had laid out. Like the work of his predecessors, though, it was objective only to the degree that market capitalism would let it be. Gallup saw his work as a means for editors to decide which parts of newspapers attracted the largest number of readers. His studies were not intended to make publications more relevant to communities or to democracy, for instance, or to make them more intellectually challenging or more accessible to the average person. The idea, at its core, was simply to give people what they wanted to see, to turn mass tastes into mass media. Publications were consumer products. The objective methods of social science were simply another, more efficient tool for promoting consumption.

The increasing use of market research set up a conflict between those who believed in natural ability, intuition and an innate sense of what the public wanted, and those who held to the beliefs of science and statistics and sought to use the scientific method to quantify decisions. That conflict played out first in advertising departments and agencies and then in newsrooms, as readership research spread to the editorial side of publications in the 1920s and 1930s.

The use of market research by magazines and newspapers set up another conflict, as well, or, rather, exacerbated one. The model newspaper was often seen, at least by journalists, as one that served democracy. It was frequently considered a public utility, providing not necessarily what the public wanted but what editors thought people needed to know to make informed choices about living in a democratic society. The new model that emerged made no such grand claims. In it, the newspaper was simply a product like any other product that was at the mercy of consumers' whims. The idea of market research was to understand the reading public better and to create a product that more people would buy.

As market research moved from advertising departments into newsrooms, it carried with it an ideal of the reader. That is, readers of different ages and different occupations, of different sexes and different ages all had at least one thing in common: they were consumers of information, entertainment and advertised products. That is important because the methods of social science, as applied to business problems, have become such a common tool today that little thought is given to what they are or how they came about. Implicit within them is the understanding that they are objective, that they provide a neutral means of gauging public sentiment, of better knowing and better understanding the thousands of readers of a mass market.

To a great extent, they do that, providing composite characteristics of audiences scattered around a city, a region or the nation. Behind the studies, though, lie the tenets of business, the goals and beliefs of market capitalism. Most journalists strive to approach individual articles with the idea of fairness and balance — with objectivity — but collectively, those articles are designed and packaged with an audience in mind. In that broader sense, objectivity becomes another piece of the business world, an ideal that can be clearly identified and thus marketed to a mass audience. News, entertainment and information have become commodities, sold just like the branded wares that appear in advertisements. Readers are studied and surveyed, analyzed and categorized, and eventually shaped into a product themselves: an audience for the manufacturers and sellers of consumer goods.

The melding of consumerism and objectivity has been both conscious and unconscious, a means of increasing profit and a means of survival in a competitive market for the attention of the public and the dollars of advertisers. It has helped push journalism toward standardization and homogeneity and has provided the justification for publications to shirk the reader-citizen in favor of the reader-consumer. Increasingly today, media chains, pressed by stockholders for larger profit margins, have insisted that journalists learn the values and expectations of business. The idea of a publication as a public utility has largely given way to the goal of a publication as a brand name.

The reality of modern publishing is that the two models of readers must coexist. The press has always marketed itself by one means or another, usually with profit in mind. In 1902, the trade journal *Fourth Estate* said that the modern newspaper no longer put political considerations above all else. Instead, the modern newspaper worried most about the bottom line. The newspaper "is a business institution," the trade journal said. "Like all other business, its success or failure depends on

FAIR AND BALANCED • *178*

its methods. It is the duty of a newspaper to find out what its patrons want, and then follow the course that will in the greatest measure fill that want."[24] That still holds true today. A press free from government control must have some means of stable income. The problem is not that the reader is viewed as a consumer. The problem today is that the reader is too often viewed *only* as a consumer.

NOTES

[1] See David Sloan's Chapter 3, "Neutrality and Colonial Newspapers," in this book for the role that the business function of printing played in ideas of objectivity.

[2] Thomas C. Leonard, *News for All: America's Coming-of-Age With the Press* (New York: Oxford University Press, 1995), 3-31, 150-1; David Paul Nord, "A Republican Literature: Magazine Readers and Reading in Late-Eighteenth Century New York," in Cathy N. Davidson, ed., *Reading in America* (Baltimore: Johns Hopkins University Press, 1989), 114-39.

[3] See various clippings and advertisements in a scrapbook, c. 1880-1890, pp. 324-40, Curtis Publishing Company papers, Special Collections, University of Pennsylvania, Box 178.

[4] William V. Alexander to Mrs. John A. Grier, January 24, 1905, Curtis papers, Box 3; George Horace Lorimer, "Business Policies of the Saturday Evening Post," in "Dope Book," ca. 1920-1923, Curtis papers, Box 130; *Selling Forces* (Philadelphia: Curtis Publishing Company, 1913), 217-8, 241-4; "The Country Gentleman," advertisement, *Advertising & Selling*, October 1912, pp. 12-3.

[5] "Clean Company," *Printers' Ink*, 13 July 1911, p. 16; "Waldo Joins New York 'Tribune,'" *Printers' Ink*, 20 August 1914, p. 12; "Ineffective Advertising," *The Fourth Estate*, 16 August 1902, p. 10; untitled advertisement, *Printers' Ink*, 9 November 1916, p. 23.

[6] Harvey Green, *The Uncertainty of Everyday Life, 1915-1945* (New York: Harper Collins, 1992); George E. Mowry, *The Urban Nation, 1920-1960* (New York: Hill and Wang, 1968); Simon J. Bronner, ed., *Consuming Visions: Accumulation and Display of Goods in America, 1880-1920* (New York: W.W. Norton, 1989).

[7] Susan Strasser, *Satisfaction Guaranteed: The Making of the American Mass Market* (New York: Pantheon, 1989); "A.N.P.A. Considers Important Question," *Printers' Ink*, 4 May 1911, pp. 78-9; Daniel Pope, *The Making of Modern Advertising* (New York: Basic Books, 1983), 6.

[8] F.R. Feland, "A Curious Place is Ad-Land," *Printers' Ink*, 28 January 1915, pp. 88-9.

[9] Quentin J. Schultze, "The Trade Press of Advertising: Its Content and Contribution to the Profession," in *Information Sources in Advertising History*, ed. Richard W. Pollay (Westport, Conn.: Greenwood, 1979), 49-62; Lawrence C. Lockley, "Notes on the History of Marketing Research," *Journal of Marketing* 14 (April 1950): 733-6; C.S. Duncan, *Commercial Research* (New York: Macmillan, 1919), 106-9; George Batten, "An Advertising Agent's Talk to Salesmen," *Printers' Ink*, 23 February 1911, pp. 23-4.

[10] George M. Burbach, "Newspaper Organization and Some Observations on Newspaper Advertising," *University of Missouri Bulletin* 35 (May 1925); Mac Martin, "Getting Responses from Dealer Questionnaires," *Printers' Ink*, 3 August 1916; "Trade Bulletins," 1914, pp. 55-6. Curtis papers, Box 37; Duncan, *Commercial Research*, 108-9, 307.

[11] "Tenth Annual Conference of the Advertising Department of The Curtis Publishing Company," Curtis papers, Box 17.

[12] John E. Kennedy, "Epistles on Advertising," *Advertising & Selling*, August 1912, p. 7.

[13] Robert H. Wiebe, *The Search for Order, 1877-1920* (New York: Hill and Wang, 1967), 181.

[14] L.B. Jones, "Why Advertisers Demand Facts About Circulation Methods," *Printers' Ink*, 12 October 1916, pp. 8-12; Charles Coolidge Parlin, "Department Store Lines: Textiles," vol. B, pp. 191, 204-5, Curtis papers, Boxes 21 and 22; Parlin, "Motor Accessory Speech," typescript, c. 1921, Curtis papers, Box 148, Folder 17.

[15] "The Public Ledger Report," typescript (Philadelphia: Curtis Publishing Company, 1920), vol. B; Edward W. Bok, *A Man From Maine* (New York: Charles Scribner's Sons, 1923), 197-212; Oswald Garrison Villard, *The Disappearing Daily* (1946; reprint ed., New York: Books for Libraries Press, 1969), 218-28.

[16] "The Public Ledger Report," vol. B, 308-59.

[17] "The Reading Habits of Saturday Evening Post Readers," Curtis *Bulletin* 68 (Dec. 25, 1925); "Reader Responsiveness," *Bulletin* 94 (Oct. 28, 1927); "The Demand for The Post," *Bulletin* 106 (December 1928); *Digests of Principal Research Department Studies* II: 31, 72, 124-5, Curtis papers, Boxes 119, 160, 161, 162.

[18] *The Saturday Evening Post* (Philadelphia: Curtis Publishing Co., c. 1930), Curtis papers, Box 140.

[19] "Looking Ahead," typescript, c. 1931, Curtis papers, Box 140.

[20] "Condensed Report of Advertising Conference," 1915, Curtis papers, Box 18; "The Home Journal Fashion Serials," Curtis *Bulletin* 13 (Dec. 6, 1922), Curtis papers, Box 158, Folder 167. "Magazine-Reading Families," J. Walter Thompson *News Letter*, 1 September 1928, J. Walter Thompson Company Archives, Duke University; "Where Do The Best Customers Live?" typescript, 1923, Curtis papers, Box 81.

[21] George Burton Hotchkiss and Richard B. Franken, *Newspaper Reading Habits of Business Executives and Professional Men in New York* (New York: New York Tribune, 1922).

[22] George Gallup, "A Scientific Method for Determining Reader-Interest," *Journalism Quarterly* 7 (1930): 1-13; Gallup, "Guesswork Eliminated In New Method for Determining Reader Interest," *Editor & Publisher*, 8 February 1930, pp. 5, 55.

[23] Williston Rich Jr., "The Human Yardstick," in John E. Drewry, ed., *Post Biographies of Famous Journalists* (Athens, Ga.: University of Georgia Press, 1942), 107-27; Gallup, "Guesswork Eliminated."

[24] "The Modern Newspaper," *The Fourth Estate*, 2 August 1902, p. 10.

CHAPTER 13

Objectivity
and Journalism Education

By Maurine H. Beasley
and Joseph A. Mirando

When the first journalism schools opened before World War I, they wanted to elevate a field tarnished by the yellow press. Walter Williams, dean of the University of Missouri School of Journalism — which started in 1908 and was the first institution to give a degree in journalism — spelled out the school's purpose: to supply "well-equipped men for leadership in journalism, with high ideals and special training."[1]

Williams and other early educators did not use the word "objectivity," but the curriculum was oriented toward accurate fact-gathering, and as his and other journalism schools became established, particularly in the period between World War I and II, they clearly embraced the concept. Commitment to an ideal of objectivity suited several purposes: it appeared to be "scientific," in line with social science research that was integrated with skills training at the University of Wisconsin and some other journalism schools, it could be used to distinguish journalism education from the liberal arts, and it provided a rationale for enlisting support from the leaders of the newspaper industry, some of whom were suspicious of formal education in a field long marked by apprenticeship-style preparation.[2]

The purpose of this chapter is to explore the reasons that journalism education gravitated to an ideal of objectivity in the first half of the 20th century by analyzing the references to objectivity in the journalism textbooks that attempted to describe journalism as a profession. Although in these texts, the term "objectivity" was used more often than it was defined, early journalism educators equated it with gathering and presenting consensually validated statements — the facts — free from partisan influences for newspaper readers.

This was in line with changes that had taken place in journalism in the 19th century, as newspapers moved away from patronage by political parties and toward a commercial base of advertising and circulation. Based on a belief in the existence of a neutral, verifiable reality, objectivity became identified with newswriting techniques, ways to perceive or "cover" situations and news-gathering strategies based on an assumption of journalistic impartiality.

Although the number of journalism graduates was not large (only 2,500 annually as late as 1958, compared with 42,000 who received bachelor's degrees in 2002 in journalism and mass communication), journalism instruction started in 218 institutions from 1910 to 1940 and played an important role in establishing professional standards.[3] As earlier chapters in this book have pointed out, several influences contributed to the rise of objectivity as well as to the growth of journalism schools. In adopting objectivity, educators embraced the ideas of Walter Lippmann, who argued after World War I that the public was unable to sort out truth from fiction in a world of distortions.[4] His remedy: elevate journalism into a profession and educate reporters to be as objective as possible.

Joseph Pulitzer, who endowed the Pulitzer Prizes in literature, drama and music, as well as in journalism, believed firmly in the role of the journalist as a gatherer and interpreter of facts. He specified that the Pulitzer Prize in reporting should be based on "strict accuracy, terseness, the accomplishment of some public good commanding public attention and respect."[5] As the founder of the Columbia University School of Journalism, which started in 1912, Pulitzer was one of the first influential backers of professional education for journalists.

The initial proposals for collegiate training in journalism emerged in the late 19th-century and were in line with a faith in education as a means of progress. Inexpensive, sensation-driven newspapers — both the popular penny press of the pre-Civil War era and the bold new journalism of the 1870s and 1880s — shocked the sensibilities of respectable people. Formal education for journalists was discussed in periodicals after 1870, although vilified as ridiculous by editors like E.L. Godkin of *The Nation*, who insisted that the newspapers themselves were the best journalism schools.

Some educators thought otherwise. Gen. Robert E. Lee, as president of what became Washington and Lee University in Lexington, Va., proposed formal courses in journalism in 1869. The first actual college courses grew out of a variety of pursuits. One was the printing trade. Kansas State College set up a department of printing in 1873, and it developed into a department of industrial journalism.[6] Through its correspondence school division, the University of Chicago offered training in writing for newspapers, while a course that studied the press as a social force was taught under Robert Park, a scholar of the immigrant press.[7]

Coincidentally, authors of books intended for aspirants to the growing field of newspaper work described practices generally considered part of what came to be known as objective reporting. In picturing the job of a journalist on a rural newspaper, Jesse Haney in 1867 described a version of objectivity, even if he did not quite use the whole word: "If there be a public meeting it should be reported fairly. It makes no difference if the editor differs with its object...." Haney saw an objective report as market-based: "... a newspaper is a thing made for sale."[8]

Similarly, the author of *Hints to Young Editors* (1872) offered comments on marketing, saying there was no reason why the *news* of a Republican paper should not be read by a Democrat with as much confidence as that of a paper of his own party, and *vice versa*.[9] George A. Gaskell, writing in 1884, emphasized that reporters should be impartial observers: "... in ordinary reporting it is well to lose sight entirely of the reporters. By them impersonality must be cultivated as carefully as it ought to be avoided by those whose work is of a less conventional order."[10]

In the quarter-century after Haney, the idea of objective impartiality gained further affirmation in textbooks. Edwin Shuman (1894) insisted that a journalist must report "the opinions of others, not... express his own."[11] To Nevada Davis Hitchcock (1900), a reporter "must describe conditions exactly as he found them, no matter what influences may have been brought to bear upon him."[12] To Charles Olin (1907), a reporter was "simply a recorder of separate events, of isolated circumstances, of chance occurrences, in fact a snapper-up of the unconsidered trifles of existence."[13]

Writing in 1906, James McCarthy compared writing a news story with conducting a scientific investigation.[14] The next year, Robert Luce admonished reporters to keep themselves out of their stories, telling them in regard to opinions: "your own are insignificant; those of others, if they are men whose opinions carry weight, should often be reported, but so as to put the burden on them, or if it is a general opinion you voice, let it appear as such and not your own."[15] Similarly, "Don't write out your opinion on things," Edwin Hadlock advised four years later, "Let people form their own ideas."[16]

The case for objectivity as a pivotal value can be seen in a plan for journalism instruction drawn up by Charles W. Eliot, president of Harvard University, where Pulitzer considered endowing his journalism school before giving the money to Columbia instead. Although Eliot disliked the idea of a separate school to train journalists, he proposed a curriculum concerned with marketing information intelligently so democratic government could be well served.

Pulitzer disagreed vehemently with Eliot, and insisted on separating the business side of journalism from the editorial. He wanted his school to stress improved news-gathering and writing techniques, along with the social significance of journalism and the role of editorial leadership. Pulitzer forbade the teaching of advertising and business management at the Columbia University School of Journalism. Eliot's broader plan was largely adopted at the University of Missouri, which emphasized managerial along with editorial techniques. Still, supporters of both approaches agreed on the need to teach students how to gather and present facts.

Once objectivity appeared as a professional value in education, standardized news-gathering rituals and writing techniques were soon developed to further the goal. These included pursuing official sources for direct quotations, balancing reports by obtaining information from those on both sides of an issue, presenting background information and packaging facts in an inverted pyramid form of newswriting, answering the questions "who, what, when, where and why."

More important, the idea of objectivity attributed power to journalism because it made the journalist responsible for finding out, and for telling, the truth about society so citizens could make intelligent decisions in governing themselves. J. Herbert Altschull argued that this belief system, very much a part of the investigatory aspects of American journalism, called on the journalist to serve, not only as the public's educator, but "as the citizen's eyes and ears in scrutinizing the powerful."[17]

Carried to an extreme, the idea of the journalist as an objective reporter conjured up an image of an omnipotent professional who could see through falsehood to discover the truth and soberly lay it before the public. Columnist Heywood Broun poked fun at the concept. In a column titled "The Imperfect Reporter," he noted a claim that the perfect reporter "ought to be patterned more or less along the physical and chemical lines of a plate glass window." He concluded, "I never feel minded to call for a bowl of water and ask, 'What is truth.'"[18]

Still, many educators encouraged students to see their work as a noble calling, based on an objective pursuit of facts. Members of state press associations, which backed the establishment of the first journalism schools, mainly at state universities, benefited from a steady supply of eager young graduates who had been acculturated into the field. As Altschull put it, "... by recruiting staffs from the journalism schools, publishers could eliminate the considerable cost of on-the-job training." In his view, by socializing students into the political, social and economic environment in which newspapers operated, journalism schools offered publishers "the best possible mechanism of social control, adherence to the familiar, cost-effective status quo, and at virtually no cost."[19]

By the 1920s the newspaper industry had committed itself on paper at least to public service. The Canons of Journalism, a high-minded code of ethics, was adopted by the American Society of Newspaper Editors in 1923, in part as a reaction to the flamboyant and unethical practices of the tabloid press of the day. It said, "Journalism... demands of its practitioners the widest range of intelligence, of knowledge, and of experience, as well as natural and trained powers of observation and reasoning." Three years later Sigma Delta Chi, a journalism fraternity that became the Society of Professional Journalists, adopted a similar code. Until a revision in 1996 removed the word altogether, the code declared that "objectivity" was "another goal, which serves as the mark of an experienced professional."[20]

The image of the reporter as an omniscient observer defied other depictions of the journalist at work. As a group, reporters were known for raffish behavior, as characterized in the 1928 play *The Front Page*, written by Ben Hecht and Charles MacArthur, who drew from their experience as Chicago reporters. Subsequently made and remade as a movie, it became Hollywood's first and prototypical newspaper film. Screen journalists were, as Thomas H. Zynda has pointed out, "streetwise, hard-driving, utterly unscrupulous characters who will do anything for a story," awed by nothing except, perhaps, their city editors. This caricature of the reporter merged into social criticism in such films as *Citizen Kane* (1941), which pictured journalists as willing to write whatever was desired as long as the price was right.[21]

To some observers the idea of objectivity as the basis for a profession of journalism ran contrary to what seemed obvious. As a commercial medium, newspapers fed the public's appetite for entertainment as well as knowledge. That dual role led to a peculiar split in journalism education. Aspiring journalists were told to "get the facts," but in writing articles, to "make it interesting."

In an academic setting, the concept of objectivity meshed with the idea of logical positivism, which dominated social science research. It became a hallmark of journalism education at the University of Wisconsin and other research schools. Under the leadership of Willard Bleyer, Wisconsin organized a journalism department in 1912 that became a school in 1927. Its graduates, urged to earn advanced degrees in political science, sociology or history with minors in journalism, headed journalism schools at major universities, including Minnesota, Northwestern, Stanford, Illinois and Michigan State.[22] In contrast with Wisconsin, the Missouri and Columbia schools were seen as vocationally oriented.

Bleyer sought academic respectability by teaching journalism from a social science perspective, in line with Eliot's ideas on curriculum.[23] Bleyer moved into the new area of public opinion research, an empirically based domain that relied, like other social science research, on the positivist school of thought. Convinced that human behavior could be objectively measured, sociologists and other researchers who used this mode of inquiry emphasized observable behavior — thus, they were interested in "facts," not questions of motivations.[24]

In line with this approach, Bleyer conducted some of the initial survey research that laid the groundwork for the communications research associated with schools of journalism and mass communication today. For example, he carried out a newspaper readership study in Madison in 1928 in hopes of determining the effect of newspapers on their readers.[25] In common with other early journalism educators, Bleyer was influenced by the work of Lippmann, whose classic 1922 book, *Public Opinion*, offered an authoritative stand on objective reporting.

Lippmann contended that journalism needed a standard system of observation like the scientific method, which relied on documented evidence, and an impersonal, detached perspective to produce a shared meaning. With journalists exposed to a training system "in which the ideal of objective testimony is cardinal," Lippmann wrote, readers could easily separate good journalism from bad and democratically make up their minds solely based on the facts presented.[26]

Bleyer emphasized the need for newspapers to give factually correct information. He deplored the partisanship of early political newspapers, citing Thomas Jefferson's despairing observation: "Nothing can now be believed which is seen in a newspaper."[27] It was clear to Bleyer that professional journalists could — and should — find the truth and report it in their newspapers. He praised the work of well-known editors, establishing a "great man" perspective that long dominated the teaching of journalism history. Nevertheless, he remarked on the "skepticism of leading newspaper editors" regarding the establishment of journalism schools. He also called attention to the relative weakness of the individual reporter and editor. He said that efforts to organize professional societies of reporters and editors had not succeeded "partly through the lack of interest of the members and partly because of the hostility of newspaper publishers."[28]

The idea of objective fact-gathering without regard to subjective questions of meaning led to confusing expectations regarding journalistic performance that continue today. As John C. Merrill said, "Reporters are simply not able to get enough facts — in the proper context and with the correct balance — to tell the truth (or the whole truth) about some news event."[29] To illustrate, he referred to the difficulties experienced by journalists in covering the Vietnam War.

A reliance on objectivity led to the glorification of facts, which helped to spur criticism of journalism schools as offering only a "trade school education." A 1940 reporting textbook, purportedly based on the sad experiences of a youth who had started work on a daily newspaper without a journalism degree, indexed the following vignette under the heading, "Objectivity in the News": "The city editor motions him [the youth] to the desk. 'You say it was "unseasonably warm" this morning.' Call the weather observer again and find out whether it was 84 or 85 at 7 o'clock. The exact temperature is what we need."[30]

Early textbooks assumed that women were less able than men to divorce themselves from their own emotions and gather facts to serve as the basis for objective judgment. They presented reporters as members of a fraternity almost always closed to women, who were rarely mentioned except negatively.[31] The first major textbooks by journalism professors appeared in 1911 with the publication of two books by Missouri journalism faculty, one by Charles Ross and the other by Walter Williams and Frank Martin. Each attached the name "objectivity" to the elements and values of reporting that had been set forth in career guides since the days of Haney. Both reprinted an excerpt of an editorial from the *St. Louis Republic* that said, "The three notes of modern reporting are clarity, terseness, objectivity." Ross listed objectivity as one of four qualities of an ideal news article, contending: "Newswriting is objective to the last degree, in the sense that the writer is not allowed to 'editorialize.' He must leave himself out of the story."[32]

The male-oriented tone was unmistakable. Ross held a low opinion of the abilities of most women students, who he thought were frittering away their time until they could get married. He abruptly left teaching during World War I, when most of the male students had gone to war, telegraphing the *St. Louis Post-Dispatch* that he would take a job there after he saw a woman student staring out the window and munching candy during his lecture.[33] (Ross went on to become head of the *Post Dispatch's* Washington bureau and press secretary for President Harry Truman. The student, Pauline Pfeiffer, had a career as a magazine writer. She also married Ernest Hemingway.) *But — who didn't*

Advice aimed at men dominated most texts, such as a 1935 book, *The Reporter and the News*, written by Philip W. Porter, an editor on the *Cleveland Plain Dealer*, and Norval N. Luxon, an associate professor of journalism at Ohio State University. They began by debating whether journalism constituted a profession or a skilled trade, but sidestepped giving an answer. The book concentrated, however, on imparting "craftsmanship." Novices were told how to write the news according to standard formulas and how to search for truth by verifying names in the telephone book. Harsh realities were spelled out — "the long periods of working at top speed invariably under high nervous tension, the absolute necessity of trying to beat the deadline."[34]

Women were told to forget about the field: "[The] general tempo — with the deadline-fighting element always present — is such to bar many women because of nervous temperament." Furthermore, the authors stated, "Most women are incapable of covering police and court news."[35]

Within two years after the publication of Lippmann's *Public Opinion*, two influential textbooks appeared that quoted Lippmann and made objectivity into a common term. Harry Harrington and T.T. Frankenberg maintained that a reporter must be "an unbiased recorder of an *objective fact*, which is his chief function...."[36] Casper Yost argued that a newspaper's personality should be judged "objectively" because it was separate from the personalities of the owners.[37] By 1927 Dix Harwood argued the "objective method" possessed a capacity for truthtelling similar to a photographic image and that evidence of objectivity could even be found in the Bible.[38]

Opposition to objective reporting emerged in the textbooks of only three professors: Curtis MacDougall, Sidney Kobre and Chilton Bush. Like Williams and Martin in 1911, these three embraced many of the values associated with objectivity but argued that interpretation was a stronger and more appropriate model for reporting.

Bush, who taught at Stanford University, argued that reporters had carried objectivity too far and, in so doing, had made their writing dull and bland. He took issue with Lippmann, saying, "The newspaper ought not to relinquish its leadership, but it ought to invoke realism in public thinking."[39] Kobre, who taught at Florida State University, wrote that publishers needed to reorganize their staffs to seek the meaning behind news events, in line with new thinking in psychology.[40]

The most celebrated attack on objectivity came from Curtis MacDougall of Northwestern University, whose widely used text, *Interpretative Reporting*, implied that it taught a completely new reporting technique. First published in 1938, the book went through eight revisions — 1938, 1948, 1957, 1963, 1968, 1972, 1977, 1982 and 1987 (the last with Robert Reid). Like Bush and Kobre, MacDougall supported many of the aspects of objectivity, such as reliance on facts and avoidance of editorial comment. His 1938 volume grew out of an earlier book after MacDougall recognized the need to combine reporting with interpretation because of the complexities of covering the increased activities of the federal government as it coped with the Depression. Much information, however, was eminently practical. The "cub reporter" was told to accept gracefully the task of rewriting press releases marked "B.O. Must" (business office must). MacDougall rationalized that this afforded a lesson in the interrelationship of different newspaper departments.[41]

Yet no other writer was more vehement in attacking objectivity — holding that it was impossible to attain, that it was a disservice to readers who needed more explanation, that it relegated newspapers to a weak role as a news medium and that it could not provide justification for journalism education. He held that neither reporters nor readers were capable of being objective: "Try as hard as he may, no reporter or writer ever will be able to achieve complete objectivity and if he did, as often as not the result would not give a true picture.... [O]bjective fact-giving — the professed ideal of journalism in a democracy — cannot succeed." MacDougall's criticism of objectivity was based on a brand of common sense that journalists could easily accept. But they could not as readily subscribe to his statement that reporters should be "allowed the liberty of injecting their own opinions to explain, evaluate and interpret what has happened."[42]

Interpretation versus objectivity became a hot subject of debate among journalists and educators. Academics and professionals deemed it acceptable for objectivity to be combined with interpretation. Fact and opinion were to be kept separate as standard professional practice, but some argued that objectivity would not suffer if reporters included background information, watched trends, cited sociological and psychological influences, and emphasized *why* and *how* instead of just who, what and when. When news articles made extensive use of speculation or outlined possibilities, motives and outcomes, they were labeled "analysis," (a term that newsroom jargon changed into "think pieces") or displayed as personal columns. Nevertheless, objectivity remained the professional watchword. Writing in a 1947 book that described practices at the *New York Herald Tribune*, George Cornish, the managing editor, declared, "The trend now, despite the exceptions, is toward greater objectivity."[43]

In the 1940s the term "profession" appeared increasingly in textbooks. Even when ethical principles were addressed, they took second place to the specifics of standardized reporting procedures. For instance, Charles C. Clayton of the *St. Louis Globe-Democrat* began his 1947 book *Newspaper Reporting Today* by reprinting the "Journalist Creed" written years earlier by Walter Williams of the University of Missouri. "I believe in the profession of journalism. I believe that the public journal is a public trust; that all connected with it are, to the full measure of their responsibility, trustees for the public; that acceptance of lesser service than the public service is betrayal of this trust."[44] Yet, most of his book, like its many predecessors, discussed practical subjects as specifically as possible: lead writing, article organization and the coverage of meetings, speeches and politics. Whether or why such techniques elevated journalism to a profession was never debated.

Five years later Grant M. Hyde, a professor of journalism at the University of Wisconsin, stated flatly, "Material and techniques that must be presented in any book on newspaper reporting are quite standardized and unchanging through the years...."[45]

Comparatively little material related to what Burton J. Bledstein called the distinguishing quality of a profession. Bledstein defined this as the examination of nature for principles and theoretical rules "transcending mechanical procedures, individual cases, miscellaneous facts, technical information and instrumental applications."[46] Nevertheless, although the books were far longer on technique than theory, they did have an underpinning: the concept of objectivity.

By the middle of the 20th century, objectivity stood at the apex of journalistic values in the United States. In 1943 Kent Cooper, general manager of the Associated Press, went so far as to call objectivity "the highest original moral concept ever developed in America and given to the world."[47] His successor, Wes Gallagher, likened it to both an intellectual and moral responsibility: "Like the priest or minister, the objective reporter is called upon to use his conscience and reason instead of his emotions."[48]

Objectivity and Journalism Education • *189*

Throughout the 20th and into the 21st century, the idea of journalists as inheritors of an empirical tradition continued to draw support. Reporters' routine preparations for writing articles have been found to be similar to the prewriting procedural pattern followed in social science research.[49] A 1989 *Journalism Educator* commentary drew parallels between journalists and scientists.[50]

On the other hand, objectivity has faced mounting opposition. In the early 1950s, Senator Joseph McCarthy of Wisconsin demonstrated that the techniques of objectivity could be used to manipulate the press into running unsubstantiated accusations that Communists had infiltrated the federal government. At the same time the United States was engaged in a nuclear arms race with the Union of Soviet Socialist Republics and fighting an undeclared war in Korea. In the shadow of these events, opponents contended that objectivity was not an appropriate rationale for reporting on complex developments. As the Hutchins Commission had declared in 1947: "It is no longer enough to report *the fact* truthfully. It is now necessary to report *the truth about the fact.*"[51]

During the later decades of the century, objectivity came under increasing fire, particularly from sociologists who disputed its rituals of reporting and writers who wanted to employ literary techniques. By the 1970s and 1980s the dominant view of journalism textbooks on the subject was that objectivity represented a noble attitude and goal, but that it could seldom be achieved. In a 1979 text Ken Metzler delayed mentioning the word "objectivity" until almost the final page because it had become so emotionally charged.[52] But Melvin Mencher, a Columbia professor, continued to uphold sweeping claims for objectivity: "The idea that through experience, the amassing of facts, a person may find truth reflects the American style of life. Journalists came naturally to adopt the objective approach of American empiricists and pragmatists."[53]

Whatever else can be said about objectivity, it has become ingrained in the language and culture of American journalism, if only as a point of attack. As succinctly stated in a 1997 book, "Objectivity is the enduring myth of journalism."[54]

NOTES

[1] Sara Lockwood Williams, *Twenty Years of Education for Journalism* (Columbia, Mo.: Stephens Publishing Co., 1929), 53.

[2] For a synopsis of the debate over the establishment of journalism schools, see Albert A. Sutton, *Education for Journalism in the United States from its Beginning to 1940* (Evanston, Ill: Northwestern University, 1945), 108-9.

[3] "Recruiting Young Journalists," *The Matrix* (journal of Theta Sigma Phi) 44 (September-October 1959): 10; Sutton, *Education for Journalism in the United States...*, 17-8.

[4] Walter Lippmann, "The Basic Problem of Democracy: What Modern Liberty

Means," *Atlantic Monthly* 124 (November 1919): 624.

[5] Quoted in John Hohenberg, *The Pulitzer Prizes: A History of the Awards in Books, Drama, Music, and Journalism Based on the Private Files over Six Decades* (New York: Columbia University Press, 1974), 20.

[6] De Forest O'Dell, *History of Journalism Education in the United States* (New York: Teachers College, Columbia University, 1935), 5-20, 21.

[7] See both O'Dell, *History of Journalism Education in the United States*, and Sutton, *Education for Journalism in the United States...*, who offer detailed overviews of the origins of journalism education.

[8] Jesse Haney, *Haney's Guide to Authorship* (New York: Haney, 1867), 92, 84.

[9] "An Editor," *Hints to Young Editors* (New Haven, Conn.: Chatfield, 1872), 17.

[10] G. A. Gaskell, *How to Write for the Press* (New York: Penman's Gazette, 1884), 11-2.

[11] Edwin Shuman, *Steps into Journalism* (Evanston, Ill.: Correspondence School of Journalism, 1894), 65.

[12] Nevada Davis Hitchcock, *What a Reporter Must Be* (Cleveland: Ralph Hitchcock, 1900), 8.

[13] Charles Olin, *Journalism* (Philadelphia: Penn, 1907), 121.

[14] James McCarthy, *The Newspaper Worker* (New York: Press Guild, 1906), 67.

[15] Robert Luce, *Writing for the Press*, 5th ed. (Boston: Clipping Bureau, 1907), 170-1.

[16] Edwin Hadlock, *Press Correspondence and Journalism* (San Francisco: United Press Syndicate, 1910), 18.

[17] J. Herbert Altschull, *From Milton to McLuhan: The Ideas Behind American Journalism* (New York: Longman, 1990), 263.

[18] Heywood Hale Broun, *Collected Edition of Heywood Broun* (New York: Harcourt, Brace, 1941), 397.

[19] J. Herbert Altschull, "The Origins of Journalism Education: A Cross-National Perspective," paper presented to the Association for Education in Journalism national convention, 7 August 1983, Corvallis, Ore., 3.

[20] See John L. Hulteng, *The Messenger's Motives: Ethical Problems of the News Media* (Englewood Cliffs, N.J.: Prentice-Hall, 1976), 18-9, 21.

[21] Thomas H. Zynda, "The Hollywood Version: Movie Portrayals of the Press," *Journalism History* 6 (Spring 1979): 17.

[22] Everett M. Rogers, *A History of Communication Study: A Biographical Approach* (New York: The Free Press, 1994), 19-20.

[23] Ibid., 20.

[24] For a concise description of positivism, see Kenneth McLeish, ed., *Key Ideas in Human Thought* (Rocklin, Calif.: Prima 1995), 583-4.

[25] Rogers, *A History of Communication Study...*, 20.

[26] Walter Lippmann, *Public Opinion* (New York: Macmillan, 1922), 82.

[27] Quoted in Willard G. Bleyer, *Main Currents in the History of American Journalism* (Boston: Houghton Mifflin, 1927), 138.

[28] Bleyer, ibid., 427, 428.

[29] John C. Merrill, *Journalism Ethics: Philosophical Foundations for News Media* (New York: St. Martin's Press, 1997), 106.

[30] Robert M. Neal, *News Gathering and News Writing* (New York: Prentice-

Hall, 1940), 13.

[31] For a full discussion, see Linda Steiner, "Construction of Gender in Newsreporting Textbooks: 1890-1990," *Journalism Monographs* 135 (1992).

[32] Charles Ross, *The Writing of News* (New York: Holt, 1911), 17; Walter Williams and Frank Martin, *The Practice of Journalism* (Columbia, Mo.: Lucas Brothers, 1911), 79, 20.

[33] Ronald T. Farrar, *Reluctant Servant: The Story of Charles G. Ross* (Columbia: University of Missouri Press, 1969), 68-70.

[34] Philip W. Porter and Norval N. Luxon, *The Reporter and the News* (New York: Appleton-Century, 1935), ix and 4.

[35] Ibid., 8.

[36] H. F. Harrington and T. T. Frankenberg, *Essentials in Journalism*, rev. ed. (Boston: Ginn, 1924), 31.

[37] Casper Yost, *The Principles of Journalism* (New York: Appleton, 1924), 63, 142.

[38] Dix Harwood, *Getting and Writing the News* (New York: Doran, 1927), 101.

[39] Chilton Bush, *Newspaper Reporting of Public Affairs* enl. ed. (New York: Appleton-Century, 1940), 327-8.

[40] Sidney Kobre, *Backgrounding the News* (Westport, Conn.: Greenwood, 1939), 12.

[41] Curtis MacDougall, *Interpretative Reporting* (New York: Macmillan, 1938), 141, 251, and 73-4.

[42] Ibid., 13-4.

[43] Quoted in Joseph G. Herzberg and Members of *The New York Herald Tribune* Staff, *Late City Edition* (New York: Holt, 1947), 233-5.

[44] Charles C. Clayton, *Newspaper Reporting Today* (New York: Odyssey Press, 1952), ix.

[45] Grant M. Hyde, *Newspaper Reporting* (New York: Prentice-Hall, 1952), iii.

[46] Burton J. Bledstein, *The Culture of Professionalism* (New York: Norton, 1976), 90.

[47] Quoted in William B. Blankenburg and Ruth Walden, "Objectivity, Interpretation and Economy in Reporting," *Journalism Quarterly* 54 (Autumn 1977): 591.

[48] Quoted in Ralph S. Izard, Hugh M. Culbertson and Donald A. Lambert, *Fundamentals of News Reporting*, 2nd ed. (Dubuque, Iowa: Kendall/Hunt, 1973), vii.

[49] Elise Keoleian Parsigian, "News Reporting: Method in the Midst of Chaos," *Journalism Quarterly* 64 (Winter 1987): 721.

[50] Lawrence Cranberg, "Plea for Recognition of Scientific Character of Journalism," *Journalism Educator* 44 (Winter 1989): 49.

[51] Commission on Freedom of the Press, *A Free and Responsible Press* (Chicago: University of Chicago Press, 1947), 22.

[52] Ken Metzler, *Newsgathering* (Englewood Cliffs, N.J.: Prentice-Hall, 1979), 313.

[53] Melvin Mencher, *Basic News Writing* (Dubuque, Iowa: Brown, 1983), 174.

[54] Rob Anderson, Robert Dardenne and George M. Killenberg, *The Conversation of Journalism: Communication, Community, and News* (Westport, Conn.: Praeger, 1997), 47.

CHAPTER 14

Objectivity in Broadcast Journalism
by Lynn Boyd Hinds

Broadcast journalism was born in the "Golden Age" of radio — the three decades between 1920, when commercial radio was born, and about 1950, when television caught on with the public. The mores and values that evolved during that formative period would come to be accepted as normative for radio news. By the time television eclipsed radio, the assumptions of broadcast journalism were well established.

The nature of the electronic medium was such that objectivity was not an issue in the beginning. News was reported live, by necessity in the early years, by habit later. The immediacy of radio was somehow equated with the notion of the transparency of the medium. News reports were simple recitation of facts, as gleaned from the standard sources of newspapers or wire services. The live announcers gave every appearance of objectivity. There was little reason to think otherwise.

The rise of network news would heighten the human element, as commentators added their personalities to the news. The audience for each commentator at the end of radio's second decade would find the news to be an objective presentation because of the high degree of credibility attributed to the commentator. The ethos of the presenter, combined with the immediacy of the medium and the factual basis of news would form the basic tenets that would prevail in broadcast journalism. Those tenets evolved, perhaps ineluctably, from the earliest days of broadcasting.

For most of its first decade, all radio was local. Soon after KDKA's first broadcast of election results on November 2, 1920, radio stations proliferated nationwide. What passed for news, in that period, was mostly limited to announcers "whose idea of legwork," as Robert Kintner, who was director of news at ABC during the early days, remembered it, "was to run out and buy all the newspapers so they could read the headlines over the air."[1] Announcers would often add, "For further details, consult your local newspaper." The standard for news on most local stations up until the coming of television would continue to be "rip and read." Quincy Howe, who was a prominent radio commentator in the prewar era, reflecting on the news practices of the 1930s, advised that "most of what you hear over the radio is the same news you read in the newspaper, gathered by the same people...."[2] On local radio stations the men[3] who reported the news were announcers, who were selected for their pleasant voices more than for journalistic skills and told to "read it straight."[4]

Thus when an announcer sat in a studio and read copy gleaned from the pages of a wire service or a local paper, what was transmitted to listeners were facts as reported by common sources. Since radio reported what listeners could find confirmed in their newspapers, there was little reason to question objectivity. There was a sharing of official reality on the part of newspapers and radio, resulting from a reliance on what the journalist Tom Wicker called "official, conventional wisdom," passed on "in the guise of objectivity."[5]

There was good reason for local radio to play it safe on news. The Federal Communications Commission was, in those days, the "dreaded FCC." The threat of losing the license to broadcast, and thus the privilege of doing business, posed a threat of draconian proportion to a young industry that was treated by the government as a public utility. The Communications Act of 1934, which had created the FCC as a federal watchdog, mandated that radio would broadcast in "the public interest, convenience, and necessity."[6] The vague language served only to intensify the threat, for the interpretation about what those words meant rested solely with the FCC.

The creation of networks during the second decade would change the nature of radio news. The FCC had no authority over network radio because networks were not and are not licensed since the networks do not broadcast, but simply relay their signal to local affiliates, which then broadcast the programs to listeners. So it was on network radio that the neutral voices of local radio announcers were replaced by the strong personalities of radio "commentators."

Audiences came to trust the commentators; and, as the historian Irving Fang observed, the commentators came to exercise considerable influence on America for the two decades between 1929 and 1948. "For whatever reason," Fang wrote, "Americans came to trust radio commentators more than they did newspapers.... These were troubled times. The commentators brought explanations, sometimes along with delivering the day's news.... The radio commentators helped to clarify it all, letting others see matters as they saw matters, talking to their fellow Americans.... [O]ur favorite radio commentator was there to sort it all out."[7] It was perhaps inevitable that the credibility of the speaker would play a significant role in establishing the acceptance of the message as objective truth.

It was apparent from the start of the networks. In 1930, NBC and CBS, both about two years old, each sent a commentator to London for the Five Power Naval Conference. Both William Hard of NBC and Frederic William Wile of CBS had been Washington newspaper correspondents. Wile took along his friend, Cesar Saerchinger, whom he would hire to represent CBS in England after Wile returned to America. (Saerchinger would be replaced seven years later by Edward R. Murrow.) Saerchinger, who had never even seen a microphone until then, provided a pristine description of the effect the new medium had on the task of the two commentators:

> Their business was to report every few days, by radio, on the progress of the Conference, speaking by way of a nation-wide 'hook-up' direct to the radio audience of the United States and Canada. This was, essentially, no different from the daily cable reporting by newspaper correspondents, except for the medium employed. In effect, they were to telephone their observations from what amounted to little more than a telephone booth within a mile of St. James's Palace, where the Conference met, to a radio control-room in New York, whence their voices were instantaneously retransmitted to the sixty or more broadcasting stations constituting a radio 'chain' and simultaneously broadcast from these stations.[8]

Thus the basic elements contributing to credibility were present: reporters narrated the same facts being reported by newspaper correspondents. But radio offered advantages: not only its live nature, but the personality of the reporter, "the superior power of the spoken word over the written word," as Saerchinger put it. "They could convey, by inflection and emphasis, what no amount of punctuation could suggest; they could capture and hold the interest of their audience by the appeal of their voices instead of relying upon words in cold print."[9]

The introduction of the personality of the reporter or commentator was, given the nature of the medium, inevitable in broadcast journalism. Since Aristotle's *Rhetoric* in the fourth century B.C., ethos has been considered a key element in the credibility of the speaker. A person who sounds intelligent, of good character and with good will toward the audience is more likely to be trusted to tell the truth. Thus a reporter who has high ethos with the audience will appear credible and, by implication, objective. The credibility or ethos of the commentator, noted so early by Cesar Saerchinger, would play a major role in the controversy over objectivity that would arise during the war.

Networks were slow to develop the capacity to gather news, and in 1934 Lowell Thomas told an interviewer that there really were not any news broadcasters. "We're really entertainers," he said. Broadcast news as we know it today — with more emphasis on reporting and less on commentary — only slowly took shape.

The early efforts of NBC and CBS to gather as well as disseminate

Objectivity in Broadcast Journalism • 195

news are instructive. A. A. Schechter revealed some interesting observations, pertinent to objectivity, in his anecdotal memoir of his years at NBC. There was an insistence on staying with facts during that early era. "A member of the news staff consults me on a 'dangerous' line in a broadcast to be delivered in less than an hour by a well-known commentator," Schechter wrote. "The line *was* dangerous — because there were no supporting facts." He added, "I killed it, of course."[10] Not only was there an effort to "stay with the facts," but the facts were those of official reality, congruent with the expectations listeners had from other news sources. When Schechter got the idea to broadcast citizens' reactions to the Second Inaugural Address of President Franklin D. Roosevelt, he decided to show off the technology by broadcasting live from the ocean liner *Rex* off the coast of Gibraltar. The citizen passengers who chose to participate in the live broadcast had to write a script of what they intended to say for approval before they were allowed to give their "spontaneous" reactions into a microphone.

Broadcasting live meant taking the risk of having participants stray from official reality. Schechter tells the story, during the coverage of the 1937 flood in the Ohio Valley, of interviewing a boy who said, "Aw, it's nothin' ... every year we have some kind of flood trouble." Schechter added, "On the whole, we've been lucky with our broadcasts involving statements from survivors, so we're philosophic about our flops."[11] He added a note about a discussion with a panel of experts on ways to prevent floods. "This inevitably means stepping on a few Congressional toes; but these discussions have been so objective that in the main reaction has been favorable." "Objective" here is clearly meant to indicate remaining within the parameters of acceptable facts, which conform to the expectations of official reality.

Before the Munich crisis of September 1938, when Hitler demanded that Czechoslovakia cede the Sudetanland to Germany, neither radio news nor commentators attracted widespread attention. Much news was considered "sustaining," a designation indicating that stations were donating the unsponsored time to demonstrate their respect for the FCC's concern with broadcasting in the public "interest, convenience and necessity." Entertainment was what drew public attention. When a news event was dramatic enough to provide entertainment, the public tuned in, and that might mean that a fresh news personality was born. Gabriel Heatter, for example, gained overnight fame with his reporting of the trial of Bruno Hauptmann for kidnapping the Lindbergh baby. By 1935 CBS was presenting a Friday evening program called "Kaltenborn Edits the News," which opened with the announcement: "What the news means is even more important than the news itself. H.V. Kaltenborn, editor, author, dean of radio commentators, tells you what's back of the headlines.... You hear the voice of authority when Kaltenborn edits the News."[12] The temptation to make news entertaining was

FAIR AND BALANCED • *196*

strong early on.

Events on the continent would attract public attention to radio news. CBS and NBC had begun to focus on Europe in the early 1930s. (Mutual, founded in 1934, had a news director, but contributed little to foreign broadcasts until later.) CBS had Saerchinger in London, where he arranged to broadcast "talks" by noted personalities. Often "arranging" meant that the network paid for the privilege. NBC outbid CBS, for example, for the rights to broadcast Hitler's first speech after his election.[13] Most informational programs broadcast from Europe were planned events or a restrained reading of formal copy. The model seems to have been the BBC, which was not averse to having an announcer say, at the time scheduled for a brief update: "Owing to a lack of events, there is no news tonight."

Until war loomed large in Europe, Alexander Kendrick's observation is accurate: "Radio was not yet an accepted part of the world of journalism, though it purveyed news of a sort on the periphery of its daily serials and musical programs."[14] The Munich crisis changed public perception of radio news radically. H.V. Kaltenborn set the standard, sleeping in the CBS studio for nearly three weeks, being awakened often to read the latest bulletin and interpret its meaning. From Sept. 11, 1938, through the end of the month, both CBS and NBC provided nearly round-the-clock coverage of the events in Munich. News soon became a popular genre. Newscasts were added across the radio schedule both by networks and local stations, as advertisers flocked to sponsor news programs. Network commentators found themselves in demand as they combined news with the interpretation of dramatic events. Raymond Swing, Elmer Davis and H.V. Kaltenborn gained sizable followings and commercial sponsors as affiliated stations picked up their newscasts.

By the time the war ended, the public was accustomed to getting much of its news from radio. Indeed, after September 1939, most Americans listened to the news before they read it. The terse announcement, "We interrupt this program ..." had become an expected part of the broadcast day. If radio news focused public attention on foreign affairs, it is also true that foreign affairs provided the occasion for radio news to come into its own. Network commentators achieved a surge of popularity with the coming of war, and they made the most of the opportunity that radio provided to develop their ethos. Kaltenborn, one of the most popular commentators, is a prime example. The historian David Culbert's study concluded that Kaltenborn's "commentaries contained little analysis. He had a good mind, but prepared his newscasts carelessly. Using the same evidence, he often contradicted himself. He presented a great deal of unsupported opinion."[15] Yet he was especially effective. Radio listeners trusted Kaltenborn, much as television viewers would later come to trust Walter Cronkite.

The audience trusted and believed the commentator, not so much

Objectivity in Broadcast Journalism • *197*

because of what he said, for mostly it was a summary of news bulletins with an occasional editorial comment added. "What he exploits is not a point of view but a voice, a manner, a distinctive way of speaking."[16] Commentators provided what Alexander Kendrick called "the feel of the news, with something of their own personalities injected into the presentation."[17] "Some were uninformed most of the time," said David Culbert, "even if they made up in self-confidence what they lacked in preparation."[18] And Robert Kintner added that they "found support for their positions in unusual public acceptance of their personalities,"[19] in other words, their ethos.

Radio's commentators, however, did not violate the official view of reality with impunity. As events in Europe developed and radio grew into a major source of news, what David Culbert calls a "re-newal of national self-awareness" developed. Boake Carter, a prominent commentator who advocated isolationism before Munich, was gone from CBS by August 1938. Thereafter, "none of the most popular commentators opposed the foreign policy of Franklin D. Roosevelt."[20] Commentators exploited their personalities in order to provide interpretations of news events, but usually within the limits of what was perceived as official reality, especially as it related to foreign policy, agreed upon by most journalists and within the expectations of the public.

In 1943, as commentators began to rely on their credibility with listeners to express their opinions more explicitly and to stray beyond official reality, the CBS news director, Paul White, published a memorandum as a full-page advertisement in New York papers.[21] To his surprise, he claimed, the memo "touched off a minor explosion within and without the industry," and he was roundly attacked. That the memo was published in several newspapers suggests that White's expressions of surprise were exaggerated, but it also suggests that commentators were using their ethos to go beyond the bounds of reporting mere facts.

White says that he assumed that he had merely been stating long-standing principles that had first been articulated by Edward Klauber, executive vice president of CBS, in a memorandum circulated in 1939, two years before Pearl Harbor. Klauber was second only to William S. Paley, and White regarded Klauber as the godfather of radio news, partly because he had brought his years of experience as editor of the *New York Times* to CBS. Klauber's memo is worth quoting at length. Klauber noted that the network had a "no-editorial policy" and that in being "fair and factual," news presenters should not only refrain from personal opinions but also from a microphone manner "designed to cast doubt, suspicion, sarcasm, ridicule, or anything of that sort on the matter they are presenting." What news analysts *were* entitled to do was to

... elucidate and illuminate the news out of common knowledge, or special knowledge possessed by them or made available to them by this organization through its news sources. They should point out the facts on both sides, show contradictions with the known record, and so on. They should bear in mind that in a democracy it is important that people not only should know but should understand, and it is the analyst's function to help the listener to understand, to weigh, and to judge, but not to do the judging for him.

Klauber's memo drew mild praise in 1939, while White's restatement of those principles created controversy in the middle of the war. This was partly due to White's criticism of a broadcast that Cecil Brown had made. Brown had completed a quick nationwide tour, during which he had interviewed a number of people. White says that he had received letters from various cities, "which caused me to suspect prejudgment, that his questioning had invited the answers he wanted." When Brown broadcast his conclusions that citizens had lost interest in the war effort, White accused him of editorializing, and Brown resigned. White's logic is interesting. He explained:

> It would have been all right, I told Brown, for him to say, 'I have just talked with Americans all over the country and *from information I received in those interviews,* I gathered the impression that Americans are losing interest in the war.' That, I said, would be reporting. But to say something incapable of proof and to say it flatly was out-and-out editorializing....

Once again, fact was the canon against which objectivity was measured. But once again fact is interpreted to mean "official reality," the facts that are generally agreed on by journalists and that fit with the expectations of listeners. Concerns for random samples of opinion, measured with neutral instruments, the generally accepted method of scientific inquiry, were lost amid the devotion to fact. And because Brown's opinion was contrary to the common agreement with the administration's foreign policy it was, therefore, considered unacceptably nonobjective.

H.V. Kaltenborn was one critic of White's memo. In a speech in which he protested what he called "ham-stringing," he expressed a rather clear view of objectivity:

> No news analyst worth his salt could or would be completely neutral or objective. He shows his editorial bias by every act of selection or rejection from the vast mass of news material placed before him. He often expresses his opinion by the mere matter of shading and emphasis. He selects from a speech, or interview, or public statement the particular sentences or paragraphs that appeal to him. Every exercise of his editorial judgment constitutes an expression of

opinion.[22]

In his response to Kaltenborn, White observed that it was merely a matter of how one defines "opinion" or "objective." Since all journalism is human, and since all humans do not think alike, bias is present in the reporter in the field "or anywhere else a man or woman sees something, hears something, and then reports it." White admits that complete journalistic objectivity is only an ideal. But he adds that so is the Golden Rule also only an ideal, but that should not prevent one from striving to follow it.

The discussion of objectivity in broadcast journalism was extensive. Paul White participated in a CBS network discussion with John W. Vandercook, who represented the Association of Radio News Analysts. Vandercook attributed to CBS a benevolent intention, believing the network wanted to broadcast only the truth. But that, as Vandercook saw it, "is the basic fallacy. Columbia infers that it is competent to judge what is fact and what is opinion. That's an extraordinary assertion."[23] The association of analysts, he added, has the same goal: to seek the truth. But that is best achieved, not by corporate consensus, but by the intention of each analyst, who, "out of his experience, out of his personal knowledge and out of his constant study of all available opinion, out of all available so-called facts, seeks to tell you, his listeners, the truth as he sees it his own way." So long as analysts are free to tell things as they see them, the listener can choose whom to listen to, a choice "that can only be made at the point of outlet in radio and not at the point of origin." In other words, let the audience decide who is or is not credible.

White added that as the controversy died, NBC and CBS "did their best to prevent the self-designated Messiahs from spreading their messages in the guise of news analysis." Both the ABC and Mutual networks, he noted, solved the problem by attempting to balance opposing political philosophies to try to achieve a reasonable balance in points of view. But the short-lived, conscious concern with objectivity soon returned to a concern with credibility. Irving Fang reports a "friendly heart-to-heart talk" that Kaltenborn recalled having with the CBS vice president of news, Edward Klauber:

> He would explain how a smart news analyst could put his personal opinions over to the public without being too blatant about it. "Just don't be so personal," he'd say to me. "Use such phrases as 'It is said...,' 'There are those who believe...,' 'The opinion is held in well-informed quarters...,' 'Some experts have come to the conclusion....' Why keep on saying 'I think' and 'I believe' when you can put over the same idea much more persuasively by quoting someone else?"[24]

Despite the public debate about objectivity, the concern of broadcast journalism soon shifted back to a focus on credibility.

If there was an individual who embodied that idea of the reporting of facts in a live format by a reporter with considerable ethos, it was Edward R. Murrow. He rose to prominence during World War II, when radio journalism was reaching maturity, and his career personified the transition from radio news to television news. Quincey Howe once observed that "the one completely distinctive contribution that radio has made to news coverage is the eyewitness report of current happenings."[25] The term "eyewitness report" conjures the name of Murrow, who is often celebrated as the person most responsible for creating modern broadcast journalism. Perhaps it was because he was not limited by the practices of professional journalism that he was able to utilize to the fullest the dramatic potential inherent in radio reporting.

In deciding how to shape a story, most of the commentators shared an understanding that came from the journalism profession, for most had come to radio with a newspaper background. H.V. Kaltenborn began providing informational talks in 1922 while he was a reporter for the *Brooklyn Eagle*. Edward Klauber came to CBS from the *New York Times* in 1930. Paul White of CBS and Abe Schechter of NBC both came with newspaper backgrounds. Boake Carter, one of the first news readers on CBS, quit his job at Philadelphia's *Daily News* to join WCAU. Raymond Gram Swing worked for several newspapers before becoming a commentator for the Mutual Network. These men brought with them assumptions about what did and what did not constitute news and about how to construct a news article, whatever the medium. Douglas Edwards, speaking of early television, reflected this viewpoint when he said, "Our philosophy was to put on a real news show, news being just that, whether in cuneiform or smoke signals, print or picture."[26] Professionalism and objectivity have long been intertwined. The print journalists brought to the new medium a "news sense" that they had acquired through college journalism programs and on the job.[27]

But Murrow had no newspaper background. Thus, unhampered by many of the assumptions adhered to by news professionals, he was free to use the dramatic opportunities inherent in radio. The live broadcasts he did during the 27 months between the start of World War II on Sept. 1, 1939, until Pearl Harbor, on Dec. 7, 1941, used radio in "a brilliantly creative fashion."[28] Murrow achieved a synthesis of live reporting with an enormously high ethos to elevate the credibility of broadcast journalism to its zenith. Questioning the objectivity of his eyewitness reports simply did not occur to his listeners.

Although highly credible, the Murrow broadcasts were not meant to be objective. He admitted that his goal was to promote American intervention in the war. He accomplished this indirectly by his choice of which facts to report and by the dramatic way he reported. With his

Objectivity in Broadcast Journalism • 201

magnificent voice, night after night he narrated the sounds of the British people as they continued the quotidian tasks of life in the midst of daily and nightly bombing raids, within the context of the pervasive threat of invasion. His reports made events immediate and compelling in a way in which newspaper reports could not. Americans got the sense that what they heard about London could soon be happening in New York or Philadelphia. Murrow stuck to the facts, but the facts he chose to narrate created the meaning that he intended. A typical example is a broadcast from August 1940. He "reported":

> I spent five hours this afternoon on the outskirts of London. Bombs fell out there today. It is indeed surprising how little damage a bomb will do unless, of course, it scores a direct hit. But I found that one bombed house looks pretty much like another bombed house. It's about the people I'd like to talk, the little people who live in those little houses, who have no uniforms and get no decorations for bravery. Those men whose only uniform was a tin hat were digging unexploded bombs out of the ground this afternoon. There were two women who gossiped across the narrow strip of tired brown grass that separated their two houses. They didn't have to open their kitchen windows in order to converse. The glass had been blown out.[29]

True, Murrow injected an explicit opinion from time to time. He concluded his August 1940 broadcast, for example, this way: "If the people who rule Britain are made of the same stuff as the little people I have seen today.... then the defense of Britain will be something of which men will speak with awe and admiration so long as the English language survives." After hearing the dramatic simplicity of his narration, it was difficult to distinguish opinion from fact.

Murrow's ability to persuade by the simple narration of an eyewitness account was the consummation of credibility for radio news. It was also a harbinger of television news. The difference between a recitation of facts and a narration of the facts, especially from the scene, along with the ambient sounds of airplanes dropping bombs, is a vast difference. David Culbert provides a salient example: "On September 23, 1940, Fulton Lewis, Jr. offered a dull recital of detail to prove that Nazi bombing raids had hardly damaged London.... The next night Murrow stood on a rooftop in London. As air raid sirens sounded, listeners heard bombs dropping on unknown points."[30] The difference in credibility could hardly be more stark.

Murrow sometimes avowed that he could analyze the news without advocacy, but a close reading of his broadcasts reveals a partisanship on important issues. He accomplished his advocacy by making his listeners feel that they had actually stood with him on a London rooftop. "I have an idea," he once said, "that radio's job is more than that of a mere translator. If it is to be effective, it must transport the listener to the country from which the broadcast is originating and say to him: 'Look, Joe, if you were here this is what you would see and hear and smell and taste.'"[31] His broadcasts were effective in creating a climate that was favorable toward Britain and toward American intervention in the war. He was not unaware of what he was doing, both in the effects of his broadcasts and how they were achieved. There is even testimony to his using recordings to create the desired effect. William Shirer admitted that the CBS crew did make limited use of recordings during their "live" broadcasts from Europe, mainly because the Germans didn't always time their bombing raids to coincide with Murrow's broadcasts.[32]

Robert Kintner said that Murrow (and Elmer Davis) had injected opinion into their reports, but that "their basic commodity was hard news, carefully interpreted, and such opinion as they did express was based solidly in fact. Both found support for their positions in unusual public acceptance of their personalities."[33] Implicit within the facts that Murrow reported and the way in which he wove his narrative was his view of political reality. So long as he was credible, the objectivity of his reports would not be questioned. He had written, in a letter to his parents, that he knew they had wanted him to become a preacher: "But now I am preaching from a powerful pulpit. Often I am wrong but I am trying to talk as I would have talked were I a preacher. One need not wear a reversed collar to be honest."[34] Edward Bliss concludes that examples of Murrow's breaking the CBS commandment regarding objectivity are not difficult to find. He reported what he thought to be right. "He got away with it because of his prestige and because, deep down, enough people knew he was right."[35] Murrow had such high ethos with his listeners that his credibility obliterated any question of objectivity.

Television would inevitably replace radio as the primary medium for broadcast journalism, and with the addition of the visual element the ethos of the reporter would be further enhanced. Murrow became a television news pioneer, transferring his enormous credibility from radio to the new visual medium. The kind of live contemporary account he did on radio, an "eyewitness" account, would be strengthened as broadcast journalism developed through television. Seeing became synonymous with objectivity. Walter Lippmann had foreseen this in 1922, when he spoke of photographs having "the kind of authority over imagination to-day, which the printed word had yesterday, and the spoken word before that. They seem utterly real."[36] Lippmann projected that motion pictures, with "the talking picture," would only enhance that tendency. Television pictures showing events would complete that appearance of objectivity that live broadcasts on radio had begun. Seeing would equal believing.

Objectivity in Broadcast Journalism • *203*

Above all, television reporters must have ethos with the viewer. "Anchorpeople must be attractive, likable, and convincing. Indeed, journalistic ability is often subordinate to performance skills," according to the author of a recent book.[37] An excellent example is provided by a front-page obituary written by a *Miami Herald* senior writer, Martin Merzer, on the death of a pioneering broadcast journalist. "Ann Bishop wore credibility like a cloak," he writes. "She gazed into a camera and transmitted not only the news, but also integrity.... Viewers instinctively knew they could trust Ann Bishop. Something indefinable in her eyes, her voice, her manner.... You always had the sense that she had it right."[38] Ann Bishop had high ethos with her audience. "Blessed with the ability to remain unflappable on the air, to speak extemporaneously, to connect with viewers, she particularly excelled during great crises and other big stories." Public trust, the ethos of the reporter, remains a central ingredient in making broadcast journalism credible, and thus accepted as objective.

In conclusion, local radio adhered to live reports of facts that represented the consensus of the journalistic profession, presented by announcers who were news readers. As network radio news evolved, it progressed through stages. Early on, commentators such as Lowell Thomas avoided controversial subjects, preferring to emphasize drama and personalities in their reports, so the question of objectivity was quiescent. In the prewar years, H.V. Kaltenborn could not have avoided controversy even if he had wanted to. "To him," Quincy Howe concluded, "the news is not a spectacle to be dramatically reported but a succession of moral issues to be conscientiously expounded."[39] Numerous such commentators would follow. Such exuberance created a minor flap over objectivity, which was soon forgotten. In the culminating period of radio news, Edward R. Murrow "created an entirely new type of reporting which combines news, opinion, and local color."[40] That reporting was brilliantly constructed out of the elements that provided a natural credibility for the electronic media: it was factually based, eyewitness news, presented live by a person who had the trust of the audience. These tenets create a credibility — an impression of objectivity — for modern broadcast journalism that too often substitutes for objectivity itself.

NOTES

[1] Robert E. Kintner, *Broadcasting and the News* (New York: Harper & Row, 1965), 1.

[2] Quincy Howe, *The News and How to Understand It, In Spite of the Newspapers, in Spite of the Magazines, in Spite of Radio* (New York: Simon & Schuster, 1940), 159.

[3] The use of "men" reflects the bias of the early days of broadcasting, when it

was not exclusively, but overwhelmingly, a male-dominated occupation.

[4] Joseph Julian's memoir says that he was firmly instructed to stop using his interpretive talents because "news reports are supposed to be dispassionate and objective." *This Was Radio; A Personal Memoir* (New York: Viking, 1975), 26.

[5] Tom Wicker, "The Tradition of Objectivity in the American Press – What's Wrong with It" *Massachusetts Historical Society* 71: 83-100.

[6] The Communications Act of 1934 simply repeated the language of the Radio Act of 1927, intended to establish a discretionary licensing standard. Frank J. Kahn, ed., *Documents of American Broadcasting*, 4th ed. (Englewood Cliffs, N.J.: Prentice-Hall, 1984), 40-56.

[7] Irving Fang, *Those Radio Commentators*. (Ames: Iowa State University Press, 1977), 3-4.

[8] Cesar Saerchinger, *Hello America; Radio Adventures in Europe* (Boston: Houghton Mifflin, 1938), 4.

[9] Ibid., 5.

[10] A.A Schechter, with Edward Anthony, *I Live On Air* (New York: A. Stokes, 1941), 99.

[11] Ibid., 165-6.

[12] Fang, *Those Radio Commentators*, 28.

[13] David H. Hosley, *As Good As Any: Foreign Correspondennce on American Radio, 1930-1940* (Westport, Conn.: Greenwood Press, 1984), 24.

[14] Kendrick, *Prime Time...*, 139.

[15] Culbert, *News For Everyman...*, 205.

[16] Howe, *The News and How to Understand It...*, 170.

[17] Kendrick, *Prime Time...*, 140.

[18] Culbert, *News For Everyman...*, 201.

[19] Kintner, *Broadcasting and the News*, 9.

[20] Culbert, *News For Everyman...*, 5.

[21] For White's account of the episode, see Paul W. White, *News On the Air* (New York: Harcourt, Brace and Co., 1947), 198-207.

[22] Quoted in ibid., 204.

[23] Quoted in ibid., 205.

[24] Fang, *Those Radio Commentators*, 38-9.

[25] Howe, *The News and How to Understand It...*, 159.

[26] Edward Bliss Jr., *Now the News; The Story of Broadcast Journalism* (New York: Columbia University Press, 1991), 228.

[27] See, for example, Barbara Kelly's chapter 11, "Objectivity and the Trappings of Professionalism, 1900-1950," in this book.

[28] Culbert, *News For Everyman...*, 180. Culbert provides a summary of the characteristics of the broadcasts of Murrow on pp. 179-200.

[29] *In Search of Light; The Broadcasts of Edward R. Murrow, 1938-1961*, Edward Bliss, Jr., ed. (New York: Da Capo Press, 1997), 30.

[30] Culbert, *News For Everyman...*, 207.

[31] Quoted in White, *News On the Air*, 368.

[32] Hosley, *As Good As Any...*, 138.

[33] Kintner, *Broadcasting and the News*, 9.

[34] Kendrick, *Prime Time...*, 195.

35 Bliss, *Now the News...*, 207.

36 Walter Lippmann, *Public Opinion* (New York: Macmillan, 1922), 61.

37 Art Silverblatt, *Media Literacy; Keys to Interpreting Media Messages* (Westport, Conn.: Praeger, 1995), 16.

38 Martin Merzer, *Miami Herald*, 15 November 1997, A1.

39 Howe, *The News and How to Understand It...*, 171.

40 Ibid., 175.

CHAPTER 15

The Challenges of Civil Rights and Joseph McCarthy

By David R. Davies

Senator Joseph R. McCarthy often gets the credit — or the blame — for weakening journalists' faith in objectivity after World War II. And indeed, his mastery of the news media did help undermine the foundations of what had been journalism's most hallowed principle for decades. But McCarthy's anti-Communist crusade of the early 1950s was only one of the journalistic challenges that led journalists to question objectivity in the early postwar years. In fact, a succession of events between 1945 and 1960, including the events of the civil rights movement, fostered increasing doubts about objectivity; the long-running McCarthy story was just one of them.

The events that challenged objectivity, defined then as reporting free of interpretation, came from both inside and outside journalism. The efforts inside journalism came just as World War II ended and were manifested primarily in the journalism profession's efforts at self-improvement, including a renewed emphasis on interpretation that acknowledged the shortcomings of objectivity. Critics outside journalism were also heard, as in the 1947 report of the Commission on the Freedom of the Press, the so-called Hutchins Commission. These critics assailed objectivity directly and called for change in journalistic practices. Then, in the 1950s, several long-running news stories helped demonstrate the critics' prescience. To their dismay, reporters found that just-the-facts journalism was ill suited for explaining the complex news about McCarthy and school desegregation.

So by 1960, journalists' faith in objectivity was substantially weaker than it had been in 1945. Objectivity was much more open to question, and interpretation was more readily accepted. While journalists continued to define objective news articles as those that presented the facts of a news article without benefit of the reporter's opinion, they were coming to understand that this journalistic ideal was not always suited to imparting the truth of an event. By 1960 reporters were much more willing — even eager — to include interpretive elements in news stories.

The seeds of an increasing acceptance of interpretation were rooted in the postwar drive to improve America's newspapers. Economic and industrial news crowded newspapers after the war and seemed to demand a higher quality of newswriting. Efforts to improve journalism blossomed after the war both at individual newspapers and on a national scale through newspaper organizations, particularly the American Society of Newspaper Editors, the Associated Press Managing Editors and the wire services. Before the turmoil of two world wars, "People were interested in love, murder, and money," observed *Detroit Free Press* editor Malcolm W. Bingay shortly after World War II ended. "Today even the poorest of our newspapers give over 70 percent of space to economic and industrial problems."[1] Editors and publishers believed that they had a responsibility to make such important information understandable to the public. Lester Markel, Sunday editor of the *New York Times*, said, "[N]ever has the news been so complex and the need of understanding it more urgent."[2]

In his presidential address to the American Association of Journalism Teachers in early 1946, the journalism educator Frederic E. Merwin, director of the Rutgers University School of Journalism, defined interpretation as newswriting that explained the "how" and "why" of news events:

Interpretation means clarification, integration, and logical generalization. It merges background, present, and likely future. It always must be considered as a reporting not only of the bud that has just broken through the ground but also with the roots underneath which forced the bud out into the air.[3]

Curtis D. MacDougall, a Northwestern University journalism professor and longtime advocate of interpretive reporting, said in January 1947 that both World War II and the Depression had increased journalists' emphasis on the "why" in news articles. MacDougall, whose textbook on interpretive reporting was first published in 1938, even claimed that interpretation had overtaken objectivity. "So-called objectivity," he said, "has been discovered to be what it always was — impossible and, if possible, undesirable."[4]

A vocal exponent of interpretive reporting was James Reston, diplomatic correspondent of the *New York Times*, who once said he was "nuts about the subject of explanatory reporting." He saw interpretation as necessary both for public understanding and for the survival of newspapers because it allowed newspapers to serve a need unfilled by any competitor.[5]

In the early 1940s, the Associated Press announced that it would step up its use of interpretive reporting, and increasing acceptance of the practice was evident at meetings of AP managing editors in the late 1940s.[6] The AP managing editor Alan Gould saw interpretation and objectivity as compatible, circulating a memo to his staff in 1947-1948 to tell reporters that interpretation was expected in daily news articles, yet they should also be objective.[7]

As part of a 1948 self-study, the APME called for more interpretive reporting on the AP news wires:

> The essence of the problem has been, and still is, this: Should AP writers have latitude to interpret the news? Should they be permitted to appraise the cause and effect (and thereby the significance) of news developments? Should they be permitted to state as facts what they know from their own experience and observations to be true, without giving the source for their statements? The committee believes the answer to all of these questions is 'Yes,' assuming that certain safeguards are established to preserve fundamental AP objectivity.[8]

The trend toward interpretation was reinforced by the Hutchins Commission report of March 1947, part of a wave of postwar press criticism. Founded by Henry Luce, publisher of *Time* and *Fortune*, and chaired by the University of Chicago president Robert M. Hutchins, the Hutchins Commission took testimony and interviews from more than 275 journalists and experts in the course of a four-year study. In its final report, published as a book and also in a special edition of *Fortune* in April 1947, the commission called on the press to better meet its responsibilities to society and to democracy. It said that many newspapers were falling far short of that goal and that the entire newspaper industry was subject to a growing monopoly that threatened newspapers' ability to serve the public. "Today our society needs, first, a truthful, comprehensive, and intelligent account of the day's events in a context which gives them meaning," the commissioners wrote.[9] In other words, the Hutchins Commission was joining the call for more interpretive reporting.

Journalists accused the commission of unfairly failing to include a working journalist on the panel, of inviting government regulation, of unfairly lumping in radio and movies with the print press and of failing to conduct elaborate research. Louis M. Lyons of the Nieman Foundation, summarizing press reaction in an article for *Atlantic Monthly*, said that most newspapers ignored the commission's report, underplayed it or misrepresented its findings.[10] For all of its importance to journalism historians as a bellwether for increasing press responsibility, the report was largely ignored in 1947.

While interpretation was on the rise in the late 1940s, it remained controversial. The debate was evident in a University of Oregon poll of 50 editors across the country in 1947. Most respondents favored the use of some interpretive news articles, the survey found, but most also believed that such articles should be signed and that the use of objective news articles, without interpretation, should be preferred. The editors surveyed also disagreed on the definition of interpretation. Some believed it was an objective accounting of events with additional background. Others took interpretation as including "the writer's definition of what a given development or statement may mean," noted George E. Stansfield of the *Hartford Courant*. [11]

But in the late 1940s and early 1950s, journalism's opinion leaders were nearly unanimous in calling for the increased use of interpretive reporting to bring depth and perspective to daily journalism. "[A] world war — and the thought-provoking, soul-stretching years of this peace which is no peace — have given newspapers greater depth and a broader perspective," said Oveta Culp Hobby, an executive of the *Houston Post* and president of the Southern Newspaper Publishers Association, in 1950. "Journalism is maturing. The emphasis has shifted from scoop to scope."[12]

In the early 1950s, objectivity was weakened by the challenge posed to journalism by the anti-Communist accusations of the junior United States senator from Wisconsin, Joseph R. McCarthy. McCarthy would prove a formidable challenge to the nation's editors throughout the early 1950s, from his infamous speech in Wheeling, W.Va., on Feb. 9, 1950, to his censure by his fellow United States senators in 1954.

Jack Anderson and Ronald W. May, two critics of McCarthy and his anti-Communist crusade, summarized in a 1952 book the essential dilemma that the senator's charges posed to newspapers in the early 1950s. They imagined the editor of an afternoon newspaper, worried in the last few minutes before deadline about what to place on Page 1. Then the latest charge leveled by McCarthy arrives on the wire. At last, the editor had his lead Page 1 article.

> There, in a nutshell, you have 99 percent of the reason for Joe Mc-Carthy's success. You can discount his personal ambition: that may have started the McCarthy flywheel, but it was the press that kept the wheel turning.... Any way you slice it, it adds up to the same thing: if Joe McCarthy is a political monster, then the press has been his Dr. Frankenstein.[13]

Anderson and May's view of McCarthy as "a political monster" was by no means unanimous among journalists. But the two expressed a common sentiment in the nation's newsrooms in the early 1950s: that McCarthy's newfound political power owed much to the publicity afforded him by the nation's newspapers. There was little doubt, the *Washington Post* editorial writer Alan Barth said at the height of McCarthy's power, that most newspapers' unquestioning coverage "serves Senator McCarthy's partisan political purposes much more than it serves the purposes of the press, the interest of truth."[14] Journalists, increasingly aware of the difficulty of proving many of McCarthy's charges of Communist infiltration in the State Department, the Army and the press, soon felt trapped by the journalistic conventions that required them to report every charge, no matter how outrageous.[15]

Particularly in the beginning of the senator's climb to national prominence, reporters were willing to cooperate because he was news. "McCarthy was a dream story," remembered Willard Edwards, who covered the senator in Washington for the *Chicago Tribune*. "I wasn't off Page 1 for four years."[16] McCarthy was helpful to reporters, sometimes telephoning government officials to fish for information while reporters listened in on the extension.[17] "He was the most cooperative guy in the world with the press," recalled the television correspondent George Cheeley. "That had an awful lot to do with his getting heavy press play."[18]

More significantly, the senator knew newspapers' and wire services' deadlines and timed his public releases for maximum exposure. Often he would call a morning press conference only to announce the scheduling of an afternoon press conference, doubling the publicity in the process. The *Milwaukee Journal* editor Wallace Lomoe complained that McCarthy was "a sideshow barker" in his dealings with the press. "He can get three stories instead of one. First he drops a hint. Then he gives out a name. Third, he gives out his version of what the name said or did. And the press carries all three."[19]

McCarthy's statements were automatically considered news because of his status as a United States senator. "My own impression is that he was a demagogue, but what could I do?" recalled Bob Baskin of the *Dallas Morning News*. "I had to report — and quote — McCarthy. That's all I could do. How do you say in the middle of your story 'This is a lie'? The press is supposedly neutral. You write what the man says."[20] Once when McCarthy leveled a new charge at a hearing in 1950, two reporters from large Baltimore and New York City newspapers agreed between them that the new accusation was baseless. But one reporter said with a shrug, "The people who read my story tomorrow won't know it."[21] The tradition of objective reporting required that the story be reported without qualification, no matter what. Richard L. Strout, a longtime Washington correspondent of the *Christian Science Monitor*, described the process this way: "The writer takes the statement of one man, tries to find the reply of another man, puts them competently together in one story, adds a little color and goes home to his wife and three children in the happy satisfaction of a day's work well done."[22]

The broadcast commentator Elmer Davis said in 1952 that reporters were too often writing "objective" accounts of McCarthy's charges without checking them out. "[O]bjectivity often leans over backward so far that it makes the news business merely a transmission belt for pretentious phonies," said Davis, a former *New York Times* reporter.[23]

The *Washington Post's* Alan Barth believed that reporters had done a poor job on the McCarthy story. "They may have to report the statements of a demagogue," he said, "but they do not have to leave their readers in exclusive reliance on their statements. It is part of their job to put them in perspective."[24]

What were newspapers to do about McCarthy, then? A very few newspapers simply withheld news dealing with charges of Communism. The *Claremont* (N.H.) *Daily Eagle*, for example, announced in its columns in 1951 that it was not releasing a list of prominent Americans named by the House Un-American Activities Committee as having been involved in a Communist peace initiative. The newspaper declared that it was withholding the accusations because of the committee's record for making unsubstantiated charges.[25] Other newspapers, such as the Boston-based *Christian Science Monitor*, tried to avoid overplaying McCarthy's charges. In 1953, the board of directors of the *Monitor* expressed concern to the newspaper's editors that the Wisconsin senator was using the press solely to obtain publicity for running for office. *Monitor* editors agreed to exercise caution in using McCarthy's name in headlines and in placing stories about him on the front page.[26]

Far more often, though, newspapers solved their dilemma about how to treat McCarthy by turning to greater use of interpretive writing. At the nation's most influential journalistic institutions — the large metropolitan dailies and the wire services — the McCarthy phenomenon accelerated the trend toward interpretation.

At the *Denver Post*, a memorandum instructed the staff to take special care in reporting "loose charges, irresponsible utterances and character assassination by spokesmen, official or otherwise," noted the *Post's* managing editor, Ed Dooley, in 1953. The memo, written by the editor-publisher, E. Palmer Hoyt, instructed reporters and editors to evaluate the source of the charges and to consider withholding the story until proof and/or the victim's response could be obtained. Reporters were instructed to ask themselves whether they knew the charges to be false, and then to explain any reasonable doubt in their articles.[27]

The foremost advocate of interpretation was the *New York Times*. But the publisher Arthur Hays Sulzberger urged caution. "Despite everything I have said about the need for interpretation of the news, it does not take the place of the factual news report," Sulzberger said in a speech to journalism educators in 1952. "It is supplementary and, essential as it is, it is dangerous if not watched and done correctly within rigid limits. The balance between interpretation and opinion is delicate and it must be preserved."[28]

Many reporters and editors had concrete suggestions as to how to better report McCarthy using interpretive methods. Melvin Mencher, then a reporter at the *Albuquerque Journal*, suggested in *Nieman Reports* in 1953 that newspapers should require McCarthy to submit advance copies of his speeches with supporting documents to allow reporters time to check them for accuracy. Newspapers should also put victims' responses to the charges in the lead paragraph of their news articles, Mencher said.[29]

Wire services were especially vulnerable to the senator's methods in two ways. First, their intense competition pushed reporters to get newsworthy copy onto the wires quickly, often without a response to McCarthy's charges. Second, wire services faced consistent pressure to file inoffensive, straightforward copy. But not everyone found it neutral. Some editors, such as William T. Evjue of the *Madison* (Wis.) *Capital-Times*, who was a McCarthy opponent, complained that the AP tended to run McCarthy's allegations unquestioningly. "The Associated Press," Evjue lamented in 1950, "flagrantly violates the principle of objective journalism in seeking to build up Senator Joseph McCarthy as a present-day Horatio Alger of the United States Senate." At the same time, other editors argued that the AP was anti-McCarthy. In 1950 Charles A. Hazen, editor of the *Shreveport* (La.) *Times*, filed a 66-page report with AP's management alleging 58 instances of left-wing bias within the wire service, with most of the complaints involving McCarthy.[30] The AP's Domestic News Committee investigated Evjue and Hazen's charges in 1950 and found no willful bias in either direction by the wire service.[31]

Nieman Reports, the quarterly journal published by the Nieman Foundation at Harvard University, encouraged interpretive reporting. Louis M. Lyons, curator of the Nieman Foundation and a veteran reporter for newspapers in Boston and elsewhere, argued that reporters had an obligation to set the record straight. "Who but a newspaperman can show you the record?" Lyons told a Newspaper Guild audience in 1953. "If a politician distorts it, the newspaperman needs to straighten it out for the reader."[32] Lyons credited some newspapers in particular with investigating McCarthy's charges, notably the *Washington Post*, the *New York Times*, the *Baltimore Sun* and the *Milwaukee Journal*. Most newspapers in the McCarthy era, Lyons recalled, relied heavily upon the wire services for their news about McCarthy and his charges. Few fought him.[33]

Just as McCarthy's methods had demonstrated the weakness of objective journalism, the desegregation movement later in the 1950s would undermine it further still. But while the McCarthy story was essentially a simple story of a demagogue abusing his power, desegregation was many times more complex and contentious. Editors divided sharply on how to cover black Americans' demands for civil rights and on the challenges that covering these news events posed to objectivity.

Race issues pitted North against South, conservative against liberal. Southern editors in particular concluded that strictly objective journalism was the best approach to covering school desegregation. Shortly after the Supreme Court found school desegregation unconstitutional in *Brown v. Board of Education*, a group of Southern editors formed their own reporting service to gather objective accounts and to publish them in a monthly newspaper, the *Southern School News*. Based in Nashville, the Southern Education Reporting Service was founded in 1954, as the *News* once put it, "to tell the story, factually and objectively, of what happens in education as a result of the Supreme Court ruling that segregation in public schools is unconstitutional." Correspondents from Southern and border states provided reports to the *News*, which quickly developed a monthly circulation of 30,000 among educators, journalists, public officials and libraries. The *News* and the Southern Education Reporting Service provided journalists across the nation with a clearinghouse for unbiased accounts of desegregation-related developments, serving as both a resource and a model. Reporters for the Southern Education Reporting Service prided themselves on their just-the-facts reporting of desegregation issues.[34]

The problem was that objectivity meant something different to Southern journalists than it did to Northerners. To Southerners well disposed toward segregation, objective accounts challenged *Brown*'s legitimacy but not the "Southern way of life." Northern reporters covering the South, on the other hand, approached the articles with an understanding that Southern racial mores were inherently unjust to blacks. Desegregation was simply not a subject about which journalists could be completely objective.

"Most of the press, no less than most of the politicians, responded miserably," recalled the Mississippi editor Hodding Carter Jr. of the years before and after the Supreme Court's desegregation decisions. "For many editors and publishers the response was honest: they shared the values of the land they inhabited and felt it was their duty to reflect them."[35] J. Oliver Emmerich, veteran editor of the *McComb* (Miss.) *Enterprise-Journal*, recalled that in the South "[t]he prejudices were recognized as traditions and not as prejudices. It was very difficult for some editors even to grasp."[36] James McBride Dabbs, longtime director of the Southern Regional Council, said Southern newspapers' bias was to be expected. "Local newspapers, with exceptions so small as to be negligible, are owned, published and edited by Southern whites," Dabbs once wrote. "Their subscribers are white; their advertisers are white. Is it not going a little far to expect complete objectivity and candor of a white Southern editor in discussing the duties of his subscribers and advertisers to members of a race that brings him no bread and butter?"[37]

Not surprisingly, most of the nation's daily newspapers were slow to exercise editorial leadership on the race issue. Southern editors were unanimous in condemning violence, but most had little else to say editorially.[38] *Time* magazine's media correspondent concluded in 1956 that, with a few exceptions, Southern newspapers in particular were doing "a patchy, pussyfooting job of covering the region's biggest running story since slavery." Jere Moore, editor of the weekly *Union Register* in Milledgeville, Ga., said newspapers had failed to offer leadership. "They have been weak-kneed when they should have been strong," Moore said.[39] Of the 30 largest dailies in the South and border states, the Southern Education Reporting Service concluded in 1957, all were hostile to *Brown* except for a dozen in the border states of Arkansas, Georgia, North Carolina and Tennessee. A few large and influential newspapers, such as the *St. Louis Post-Dispatch* and the *Louisville Courier-Journal*, had urged compliance with *Brown*. Others, such as the *Nashville Tennessean* and Carter's *Delta Democrat-Times*, had favored gradual integration.[40]

Journalistic battles over objectivity were fought in the South as Southerners reacted against the Northern reporters who crossed the Mason-Dixon line to cover desegregation-related stories. "There are as many Yankee reporters dropping off planes and trains as there were carpetbaggers in the 1860s," complained the self-proclaimed segregationist editor Thomas R. Waring of the *Charleston* (S.C.) *News and Courier* in 1956. The South's leading moderate, Ralph McGill of the *Atlanta Constitution*, said of the mass of incoming journalists, "It's been like waves beating on a stern and rockbound shore."[41] Many Southern editors deeply resented the influx of Northern reporters covering Southern racial news after *Brown*.[42]

Tempers flared at the 1956 meeting of the American Society of Newspaper Editors when Southern editors took the floor to complain about Northern reporters during a panel discussion on the difficulties of covering integration. "[D]own in our part of the country we wish you Northerners would ease up just a little bit on the pressure," admonished the *Texarkana* (Tex.) *Gazette*'s J.Q. Mahaffey. He charged that Northern editors habitually ignored or played down their own racial disturbances and racial disputes, a charge that prompted a spirited denial from a contingent of Chicago journalists. Then Harry M. Ayers of the *Anniston* (Ala.) *Star* took the floor to defend segregation and to lament what he described as the inferiority of blacks. The day's discussion concluded with editors agreeing that newspapers were adequately covering breaking developments about integration but failing to explain much else. "Our sins, as always, are those of apathy and provinciality, rather than venality," said Forrest W. Seymour of the *Worcester* (Mass.) *Telegram and Gazette*.[43]

Editor & Publisher noted with dismay the emotional dispute over desegregation coverage. "[W]e have rarely seen the heat that is now being generated between editors of two sections of the country over the desegregation issue," the editor Robert U. Brown observed in 1955, after the trial in the Emmett Till murder case.[44] Northern and Southern

Civil Rights and Joseph McCarthy • 215

differences, a 1957 editorial said, were compounded by the rise of interpretive reporting and by the intense emotionalism evident on both sides.[45]

Editors in both North and South wanted the wire services to cover racial problems outside their own region. In 1956, the AP assigned a staff member to survey Northern racial difficulties. His 1,800-word piece was part of a concerted AP attempt to cover the explosive desegregation issue as neutrally as possible. "It is the committee's view," the AP's Domestic News Committee concluded in 1956, "that in this situation the AP walked reasonably straight along the Mason-Dixon line."[46] At the urging of Southern editors, the United Press agreed in 1958 to send a Georgia-born correspondent to assess school segregation problems in the North.[47]

A Southern-born AP reporter who had worked during the 1950s in bureaus in Jackson, Miss., and Little Rock, Ark., grew increasingly exasperated at the conflicting demands of AP's member newspapers. Each time he had filed an article involving race from Jackson or Little Rock, the correspondent recalled, Northern editors telephoned him to complain that he had failed to tell the entire story and that he was imposing a white supremacist interpretation on his account. After transferring to an AP bureau in the North, the same correspondent was subject to complaints from Southern editors. "The whole process is reversed up here," the correspondent complained to his superiors in 1957. He added, "If the newspapers in both sections would concentrate more on objectivity instead of making us — the AP — prove that the Negro is treated worse in a different section than he is in their own backyard, all of us would be better off."[48]

The challenge the Southern beat posed to objective journalism was apparent in the widespread press coverage afforded the largest desegregation story of the decade, the desegregation of Little Rock Central High School in 1957. President Dwight D. Eisenhower eventually enforced integration with federal troops. Little Rock was "transformed into a kind of giant press room," said NBC reporter John Chancellor.[49]

At various times, members of the mob taunted journalists, called them "nigger lovers," jostled them and rocked telephone booths when reporters tried to make calls. "Bigots and psychopaths don't like outsiders watching them," Chancellor reflected. In all, six white reporters and four blacks were beaten while covering the Central crisis.[50]

A Scripps-Howard reporter, Dickson Preston, said that while most reporters had acted with restraint at Little Rock, some "extremists" had acted irresponsibly. On occasion television camera crews had incited crowds to demonstrate for the cameras. And some reporters, such as the *New York Times*'s Benjamin Fine, had appeared openly sympathetic to the nine black students and had angered crowds with pointed questions. "Fine asked the kind of questions that would get anybody's hackles up," Preston said. "He symbolized to Southerners the kind of 'Yankee reporting' they dislike."[51] In fact, Fine was sympathetic to integration and had often tangled with crowds. "They hurled insulting remarks and told me to go back North where I came from," Fine reported after one encounter with a mob.[52] Fine's emotional involvement in the desegregation story prompted *Times* editors to remove him as the newspaper's education editor in the months after the Central crisis.[53]

At a 1957 panel discussion on the press coverage at Little Rock, reporters agreed that journalists had improperly made news by staging pictures and by getting attacked by the mob. Even worse, many reporters — not just Fine — had taken sides. "The Northern newspaper reporter," Bob Allison of CBS News concluded, "has been definitely tied in with the machinery of enforcing integration."[54]

But once again, objective news accounts were proving ill suited to explaining complex events. "The desegregation story," noted the longtime *Hartford Times* editor Carl E. Lindstrom in 1960, "is as thorny a challenge as the American press has ever faced." Lindstrom said newspapers were forgoing interpretive reporting that would illuminate the social revolution of school desegregation in favor of day-by-day, factual accounts of desegregation-related crises.[55] C.A. McKnight, the first executive director of the Southern Education Reporting Service, told the American Society of Newspaper Editors' 1955 convention that articles about racial issues often lacked context and emphasized conflict rather than progress, even though many of the earliest desegregation efforts in border states had been successful. "It is my impression that many of our regional newspapers are still looking at the desegregation issue as something apart from the context of a rapidly changing region," McKnight said. The story, he said, deserved better.[56]

Desegregation seemed, after all, to be a story that demanded interpretive reporting. As Harry Ashmore of the *Arkansas Gazette* put it in 1958: "I think we have got to get over the notion that objectivity means giving a villain equal space with a saint — and above all of paying the greatest attention to those who shout the loudest. We've got to learn that a set of indisputable facts do not necessarily add up to truth."[57]

To conclude, though objective news accounts continued to dominate the pages of most American newspapers, by 1960 journalists had gradually become more cognizant of the weaknesses of objectivity when it was defined as free of interpretation. Myriad factors had accelerated the acceptance of interpretation in the 1940s. Joseph McCarthy had demonstrated how a demagogue could capitalize on journalists' practice of reporting unquestioningly the words of public officials. Then one of the most significant running domestic news events of the 20th century — school desegregation — had emerged as a thorny journalistic issue. Objectivity had fallen short and been weakened as a journalistic principle. Other factors were undermining objectivity's effectiveness in the

Civil Rights and Joseph McCarthy • 217

1950s and changing the way it was perceived. A growing government, increasingly secretive because of cold war imperatives, would undermine journalistic faith in public officials. Moreover, television's rise in the 1950s eroded newspapers' importance as a source of spot news, fueling the shift toward interpretation. The Cleveland *Plain Dealer* editor W.G. Vorpe said in 1952 that television had convinced the newspaper industry that "more than ordinary reporting was necessary on events of national importance." Newspapers, he said, should not simply report the facts of a news events but should "analyze the actions, tell the background and the aims of the strategy employed."[58] Vorpe's remarks reflected wide agreement among editors and reporters that print journalism would have to change in response to electronic competition.

Old habits die hard, however, and journalists were slow to come to terms with the ramifications of interpretation in the 1940s and 1950s and what it meant for the idea of objectivity. "The interpretive approach to news reporting is here, and here to stay," commented Newbold Noyes Jr., of the *Washington Evening Star* in 1953. "That doesn't mean, however, that our profession has learned to live comfortably with this new phase of its job. It has not; it still is acutely uncomfortable about the whole business."[59] Still, the stage was set for the turbulent 1960s, which would bring further, more intense challenges to objectivity.

NOTES

[1] Malcolm W. Bingay, "Bingay Says War's End Alters News Concepts," *Editor & Publisher*, 27 October 1945, p. 28.

[2] Lester Markel, "The Newspapers," in *While You Were Gone: A Report on Wartime Life in the United States*, ed. Jack Goodman (New York: Simon and Schuster, 1946), 373.

[3] Frederic E. Merwin, "The Journalism Teacher Faces the Atomic Age," *Journalism Quarterly* 23 (March 1946): 1-3.

[4] Curtis D. MacDougall address to American Association of Teachers of Journalism, 11 January 1947, reprinted in "What Newspapers Publishers Should Know About Professors of Journalism," *Journalism Quarterly* 24 (March 1947): 3.

[5] James Reston quoted in "Papers Must Excel in Explanatory Reporting," *Editor & Publisher*, 20 November 1948, p. 9.

[6] *APME Inc. 1948* (New York: Associated Press, 1949), 134. This book, the first of yearly summaries of the APME annual convention, changed its name to *APME Red Book* beginning in 1949.

[7] Gould memo quoted in ibid., 134-5.

[8] *APME Inc. Book*, 133-4.

[9] Commission on Freedom of the Press, *A Free and Responsible Press: A General Report on Mass Communication, Newspapers, Radio, Motion Pictures, Magazines, and Books* (Chicago: University of Chicago Press, 1947), v, 1-2, 90, and 20.

[10] Louis M. Lyons, "The Press and Its Critics," *Atlantic Monthly*, July 1947, pp. 115-6. A perusal of newspapers from the day after the report was released demonstrates the brevity and similarity of most newspaper accounts of the report's release on March 26, 1947. Despite its significance to journalists and historians, the Hutchins Commission report constituted only routine news in its day. See, for example, "Press Freedom in Peril, Educator Group Declares," *Atlanta Constitution*, 27 March 1947, p. 3, and "U.S. Free Press Held Periled," *New Orleans Times-Picayune*, 27 March 1947, p. 12.

[11] George E. Stansfield quoted in George Turnbull, "Interpretive Reporting Debated Among 50 Editors," *Editor & Publisher*, 12 April 1947, p. 11.

[12] Hobby's speech is reprinted in the *Congressional Record*, 11 May 1950, A3531-33.

[13] Jack Anderson and Ronald W. May, *McCarthy: The Man, the Senator, the Ism*, (Boston: Beacon Press, 1952), 266-7. Anderson was an assistant to the columnist Drew Pearson, an early McCarthy ally who later engaged in a celebrated feud with the senator.

[14] Alan Barth speech before Association for Education in Journalism, quoted in "Better Reporting Held Modern Need," *New York Times*, 27 August 1952, p. 21.

[15] Secondary works on McCarthy and cold war anti-Communism abound, but the only book-length work on McCarthy's relationship with newspapers is Edwin R. Bayley, *Joe McCarthy and the Press* (Madison, Wis.: University of Wisconsin Press, 1981). See also David M. Oshinsky's biography, *A Conspiracy So Immense: The World of Joe McCarthy* (New York: The Free Press, 1983), 179-90; and Jean Franklin Deaver, "A Study of Senator Joseph R. McCarthy and 'McCarthyism' as Influences upon the News Media and the Evolution of Reportorial Method," Ph.D. dissertation, University of Texas, 1969.

[16] Quoted in Oshinsky, *A Conspiracy So Immense*, 118.

[17] Anderson and May, *McCarthy*, 267.

[18] Quoted in Deaver, "A Study of Joseph R. McCarthy...," 87.

[19] Quoted in *APME Red Book*, 1953, p. 53. McCarthy's skill with the media was by no means unique; the House Un-American Activities Committee showed similar savvy in scheduling news conferences and public hearings for maximum media exposure.

[20] Quoted in Deaver, "A Study of Joseph R. McCarthy...," 91.

[21] Quoted in Strout, "Ordeal by Publicity," 5.

[22] Ibid.

[23] Elmer Davis, "News and the Whole Truth," *Atlantic Monthly*, August 1952, pp. 32, 35. Davis' article received wide notice. See "The Whole Truth?" *Time*, 28 July 1952, p. 51.

[24] Alan Barth, *Government by Investigation* (New York: Viking Press, 1955), 195. Also see Alan Barth, *The Loyalty of Free Men* (New York: Viking Press, 1952), 11.

[25] *Claremont* (N.H.) *Daily Eagle*, 5 April 1951, cited in "Notice," *Nieman Reports*, July 1951, p. 34.

[26] Erwin D. Canham memorandum to Saville R. Davis, 12 June 1953; Saville R. Davis memorandum to American News Department, 15 June 1953, in per-

sonal and professional papers of Richard L. Strout, in possession of Alan Strout, Weston, Mass. Strout was a longtime Washington correspondent of the *Christian Science Monitor*. His papers are held by his son, Alan Strout. Copies of these memoranda are in possession of the author.

[27] *APME Red Book*, 1953, pp. 51, 53. The memo and a 1953 speech by Hoyt justifying it are reprinted in Palmer Hoyt, "New Dimensions in the News," in *The Press and the Public Interest: The William Allen White Lectures*, ed. Warren K. Agee (Washington, D.C.: Public Affairs Press, 1968), 39-48.

[28] Arthur Hays Sulzberger speech to Association for Education in Journalism, quoted in "Better Reporting Held Modern Need," *New York Times*, 27 August 1952, p. 21. Bayley, in *Joe McCarthy and the Press*, 77, reports that his analysis of the *Times'* news articles about McCarthy found that, indeed, they were mostly reported "straight." Interpretation was limited to separate news articles analyzing the day's news.

[29] Melvin Mencher, "McCarthy: Who Made Him?" *Nieman Reports*, January 1953, p. 47.

[30] *APME Red Book*, 1950, pp. 69-76.

[31] Ibid., 63-79. Hazen appealed to the APME membership to reopen the investigation, but members refused.

[32] *Proceedings, Twentieth Annual Convention* (New York: American Newspaper Guild, 1953), 72.

[33] Ibid., 317. Bayley, in *Joe McCarthy and the Press*, 125-75, also named the above newspapers as McCarthy opponents as well as the *Madison* (Wis.) *Capital-Times*, *St. Louis Post-Dispatch*, *Denver Post* and *Christian Science Monitor*.

[34] "The Reporting Service ... and How it Grew," *Southern School News*, 4 May 1955, p. 1; "SERS Reference Library Now Has 55,000 Items," *Southern School News*, March 1957, p. 1.

[35] Hodding Carter, *Their Words Were Bullets: The Southern Press in War, Reconstruction, and Peace* (Athens: University of Georgia Press, 1969), 64. A 1956 Gallup poll found that only one in 17 Deep South whites favored desegregation. John M. Fenton, "Only 1 in 17 Deep South Whites For Integration," *Jackson* (Miss.) *Clarion-Ledger*, 27 February 1956, p. 3.

[36] Interview with J. Oliver Emmerich, 1973, Mississippi Oral History Program, University of Southern Mississippi, Hattiesburg, Miss.

[37] James McBride Dabbs, quoted in Harry Ashmore, *Civil Rights and Wrongs: A Memoir of Race and Politics* (New York: Pantheon Books, 1994), 63.

[38] Church groups that monitored press opinion found that newspapers were universal in opposing violence. See *The South Speaks Out for Law and Order: A Roundup of Southern Press Opinion* (National Council of the Churches of Christ in the United States of America et al., 1958).

[39] "Dilemma in Dixie," *Time*, 20 February 1956, p. 76.

[40] Don Shoemaker, ed., *With All Deliberate Speed; Segregation-Desegregation in Southern Schools; Prepared by Staff Members of the Southern Education Reporting Service* (New York: Harper, 1957), 31-4.

[41] T.R. Waring and Ralph McGill quoted in "Invasion of the South," *Newsweek*, 2 April 1956, p. 86.

[42] See, for example, "Interviews with Southern Newspaper Editors," *U.S.*

News & World Report, 24 February 1956, pp. 44-50, 134-44.

[43] *ASNE Proceedings,* 1956, pp. 72-98. The *New York Post* wrote that Ayers' remarks "evoked visible pain among Southern and Northern editors." Ayers later defended his speech in letters to Southern newspapers. *New York Post,* 22 April 1956; Harry M. Ayers letter to editor of the *Journal,* 1 May 1956, Harry Mell Ayers collection, Wm. Stanley Hoole Special Collections Library, University of Alabama, Tuscaloosa, Ala.

[44] Robert U. Brown, "Shop Talk at Thirty," *Editor & Publisher,* 12 November 1955, p. 80.

[45] "Emotionalism in the News," *Editor & Publisher,* 19 October 1957, p. 6.

[46] *APME Red Book,* 1956, p. 87.

[47] "Southerner Studies North for the U.P.," *Editor & Publisher,* 1 March 1958, p. 59.

[48] Unidentified AP correspondent's letter to Paul Mickelson, reprinted in *APME Red Book,* 1956, pp. 79, 82.

[49] John Chancellor, "Radio and Television Had Their Own Problems in Little Rock Coverage," *Quill,* December 1957, p. 9.

[50] Ibid., 10, 21; Ray Moseley, "Northern Newsmen Withstood Mob's Abuse to Report Little Rock Story," *Quill,* December 1957, pp. 8, 18.

[51] Quoted in "Preston Raps Press Antics at Little Rock," *Editor & Publisher,* 2 November 1957, p. 66.

[52] Benjamin Fine, "Guardsmen Curb Newsmen's Work," *New York Times,* 6 September 1957, p. 8.

[53] Benjamin Fine to Hal Faber, 5 September 1957; Fine to Orval Dryfoos, 18 November 1957, in Turner Catledge papers, Mitchell Memorial Library, Mississippi State University, Starkville, Miss.

[54] Philip N. Schuyler, "Panelists Agree: Journalistic Code Violated at Little Rock," *Editor & Publisher,* 2 November 1957, p. 11.

[55] Carl E. Lindstrom, *The Fading American Newspaper* (1960; reprint ed., Glouchester, Mass.: Peter Smith, 1964), 32.

[56] *ASNE Proceedings,* 1955, pp. 81-6.

[57] Harry S. Ashmore, "The Story Behind Little Rock," *Nieman Reports,* April 1958, p. 7.

[58] Letter to the editor, *ASNE Bulletin,* 1 September 1952, p. 11.

[59] "Design for Impressionistic School of Reporting – Noyes," reprinting of Newbold Noyes Jr. speech at the University of Missouri, *Editor & Publisher,* 9 May 1953, p. 11.

CHAPTER 16

Into the 1960s —
and Into the Crucible

By Steven R. Knowlton

In the summer of 1964, while sitting in the press box of San Francisco's Cow Palace, the *New York Times* columnist Tom Wicker witnessed the biggest problem facing journalism early in the post-McCarthy era: how to remain objective while still telling the story happening right in front of you. The occasion was a routine speech by former President Dwight Eisenhower, who was exhorting the Barry Goldwater and Nelson Rockefeller factions in the Republican Party to stick together. In the midst of a perfectly ordinary speech, Eisenhower cautioned the delegates not to be divided by "those outside our family, including sensation-seeking columnists and commentators." The auditorium erupted in anger against the journalists in the building.

In his memoirs, Wicker described the pandemonium: "I was virtually within reach of the crowd as I manned a typewriter in the press section, and I can still see those shouting, livid delegates, rising almost as one man, pointing, cursing, in some cases shaking their fists.... I feared some of the delegates might actually leap over the railing separating them from the press section and attack the reporters gazing in astonishment at this sudden surge of hatred."[1] Despite the drama, one of the prime obligations of professional journalism — objectivity — prevented the reporters from putting the outburst at the top of their stories. Objectivity, lauded for half a century since Lippmann and others tied it to the quest for the best evidence and most reliable sources instead of a reliance on personal observation, demanded that Eisenhower's call for unity be the lead.

And so it was. The lead on the *Times'* story the next morning read: "Former President Dwight D. Eisenhower warned Republicans tonight that they must unite behind their convention's choice of a Presidential nominee or 'drown in a whirlpool of factional strife.'" It was four paragraphs later before the newspaper mentioned that the room had "fairly exploded" when Eisenhower mentioned the reporters.

The lead in the *Times* was virtually textbook perfect, even though it did not mention that which was — to modern eyes — the news. The old

World War I-era definition of objectivity, with its emphasis on official sources and the written record, demanded the lead the newspaper offered. "On politics and government," Wicker explained, "objective journalism reported mostly the contents of official documents or statements delivered by official spokesmen." Analysis was possible "only in the most obvious terms."

The official record, written and spoken, contained nothing of what had just happened, "so at the moment when the hostility that the free American press aroused among its own readers first became dramatically apparent to the press itself, that press had so wrapped itself in the paper chains of 'objective' journalism that it had little ability to report anything beyond the bare and undeniable fact that the Republican National Convention had 'fairly exploded' at Eisenhower's words."[2]

In the years since Wicker's observation, polling data have shown that Wicker's judgment was right when he believed that he was witnessing something new and important: a deep-seated anger at America's journalists. A 1999 survey from the Pew Research Center for the People and the Press, showed the trend:

> The only clear and consistent trend is discontent with the news media.... [T]he public continues to give the news media poor performance grades for accuracy, correcting mistakes and the way they play their watchdog role. Moreover, the new survey finds a striking decline in the public's perception of news media values since the mid-1980s. The number of Americans seeing news organizations as immoral has tripled, leaving the public evenly split (38%-to-40%) on whether the press is immoral or not. Similarly, the two-to-one belief that the press protected democracy in 1985 has evaporated. Today, the public is divided, with 45% saying the news media protect democracy and 38% saying they hurt it.[3]

The public's criticism of the news media softened after the terrorist attacks of Sept. 11, 2001, but the Pew Research Center for the People and the Press found that the negative view of journalism had returned to 1990s levels by the summer of 2002.[4]

As the preceding chapter lays out, during the period immediately after the fall of Senator Joseph McCarthy (R-Wis.), there was much hand-wringing among the working press about how they had been manipulated and abused. They concluded that an elected government official speaking in public should not automatically be newsworthy if he is speaking nonsense. But if McCarthy's transparent abuse of the press in his irresponsible anti-Communist campaign weakened the old Lippmann-era rules about objectivity, the coverage of the 1964 Republican convention showed how slowly journalism had changed its practices. It took the tumult of the 1960s to force a new sense of *ought* and obligation

Into the 1960s — and Into the Crucible • 223

among the nation's reporters.

At least three cultural-political developments led to major changes in what American journalists thought they should be doing: the civil rights movement, the Vietnam War — including both the unprecedented intimacy of the coverage in the field, and the war's protests at home — and the presidency of Richard Nixon, ending in Watergate and Nixon's forced resignation. Although there had been civil unrest, unpopular wars and presidential scandals in the nation's past, never had all three happened at just the same moment, and certainly never in front of the watchful eye of the television camera.

This chapter will examine the major intellectual, cultural, political and technological challenges to journalistic objectivity since the beginning of the 1960s. Few people today argue that perfect objectivity is possible. But then, few ever did. However, after attacks from left, right and the ivory tower, the fundamental principles have proved remarkably resilient. Changes in technology and in the behavior of the people and the institutions that journalists cover have argued for more analysis than was done in a more straightforward (and untelevised) age, but those are differences in degree, rather than in kind.

To Walter Cronkite, the CBS news anchor from 1962 to 1981, objectivity has not changed at all. "To the journalist, I can't imagine that it means anything other than what it's always meant," Cronkite said. "I don't believe that the definition of objectivity has changed, although the perception of objectivity may have changed to some degree, and the practice of achieving it has changed. Objectivity is the reporting of reality, of facts, as nearly as they can be obtained without the injection of prejudice or personal opinion."[5]

Cronkite's definition is fairly standard within the industry. A leading textbook by Fred Fedler et al., one of the few that still deal with objectivity at all, counsels young reporters in training: "Like everyone else, reporters are influenced by their families, educations, personal interests and religious and political beliefs. Nevertheless, editors believe objectivity is a worthwhile goal and journalists can be taught to be more objective."[6]

Note that two elements often mistakenly thought to be part of objectivity are absent from the definitions offered both by a popular textbook and by a highly regarded working pro: neither Cronkite nor Fedler maintains that objective journalists have no values or that objective journalists do not, cannot and must not put facts into context.

The first notion — that journalists committed to objectivity do not believe in anything except, perhaps, objectivity itself — is patent nonsense. The first line of the first statement of principles that professional journalists adopted back in the 1920s reads: "The primary function of newspapers is to communicate to the human race what its members do, feel and think." And a few lines later: "Freedom of the press is to be guarded as a vital right of mankind." Those values were and still are at the core of journalism.

Still, a great many reporters are simply not very good at explaining what values they cherish as they go about their work. So they adopt the Damon Runyon persona, at least metaphorically, of wearing broad-brim fedoras in the office, of keeping a bottle of Maalox in one desk drawer and a bottle of rye in the other, and of swearing — always swearing — that they don't care about much of anything as long as it is spelled correctly.

Journalists' protestations of neutrality as to values and outcomes have led to much derision within the academy and the broader community. But journalists have allowed, or even encouraged, this fundamental misunderstanding of their mission, and this basic error has certainly stuck. Michael Schudson, a leading scholar of American journalism and the author of a seminal book on objectivity, sees the absence of values as central to objectivity. "The belief in objectivity," he argues, "is just this: the belief that one can and should separate facts from values. Facts, in this view, are assertions about the world open to independent validation. They stand beyond the distorting influences of any individual's personal preferences. Values, in this view, are an individual's conscious or unconscious preferences for what the world should be; they are seen as ultimately subjective."[7]

It is largely in response to this misunderstanding about value-free journalism that a countermovement called "civic journalism," or "public journalism," has grown up in the last decade. According to Davis "Buzz" Merritt, the longtime editor of the *Wichita* (Kan.) *Eagle* and the movement's chief architect, journalists have done themselves and the public they serve a grave disservice by feigning indifference, or by allowing indifference to be invoked in their name:

> The ultimate ethical question for journalists, as with any person, revolves around the question, "What are journalists for?"... And that's the question public journalism seeks to answer in a deeper way. Until we face that question, we have no ethical framework in which to operate. And until we make our answer to that question a public one, our work will be forever suspect by non-journalists who know fairly clearly what they are "for" and don't for a minute buy our protestations that we're not "for" anything — except, of course, the First Amendment.[8]

By no means does everyone in the news business buy into Merritt's statements about public journalism. Many argue that public journalism could lead to advocacy journalism, to deliberate distortion and an abdication of the duty to be an honest broker of reliable information — in other words, to an abdication of the duty to remain objective. Yet the debate argues powerfully that journalists want to maintain the knife-edge balance between detachment on one side and advocacy on the other.

The other misconception is that a commitment to objectivity necessitates the presentation of news without context. A recent account of the legendary team of radio journalists who reported to Edward R. Murrow for CBS during World War II describes objectivity similarly as "reporting the news without personal prejudice, opinion, or point of view." But the authors go on to raise questions:

> Was it "objective" for [William] Shirer to suggest that Nazi propagandists were liars? Would it have been "objective" for a reporter to assert that Neville Chamberlain was a fool for trusting Hitler?... Is there a difference between "the truth" and "objective" facts? Journalists have been asking themselves these questions for as long as journalism has existed. In the end, they usually have settled on "fairness" as a better standard than cold-blooded, neutral, impossible "objectivity."[9]

Similar questions about how a legitimate concern about bias can actually distort journalism are still around. In an interview on Nov. 11, 2003, Paul Krugman, the *New York Times* columnist and Princeton economic professor, said:

> ...[T] media are desperately afraid of being accused of bias. And that's partly because there's a whole machine out there, an organized attempt to accuse them of bias whenever they say anything the right doesn't like. So rather than really try to report things objectively, they settle for being evenhanded, which is not the same thing. One of my lines in a column — in which a number of people thought I was insulting them personally — was that if Bush said the earth was flat, the mainstream media would have stories with the headline: "Shape of the Earth — Views Differ." Then they'd quote some Democrats saying that it was round.[10]

J. Herbert Altschull notes much the same point in the introduction to his reader on the philosophical principles behind American journalism. Journalists, he said, have a "tendency to provide graphic descriptions of a single tree when what the readers need is a wider view of the forest."[11] That raises a major problem, however: those "readers" are by no means a single entity. It is impossible to provide all readers with the right amount of forest description and the right amount of tree, because their needs are very different — and may even be different in the morning than in the evening.

Still, Altschull has a good point. One of the chronic tensions in responsible journalism has been between presenting demonstrable fact on the one hand (Altschull's tree) and interpreting those facts (putting that tree into an intelligible forest) on the other. Journalists have taken seriously Walter Lippmann's dictum about being held accountable for the quality of their information: "There is no defense, no extenuation, no excuse whatever, for stating six times that Lenin is dead, when the only information the paper possesses is a report that he is dead from the source repeatedly shown to be unreliable.... [I]f there is one subject on which editors are most responsible, it is in their judgment of the reliability of the source."[12]

Getting the tree part is hard enough: official sources have an undeniable credibility, but they are certainly not infallible and are highly suspect on many types of news events, especially those involving charges of official malfeasance. Getting the forest right is even harder. It is not that journalists have not thought of this broader view, and not that they do not try. It is a mandate, in the famous phrasing of the Hutchins Commission, to present "a truthful, comprehensive and intelligent account of the day's events in a context which gives them meaning."[13] But Lippmann, a generation before Hutchins, dealt with how difficult it is for the reporter to get that necessary context right: "Once he departs from the region where it is definitely recorded at the County Clerk's office that John Smith has gone into bankruptcy, all fixed standards disappear," Lippmann wrote. "The story of why John Smith failed, his human frailties, the analysis of the economic conditions on which he was shipwrecked, all of this can be told in a hundred different ways."[14]

This is not to say that the recitation of demonstrable fact is objective, while providing context inevitably is not. It is to note that one of the most enduring tensions in journalism is located exactly here. Despite this challenge, reporting and interpreting are not the "seemingly contradictory conceptions" that Weaver and Wilhoit and many other scholars make them out to be. From the very first code of conduct for journalists, the very clear obligation has been to do both.

The American Society of Newspaper Editors adopted the first code, which it called the Canons of Journalism, at its annual conventions of 1924 and 1925. The following year, the primary writers' trade group, Sigma Delta Chi (now the Society of Professional Journalists) adopted the ASNE code for itself. Note that both groups adopted the canons in the 1920s, the very height of the era of scientific positivism, when many of the social sciences were trying to harness the scientific method to human behavior. As part of the larger effort to professionalize journalism, many, including Lippmann, championed borrowing the same techniques and applying them to journalism.

The opening paragraph of the canons says journalists must have "the widest range of intelligence, of knowledge, and trained powers of observations and reasoning," the same kind of training afforded people in the hard sciences. To journalism's opportunities as a chronicler, it says, "are indissolubly linked its obligations as a teacher and interpreter." The code does not use the word objectivity, but it certainly describes it in calling for truthfulness, thoroughness, accuracy, impartiality, fairness and the avoidance of bias.

When members of Sigma Delta Chi adopted a new code in 1973, two sections in the old code, those headed "Sincerity, Truthfulness, Accuracy" and the next section, headed "Impartiality," were combined into one, labeled "Accuracy and Objectivity." Right after saying, "Truth is our ultimate goal," the 1973 code reads, "Objectivity in reporting the news is another goal, which serves as the mark of an experienced professional. It is a standard of performance toward which we strive. We honor those who achieve it." The same phrasing was retained through the 1987 revision of the society's code but was eliminated from the most recent version on the code, adopted in 1996.

Cronkite's definition — "Objectivity is the reporting of reality, of facts, as nearly as they can be obtained without the injection of prejudice or personal opinion" — has held up well for generations of journalists. The influence of science is seen in this definition from Philip Meyer, author of *Precision Journalism* and the Knight Professor of Journalism at the University of North Carolina-Chapel Hill: "Objectivity is freeing yourself from your personal prejudices and wishful thinking and first impressions to produce an account or interpretation that would be replicated by another observer."[15]

It is that last element of replicability that ties objectivity to its roots in the 1920s. It was then that social scientists made a concentrated effort to adopt the scientific method — detached observation, testing and replicability — to the whole range of "soft sciences," including sociology, political science and journalism.

So why has the concept of objectivity in journalism seemed to have fallen on such disfavor over the last generation? One recent study concludes: "Few journalists or journalism scholars today would hazard calling upon the principle or ideal of objectivity. On the contrary, the majority reject or denounce the concept in almost total unanimity."[16] Another scholar puts it this way: "Among all the clichés that clutter up human minds, there is one which gives rise to a stir of approval in its audience each time it is sententiously pronounced: 'Objectivity does not exist — in reporting.' In politics, labor unions, diplomacy, business, culture, and justice, its existence is not questioned. But in the very profession that tries to establish a truthful report, objectivity is considered a theoretical impossibility."[17]

Journalism reflects society as much as it informs it and certainly far more than it reforms it. So people's faith in journalism's integrity was shaken in the 1960s, along with their faith in other institutions. The turbulent years of the 1960s, roughly during the administrations of John Kennedy, Lyndon Johnson and Richard Nixon, were among the most convulsive in the nation's history. Almost every value Americans held dear was challenged, and reverence for institutions was assaulted. Since a commitment to fair and neutral reporting is the lynchpin of First Amendment journalism, it is hardly surprising that this institution, and its principle of objectivity, would come under scrutiny and be found wanting.

Another reason for a declining faith in objectivity was the development of an adversarial relationship between those who govern and those who report on the governors, a relationship that grew out of growing distrust of the information coming from government.

David Wise has concluded "in a modern context, 1960 was a watershed.... It marked the first time that many Americans realized that their government lied."[18] That was the year that Francis Gary Powers, working for the Central Intelligence Agency, was shot down in his U-2 spy plane inside the Soviet Union. The United States at first maintained that Powers was a civilian flying a weather plane. Then Eisenhower was caught in the lie.

After leaving office in 1961, Eisenhower said his "greatest regret" as president was "the lie we told about the U-2. I didn't realize how high a price we were going to pay for that lie." Max Frankel, now retired as the executive editor of the *New York Times*, also says that the U-2 incident was pivotal. "Probably for the last time in the Cold War," he wrote in his memoirs, "American reporters assumed that their government was telling the truth."[19]

Two years after the U-2 incident, official lying, or at least the right to do so, became official U.S. policy. In December 1962, at a convention of Sigma Delta Chi, Arthur Sylvester, the assistant secretary of state for public affairs, answered a reporter's question about government misstatements over the Cuban missile crisis of a few months before this way: "It's inherent in [the] government's right, if necessary, to lie to save itself when it's going up into a nuclear war. That seems to me basic — basic."[20] Over time, the "right to lie" became entrenched.

Then came the Johnson administration and Vietnam, including the "Tonkin Gulf incident that emerged as the most crucial and disgraceful episode in the modern history of government lying."[21] Except for one machine-gun bullet, there is no evidence that U.S. ships were ever really fired upon by North Vietnamese in the Tonkin Gulf in August 1964, and President Johnson knew it, but he nonetheless got from Congress the Tonkin Gulf resolution, which authorized him to take "all necessary steps" in Southeast Asia. That resolution proved to be the legal authorization for the entire Vietnam War.

Such deception became commonplace in Vietnam in the months and years that followed. During the war, Secretary of State Henry Kissin-

Into the 1960s — and Into the Crucible • 229

ger's famous promise that light was visible "at the end of the tunnel" became a bitter catch phrase. The term "credibility gap" entered the lexicon. And the publication of the "Pentagon papers," a secret government history of the war that had been leaked to reporters, in June 1971 demonstrated unequivocally how the government had deliberately deceived the American people — and used the press to do so.

In a recent book, Eric Alterman outlines the results of the Red Scare paranoia in the Cold War and concludes, "Perhaps the greatest loss to American democracy from the Cold War was the destruction of the people's trust in their leaders."[22]

The Johnson administration took to lying with a relish, so by the time of the Nixon administration in 1969, government lies were considered the order of the day. As has been well documented, Richard Nixon hated the press, and the press hated Richard Nixon. Reporters would have had to be far nobler than they are not to be affected. The zeal to expose the liar is easy to fathom. Jimmy Breslin, a popular New York columnist, nailed the mood of many journalists with the title of his book on Nixon's resignation to avoid impeachment in 1974: *How the Good Guys Finally Won: Notes from an Impeachment Summer.*[23]

What did the world look like for the journalist? Two young *Washington Post* reporters, Bob Woodward and Carl Bernstein, had become such national heroes that they became collectively known as Woodstein, an emblem of a new and aggressive form of journalism. The guy in tights who can fly and look through walls had apparently ducked into a phone booth and emerged as a newspaper reporter (or two) who had saved the republic. It was heady stuff. Enrollment in journalism schools exploded, and it is no wonder that many of those students chose to emulate Woodstein's more derring-do tactics. The rage toward investigative reporting was on.

Walter Cronkite explained what happened next: "Nearly every newspaper followed, and every radio and television station, no matter how small, had to have an investigative team with investigative reporters.... Instead of doing the job of making sure that we knew the facts that were happening, we became devoted to finding out what was wrong with an organization.... It became a self-aggrandizing business, which I think loosened the editorial function of being sure that it was fair, that it was right, that it was accurate. Accuracy and fairness still should be the words that accompany objectivity."[24]

Meanwhile, reporters were regularly manipulated by increasingly skilled spinmeisters of both left and right. Masters of radical political theater, such as Abbie Hoffman, had a keen knack for tweaking authority and doing it with a flair that made good television. Running a pig for president, throwing dollar bills onto the floor of the New York Stock Exchange — all sorts of outrageous acts of political defiance were carefully designed. "The point was to get reported... the more offensive, the better."[25]

Also during this same 15-year period, roughly 1960 to 1975, the newspaper journalist's job description changed sharply. Television came to be the dominant medium by which reporters could tell people what was going on that day. It became, in other words, the prime means of conveying hard news. Newspapers were left with trying to tell why something happened — and no one has ever argued that it is easier to explain why something happened than to note that it did.

It was not just journalism that found its claim to objectivity challenged during this period — science did as well. And since much of the rationale for objectivity in journalism grew out of the idea that it could employ scientific methods to ferret out information, the attack on the idea's credibility in science undermined it in journalism as well. Journalism's wagon was firmly hitched to science when Thomas Kuhn wrote *The Structure of Scientific Revolutions* in 1962, a widely influential book that cast serious doubt on the presumed objectivity of the scientific researcher. Rather than making a bold foray into the unknown to find what is there, Kuhn argued, the scientist has preconceived ideas about what is out there to be found and adjusts his methods accordingly:

> The man who is striving to solve a problem defined by existing knowledge and technique is not, however, just looking around. He knows what he wants to achieve, and he designs his instruments and directs his thoughts accordingly. Unanticipated novelty, the new discovery, can emerge only to the extent that his anticipations about nature and his instruments prove wrong.[26]

If science's image lost some of its presumed purity after Kuhn, so did journalism's. Both scientists and journalists, chastened, grew somewhat embarrassed to use the term objectivity and began using synonyms more frequently. There is little evidence, however, that scientists — or journalists — changed the research methods they had long considered objective.

Meanwhile, over on the television side for at least a generation and perhaps even longer, political manipulators showed a vastly greater understanding of the true power of the visual medium than did television's own practitioners. In his classic book *The Image: A Guide to Pseudo-Events in America*, the historian Daniel Boorstin foresaw the arrival of this image-as-reality world even before television became ubiquitous.[27]

A CBS White House correspondent, Leslie Stahl, said that as late as the mid-1980s, neither she nor the network executives fully understood how badly she and her network were being manipulated. She did a long piece on the spinmeisters at the White House, contrasting the positive image that Ronald Reagan's White House was projecting on matters such as housing for the elderly and aid to the handicapped with

Into the 1960s — and Into the Crucible • 231

Reagan's policy of slashing funds for just those programs. "I thought they'd be mad at me," Stahl said. "But they weren't. They loved it."[28]

Michael Deaver, the chief image-maker in the Reagan White House, explained why. "She had to put on during her piece all those wonderful visuals we had created," he said. "And if you really believe that the visual is going to outlast the spoken word in the person's mind, we were delighted with it. We had gotten one more shot of all the things we had created that we wanted on television."[29]

Another assault on objective journalism in the 1960s was the advent of an approach called New Journalism, which featured fancy writing of all sorts: delayed leads, long narratives, lots of descriptive color and a style that had its roots in fiction. Two techniques used by some practitioners were most suspect to traditionalists: composite characters and the use of quoted material that the writer could not verify. For composite characters, the writer observed and interviewed many different people and then used that to create an imaginary character. The suspect quotations were often for internal monologues of a subject of an article, which the reporter was obviously not able to check, or for presumed conversations, usually including quotation marks, for words that the writer never claimed to have heard spoken or read. Many extremely talented writers took to this form, most notably Tom Wolfe, Jimmy Breslin and Hunter Thompson. Wolfe described what New Journalists were doing as well as anyone: "The kind of reporting they were doing... was more intense, more detailed, and certainly more time-consuming than anything that newspaper or magazine reporters, including investigative reporters, were accustomed to do.... Eventually I, and others, would be accused of 'entering people's minds'... but exactly! I figured that was one more doorbell a reporter had to push."[30]

Nonetheless, the field lost much of its luster in 1981 when the *Washington Post* had to return a Pulitzer because the central character in the prize-winning "Jimmy's World" series, about a young heroin addict, turned out to not exist. The National News Council, a short-lived media watchdog group, studied what had happened and issued a report. The council's chairman, Norman Isaacs, a highly regarded newspaper editor, wrote, "I would like to think that the views of the editors contained in these pages signal an end to the permissiveness and arrogance of the 'New Journalism.'"[31] Isaacs was right: defenders of the journalism that produced Jimmy aren't heard from much anymore. At the academic level, the New Journalism more or less evolved into Literary Journalism, with the emphasis on the literary.

The discussion so far has centered on real-world events (and some real-world fictions) that put a strain on the journalistic commitment to objectivity. At the nation's colleges and universities, there arose another challenge. This is hardly the place to attempt a full-blown explanation of the academic movement championed by the likes of Stanley Fish and

Jacques Derrida. Part of it is called postmodernism, part deconstructionism. Above all, this whole intellectual movement is profoundly suspicious of rational thought — that is, reason. Here is an explanation from Fish in a recent book: "Reasons do not confirm or shore up your faith; they are extensions of your faith and are reasons *for you* because of what you already believe at a level so fundamental that it is not (at least while you are in the grip of belief) available for self-conscious scrutiny."[32]

To people who have to monitor the workings of the justice system and ferret out bid-rigging in highway contracts, following Fish's mind is something like gazing at an M.C. Escher print. It is whimsical and clever, and perhaps even mildly instructive in its admonition that things are not always what they seem. But despite the wit, Fish's arguments, like Escher's staircases, do not go anywhere.

A different kind of criticism is represented by Jeremy Iggers. "Objectivity may be dead, but it isn't dead enough," he wrote. His book *Good News, Bad News* argues that the journalism of detachment has produced a sort of ignorance of, and even contempt for, the citizenry, obviating the public-good purpose that brought American journalism into existence."[33]

While Iggers, the restaurant critic of the *Minneapolis Star-Tribune*, assails objectivity because of what he takes to be its detachment, Merritt, one of the leading proponents of the sort of involvement that Iggers champions, maintains that this kind of anti-detached journalism can still be expressly objective. Merritt, the longtime editor of the *Wichita* (Kan.) *Eagle*, caused quite a stir in journalism circles in 1995 when he published *Public Journalism and Public Life: Why Telling the News Is Not Enough*,[34] in which he argued that journalists' commitment to detachment was harming, rather than helping democracy. Helping democracy work, Davis points out, has historically been inextricably tied into journalism. Here is an excerpt from a college address by Merritt: "So let's go to the core of the matter of public journalism. The core is the interdependence of journalism and democracy, and that journalists have an obligation to accept its centrality and incorporate a concern for it into the ethical framework in which we operate."[35]

Still, Merritt is adamant about maintaining objectivity, as he defines it. Public journalism, rather than abandoning objectivity, "is the sense of being honest with ourselves and others about the facts, clear-eyed and unburdened by bias or extraneous concerns, fair, balanced — all of those vital things," Merritt said.[36] Many journalists, probably most, agree with Merritt that they care about what happens to the people and institutions they write about. What many journalists object to is the activist role that some news organizations are playing in the name of public journalism. A typical example involves a news organization's sponsorship of community forums to deal with major civic problems like race

Into the 1960s — and Into the Crucible • 233

relations or declines in voting rates.

Some journalists prefer not to use the term objectivity at all. Allan M. Siegal, an assistant managing editor of the *New York Times*, prefers "impartiality" instead. Impartiality, he said, means that "you are exercising the discipline of reporting all sides of a disputed issue with intellectual honesty, finding out as much as you can about the arguments on all sides and presenting them, and not giving your own opinion. That's what we demand of reporters."[37]

Michael Gartner, a former president of NBC News, former editor of the *Louisville Courier-Journal* and subsequently the owner and publisher of the *Tribune* in Ames, Iowa, (where he won the Pulitzer Prize for editorial writing in 1998), will not define the term, saying he has no idea what objectivity means. But his description of good journalism is almost a textbook definition of objectivity. "You make your own judgments about what is important to your readers, and you try to explore those subjects in a way that is as thorough and as accurate as you know how to be," Gartner said.[38]

In the end, objectivity in journalism has proved to be a remarkably resilient concept, given the pressures placed upon it from almost every conceivable direction — intellectual, political, technological. But objectivity is far more sophisticated than it used to be.

In his memoir, Max Frankel cites his frequent railing against the constraints that the *New York Times'* standards of objectivity put upon him. Yet throughout, he makes it clear that he was not interested in inserting his own opinion into an article. When he was posted to Moscow, he learned that what politicians said was not often what they meant and that for a reporter to get to the truth, it often took much more analysis than straight reporting. "A willingness to trust my analytical imagination," he declared, "proved to be the lasting benefit."[39]

Frankel's informed judgment lies at the very heart of journalistic objectivity, a vital point to keep in mind as the journalistic world hurtles into cyberspace. It is too soon yet to see what the wired world of the Internet will mean for journalism in the 21st century. It is possible that the Internet will bring back the old idea of the marketplace of ideas. That was the pre-objectivity idea that if a dozen different people recounted an event with a dozen different points of view, the truth would emerge. But there are at least two reasons to be skeptical of expecting an information free-for-all from returning and ushering in with it a better democracy. First, as shown in the early chapters of this book, readers have placed a premium on reliable information since the earliest Colonial days, so they are likely to rely upon brand-name journalism when they go to the Internet for news. And second, the truth-from-Babel model presumes that readers (and viewers) will take the time to wade through a dozen different, highly colored versions of the same thing to arrive at some Miltonic truth. But all the evidence is that most people

FAIR AND BALANCED • *234*

spend less time, not more, with news than in earlier days.

It is possible that the age of the Internet will usher in an entirely new information model for journalism, but there is little evidence so far that it will. For the foreseeable future, responsible news organizations seem most likely to find for themselves and their readers a spot on that continuum of attachment-detachment at which they and their audience are most comfortable and will report the world from there. Some will continue to call what they do objective, while others will substitute terms like impartial, replicable, fair, balanced or evenhanded. But the principle of journalism that honestly tries to make the world comprehensible to its citizens need not change.

NOTES

[1] Tom Wicker, *On Press: A Top Reporter's Life in, and Reflections on, American Journalism* (New York: Viking, 1978), 1.

[2] Ibid., 3-4.

[3] The Pew Research Center for the People and the Press: "Public Votes for Continuity and Change in 2000," Feb. 25, 2002: http://people-press.org/reports/display.php3?ReportID=699.

[4] The Pew Research Center for the People and the Press: "News Media's Improved Image Proves Short-Lived," Aug. 4, 2002: people-press.org/reports/display.php3?ReportID=159.

[5] Interview with the author, October 1998.

[6] Fred Fedler et.al., *Reporting for the Media*, 6th ed. (Orlando, Fla.: Harcourt Brace, 1997), 99.

[7] Michael Schudson, *Discovering the News: A Social History of American Newspapers* (New York: Basic Books, 1978), 5-6.

[8] Davis Merritt, "Disconnecting from Detachment: Six Arguments for an Ethic of Journalistic Purposefulness," Silha lecture, University of Minnesota, November 1997.

[9] Stanley Cloud and Lynne Olson, *The Murrow Boys* (New York: Houghton Mifflin, 1996), 57.

[10] Paul Krugman, interview on 11 November 2003 conducted by Terrence McNally, "The Professor Takes the Gloves Off," published on AlterNet.org, accessed on 15 November 2003. http://www.alternet.org/story.html?StoryID=17169.

[11] J. Herbert Altschull, *From Milton to McLuhan: The Ideas Behind American Journalism* (White Plains, N.Y.: Longman, 1990), 1.

[12] Walter Lippmann, *Public Opinion* (1922; reprint ed. with an introduction by Michael Curtis, New Brunswick, N.J.: Transaction), 359.

[13] Commission on Freedom of the Press, *A Free and Responsible Press* (Chicago: University of Chicago, 1947), 21.

[14] Lippmann, *Public Opinion*, 359.

[15] Interview with the author, October 1998.

[16] Gilles Gauthier, "In Defence of a Supposedly Outdated Notion: The Range of Application of Journalistic Objectivity," *Canadian Journal of Communication* 18:4

(1993) http://www.cjc-online.ca/title.php3?page=7&journal_id=13.

[17] Jean-Francois Revel, "Le rejet de l'état," quoted in Gauthier, ibid.

[18] David Wise, *The Politics of Lying: Government Deception, Secrecy, and Power* (New York: Random House, 1973), 14.

[19] Max Frankel, *The Times of My Life and My Life at* The Times (New York: Random House, 1999), 184.

[20] Quoted in Wise, *The Politics of Lying...*, 39.

[21] Wise, *The Politics of Lying...*, 43.

[22] Eric Alterman, *Who Speaks for America?: Why Democracy Matters In Foreign Policy* (Ithaca, N.Y.: Cornell University Press, 1998), 96-7.

[23] Jimmy Breslin, *How the Good Guys Finally Won: Notes From an Impeachment Summer* (New York: Viking Press, 1975).

[24] Interview with the author.

[25] Todd Gitlin, *The Sixties: Years of Hope, Days of Rage* (New York: Bantam Books, 1987), 234.

[26] Thomas S. Kuhn, *The Structure of Scientific Revolutions* (Chicago: The University of Chicago Press, 1962), 95.

[27] Daniel Boorstin, *The Image: A Guide to Pseudo-Events in America* (New York: Atheneum, 1961).

[28] Bill Moyers, executive producer, "The Public Mind: Image and Reality in America. Illusions of News," Public Broadcasting Service, 1989.

[29] Ibid.

[30] Tom Wolfe, *The New Journalism* (New York: Harper & Row, 1973), 20-1.

[31] Ibid., 6.

[32] Stanley Fish, *There's No Such Thing as Free Speech ... and It's a Good Thing Too* (New York: Oxford, 1994), 7.

[33] Jeremy Iggers, *Good News, Bad News: Journalism Ethics and the Public Interest* (Boulder, Colo.: Westview, 1998), 91.

[34] Merritt Davis, *Public Journalism and Public Life: Why Telling the News Is Not Enough* (Hillsdale, N.J.: Erlbaum, 1995).

[35] Merritt gave this address to two college audiences in 1997 at Washington and Lee University, Lexington, Va., and the University of Minnesota in Minneapolis. I thank the university public relations offices of both campuses for providing me with copies of his address.

[36] Correspondence with the author, July 19, 1999.

[37] Interview with the author, June 19, 1998.

[38] Interview with the author, July 21, 1999.

[39] Frankel, *The Times of My Life ...*, 181.

Index

Acton, Lord Emerich Edward Dalberg 153
Adams, Henry 111
Advertisers 196
Advertising 133, 167, 169, 170-2, 174;
    defined 159
Advertising and Business Management,
    training for 182
Advertising agency 159
Advertising, News and Views 158
Advocacy journalism 224
Alienation of the worker 157
Allin, John 28
Alterman, Eric 229
Altschull, J. Herbert 225
American Historical Society 162
American magazine 42, 140-1
American Mercury 41-2
American Revolutionary press 51-61; biased
    battle coverage 58-60; reasons for bias 60
American Revolutionary printers, fate of 52
American Society of Newspaper editors
    151, 154, 158, 161-2, 183, 226
American Vine, The 55
Anabaptists 27
Anderson, Jack 209
Andover, Mass, attack on 11
Andros, Gov. Edmund 31, 38
Anglican church (Church of England) 25-6
Anglicans 37-41, 43-4
Anglo-Americans 156
Another Essay for the Investigation of Truth
    23-4, 28-9
Antigua 56
Antisynodalia 28
Apology for Printers, An 41, 43
Areopagitica 24, 27, 29
Aristotle 194
Associated Press 70, 112, 188
Associated Press Managing Editors
    Association 163
Association of Radio News Analysts 199
Atlantic Ocean as instigator of printing 25

Attribution[s] 95, 102-3, 150, 152, 159, 160,
    162
Audience studies 167, 171-7
Audiences 167-70, 172, 174-8
Ayers, Harry M. 214

Baconism 112
Bahama Gazette, The 56
Bahamas 56
Baker, Ray Stannard 138-41
Balance in reporting 90, 95-7
Bank of the United States 83-5
Baptism, infant 23, 26-9; meaning of to
    Puritans 33n1
Bay Psalm-Book 26
BBC 196
Beard, Charles A. 162
Beats, evolution of 69
Beniger, James 70
Bennett, James Gordon 69, 93-4, 100, 109-
    11, 153
Berlin Circle 162
Bernstein, Carl 229
Bethlehem, Pa. 58
Bias 64, 66, 90, 94, 97, 131; and audience 72;
    levels of 67-8, 100; medium level 67;
    phases of 72; story level 67; system level
    67; word level 67, 70-1
Bible 25, 28, 32
Bishop, Ann 20
Blair, Francis P. , as a party editor 91, 97
Bledstein, Burton J., 188
Bleyer, Willard 184-5
Bliss, Edward 202
Boorstin, Daniel 69, 159, 230
Boston Chronicle 53, 60
Boston Evening-Post 44
Boston Gazette 39-40, 61
Boston Globe 127
Boston, Mass. 9, 12, 14-5, 20, 26, 32, 37, 38-
    41, 43-5, 54, 61
Boston News-Letter 10, 26, 38-40, 60

Boston Tea Party 54
Bowles, Saumel III, advocates
    independent journalism 93
Boycotts of British goods 51, 54
Bradford, Andrew 41-2
Bradford, William (Pilgrim leader) 30
Bradford, William (printer) 32
Brandywine, Battle of (Pennsylvania),
    news coverage of 58-60
Breslin, Jimmy 231
Brisbane, Arthur 119
Briscoe, Mr. [author] 30
British colonies in North America 25
British soldiers, in the Revolution 59
Broadcast journalism 134, 192-205
Brooker, William 39
Brooklyn Eagle 200
Brown, Cecil 198
Brown, Francis 99
Brown, Richard 69
Bryan, William Jennings 127
Bryant, William Cullen 96; editor of the
    New York Evening Post 96; 1837
    statement on freedom of expression 96
Buildings as monuments 157
Burgoyne, John 59-60
Bush, Chilton 187
Business, printing as 36-8, 41-2, 44, 48,
    50n17
Byfield, Nathanael 31
Bylines 95

Campbell, John 10, 39
Canada 56
Canons of Journalism [1922] 151, 154, 158,
    161, 183, 226
Canons, as defense of autonomy 151
Carey, James 112
Carnegie, Andrew 156
Carter, Boake 197, 200
Carter, Hodding, Jr. 213
Casey, Ralph D. 98-9
Catholics and Catholicism 25, 27, 31
CBS 194-7, 199, 200, 202
Census, U.S. (1920) 156
Centralization 154-5
Charleston, S.C., 51, 53, 55-7; British victory
    (1780) 55; failed British siege of (1776) 55;
    objectivity in the press of 55
Checkley, John 37
Chicago American 127
Chicago Daily News 125
Chicago Inter Ocean 126
Chicago Record Herald 125
Chicago Tribune 99, 125-6
Cholera, epidemics 74; of 1832, 1849, and
    1866, 74, 107-14
Church of England (Anglican church) 25-6
Circulation 70
"Citizen Kane" 184

"City on a hill" 25
Civil liberties (Revolutionary era) 51
Civil War 69, 74, 111
Civil War, era prior to, 181
Civil rights movement 135
Class 156, 157
Class consciousness 155
Clayton, Charles C. 188
Cleveland, Grover 118
Cleveland Plain Dealer 186
clipping exchange system 69, 101
Code of ethics 151, 156-7
Collier's 139
Colonial press 36-50
Columbia University 156; School of
    Journalism 181-2, 184, 189
Commentators 192-7, 200
Committee on Public Information 150, 162
Conflict of interest 97
Congress, Continental 58
Connecticut 58
Connecticut Journal 58-9
Constitution, constitutional rights (British,
    applied to Americans) 51-2
Consumers 167, 170, 173-4, 176-7
Continental Congress 58
Control revolution 70
Cooper, Kent 188
Cornish, George 188
Cornwallis, Lord Charles (British
    commander, Revolution) 55-6
Correspondents 10-4, 17, 20
Cosmopolitan 139, 144
Cotton, John 13-20
Cotton, Rowland 11-3
Council of Safety [Revolutionary-era
    pressure group] 54
Council, King George's 54
Country Gentleman 169, 174
Courier and Enquirer 108-10
Craig, Daniel H. 105-6
Credibility 134, 193, 194, 197, 199-203
Creel, George 150, 162
Cronkite, Walter 196, 223, 227, 229
Croswell, Harry 90
Crouch, Charles 51, 55
Culbert, David 193, 196, 197, 201
Culture of haste 69
Curtis Publishing Company 168-9, 171-4

Daguerre, Louis 111
Darwin, Charles 111
Davenport, John 23
Davis, Elmer 196, 202
Day, Benjamin 73, 92, 100; and street sales
    of newspapers 92; founder of the *New
    York Sun* 92; institutes per-line
    advertising rate 92
Daye, Stephen 26
Deaver, Michael 231

Decentralization of the workplace 157
Deconstructionism 67, 232
Depression 187
Derrida, Jacques 232
Desegregation, coverage of 212
Detachment 107
Dewey, George 127
Disinterestedness of journalists 42-3, 46, 47
Draper, Margaret 60
Drayton, William Henry 51-2, 54
Dudley, Gov. Joseph 39
Dunlap, John 60
Duty of Standing Fast in our Spiritual and Temporal Liberties, The 55

East-Florida Gazette 56
Edes, Benjamin 61
Editorial page, development of 95
Editorializing 198
Editorials, lack of in early press 95
Editors, mutual insults of 93; roles of 95
Edwards, Douglas 200
Edwards, Jonathan 45
Election coverage: campaign of 1820, 82; of 1824, 82-3; of 1828, 83; of 1832, 83-4
Electrocution of a woman 153
Elizabeth Town, N.J. 60
Elliot, Charles W. 182
England (see also Great Britain) 25-6, 31, 57, 60
Enlightenment 132-3, 150
Ethics codes 132
Ethos 192-4, 196-7, 200, 202-3
Europe, Europeans 25
Event orientation 71
Everybody's magazine 139, 143
Eyewitness reporting 95, 200

Fact-based thinking 132
Factory system 153
Facts as concepts 180, 183-7, 189
Factual approach to history 162
False consciousness 66
Fang, Edward 199
Federal Communications Commission 134, 193, 195
Fedler, Fred 223
Feedback 70
Fine, Benjamin 215
Finney, Charles 109
Fireside chats 162
First Amendment 157, 161
Fish, Stanley 231-2
Five questions 150, 152, 163
Fleeming, John 53, 60
Fleet, Thomas 43-5
Flint, Nelson 132
Florida State University 187
Formulaic model 152
Frankel, Max 228, 233

Frankenberg, T. T. 186
Franklin, Benjamin 40-3
Franklin, James 37
Freedom of the press 44-6
Freud, Sigmund 132
Frick, Henry Clay 156
Front Page, The 184

Gaine, Hugh 53
Gallagher, Wes 188
Gallup, George H. 134, 175-6
Gartner, Michael 233
Gaskell, George A. 182
Gates, Horatio 59
General Assembly of New York 53
General Committee [Revolutionary-era protest group] 51
General Court of Massachusetts 27, 30, 32
Geography (location) 14-5
Germantown, Battle of (Pennsylvania), coverage of 58, 60
Glorious Revolution, The 31-2
Gobright, Lawrence 112
Goddard, William 53
Gospel of Wealth 156
Gospel Order revived 32
Great Britain (see also England) 51-2, 54, 61, 85-7
Great Depression 162
"Great Swamp Fight" 17
Greeley, Horace 96-7, 111
Green brothers, printers (Samuel and Thomas, 18th century) 58-60
Green Mountain Patriot 99
Green, Samuel (17th century) 23
Groth, Lynn 98

Hadlock, Edwin 182
Haile, C.M. 101
"Half-way covenant" 23, 26-9
Hampton's 139, 144
Hancock, John 60
Haney, Jesse 181, 186
Hard, William 194
Harrington, Harry 186
Harris, Benjamin 10, 32, 38, 49n2
Harvard College 23, 27
Harvard University 182
Harwood, Dix 186
Hauptmann trial 195
Hearst, William Randolph 72, 119-22, 127, 153
Heater, Gabriel 195
Hecht, Ben 184
Hemingway, Ernest 186
Higham, John 98
Hints to Young Editors 182
Hitchcock, Nevada Davis 182
Hitler, Adoph 196
Hoffman, Abbie 229-30

Index • 239

Hollywood 184
Holt, John 57
Howe, Quincy 192-3, 200, 203
Howe, William 58
Hoyt, E. Palmer 211
Hubbard, William 29-30
Hudson, Frederic 92, 95, 98; on absence of
    editorials in early press 95; on *New York
    Sun*'s place in press history 92
Hughes, Charles Evans 122
Humphrey, Carol Sue 98; on newspaper
    reading in penny press era 92
Humphreys, James Jr. 60
Hutchins Commission on Freedom of the
    Press 67, 132, 189, 208, 226
Hyde, Grant M. 188

Ideal 150
Ideology 37, 41
Iggers, Jeremy 232
Independent journalism 91, 94, 97
Independent Reflector 45-6
Indians (Native Americans) 27, 29-30
Industrial capitalism 156
Industrial press 164
Industrial Revolution 70, 152
Infant baptism 23, 26-9; meaning of to the
    Puritans 33n1
Information, abundance of 69-70, 102
Information model 91-4, 97
Information scarcity 69
Interpretative Reporting 187
Interpretive journalism 132, 135; rise of
    206-20
Interviewing 95
Inverted pyramid 107, 150, 152, 154, 163
Isaacs, Norman 231
Issue orientation 71

Jackson, Andrew 91
James II, King of England 31
Jarvis, Russell 93, 96; on editors and a free
    press 96; on editors' responsibility 93
Jefferson, Thomas 156, 185
Jesuits 27
"Jimmy's World" 231
Johnson, Marmaduke 23
Johnston, James 60
Journalism Educator 188
Journalism, as a profession 90; culture of
    189; education in 180-9; event-oriented
    95-6; graduates in 181; history of 185;
    information model of 91-4, 97;
    investigative 183; interpretative 187
    language of 189; partisan 90-1, 97;
    political model of 91-2; profession of 180-
    1, 188; responsibility 91, 93-4, 96; schools
    of 180, 188; standards 91, 94, 96-7;
    textbooks in 180-2, 185-9
Journalists Creed 188

Julian, Joseph 204

Kaltenborn, H. V. 195, 196, 198-200, 203
Kansas City Star 120
Kansas Code of Ethics for Publishers 158
Kansas Editorial Association 157, 159-60
Kansas State College 181
KDKA radio 192
Kendall, Amos partisan journalist 91
Kendall, George Wilkins 101
Kendrick, Alexander 193, 196-7
Kerner Commission 67
King George's Council 54
King's Chapel 40
King's College 45-6
Kingston, New York 59
Kintner, Robert 192, 197, 202
Klauber, Edward 197-200
Kobre, Sidney 187
Korean War 189
Krieghbaum, Hillier 98-9
Krugman, Paul 225
Kuhn, Thomas 230

Labor 154, 156
Ladies' Home Journal 139, 167, 169, 171
Lancaster, Pennsylvania 60
Latin American Revolutions: 81-2
Layers of management 155
Lee, Gen. Robert E. 181
Leslie's 139
Levy, Leonard 98
Lewis, Fulton, Jr. 201
Liberal arts 180
Licensing/licensers of the press, early
    Massachusetts 27, 29, 32
Lindbergh baby 150, 153
Lippmann, Walter 132, 152, 181, 185-7, 202,
    222, 226
*Little-Compton Scourge, The: Or, The Anti-
    Courant* 37
Local news 71
Local radio 192-3, 203
Locus of information 102
Logical Positivism 150, 162, 184
London Gazette 29
London Naval Conference 194
Lorimer, William 123, 125
Lowenstein, Ralph. L 98
Loyal Gazette 60
"Loyalists" (Revolutionary era), definition
    of 52; espousing objectivity 52, 57;
    partisanship in press 57
Luce, Henry 67
Luce, Robert 182
Luxon, Norval N. 186

MacArthur, Charles 184
MacDougall, Curtis 132, 187, 207
Madison, James 93-4, 96-9; on "one-sided"

periodicals 94; on solution to bias in newspapers 97; on truth 96; says some abuses in the press are unavoidable 93
Magazines 167-9, 171-4
Maqua Indians [Mohawks] 32
Market competition 70
Market factors 73
Market research 168, 170-7
Marketplace of ideas and objectivity 96
Martin, Frank 186-7
Marx, Karl 111, 157
Marxism 66-7
Mary, Queen of England (co-monarch with William) 31
Maryland, early press in, 32
Maryland Journal; and the Baltimore Advertiser 53
Mass-market newspaper 164
Massachusetts 25, 27-8, 31-2; early press in 25-6; General Court of 27, 30, 32
Massachusetts Spy 61
Mather, Cotton 13, 39-40
Mather, Increase 9-12, 19, 20, 23-4, 28-9, 32
Maule, Thomas 32
McCarthy, James 182
McCarthy, Joseph, Sen., 134-5, 163, 189, 222, and Associated Press 212, 215, coverage of 206-20
McClure, S.S. 138-40
McClure's Magazine 136-8
McRae, Milton 119
Medfield, Mass, attack on 15, 17-9
Mein, John 53, 60, 73
Mencher, Melvin 189
Merrill, John C. 98, 185
Merritt, Davis "Buzz" 224, 232
Merzer, Martin 203
Messages 64; balance 67; evolution of 64, 66, 73
Metacomet (King Phillip) 15
Metzler, Ken 189
Mexican War 70, 74, 100-6
Meyer, Philip 227
Miami Herald 203
Michigan State University 184
Middle manager 156
Mill, John Stuart 132
Milton, John 24-5, 29, 132
Missouri Controversy 82
Mitchel, Jonathan 28-9
Mob action, Revolutionary era 57, 60
Modernism 149
Mohawk Indians, called "Maquas" 32
"Monstrous births" 9-10
Moodey, Joshua 9-11, 19-20
Moon hoax 112
Morse, Samuel F.B 70, 100
Morton, Thomas 30
Mott, Frank Luther 64, 72, 98, 99
Muckrakers 131-3, 150, 160

Muckraking and objectivity 136-45
Multiple sources, use of 95
Munich Crisis 195, 196
Murrow, Edward R. 194, 200-3, 225
Musgrave, Philip 39
Mutual Radio Network 196, 199-200

Narragansett Indians 15
Narrative of the Trouble with the Indians, A 29
Nation 120, 181
National Intelligencer lists editors on the government payroll 91
National Journal lists editors on the government payroll 91
NBC 194-6, 199-200
Nelson, William 120
Neutral language 152
Neutrality 36-50
New-England Courant 37, 40-1
New English Canaan 30
New Haven, Connecticut 58-9
New Journalism 157, 231
New Orleans *Daily Picayune* 100-3
New technologies 131
New York 32, 53, 57, 59; General Assembly of 53; early press in 32
New York Evening Post 96
New-York Gazette 46, 53
New York Herald 69, 100, 102-3, 105, 109-12, 117, 153
New York Herald Tribune 120, 152, 188
New York Journal 57, 117, 119, 120, 123, 124, 127
New-York Mercury 45
New York Morning Herald 93
New York Post 124, 127
New York Sun 92, 112, 117, 127, 142; Frederic Hudson on place in journalism history 92
New York Times 97, 111, 113, 120, 152, 197, 200
New York Tribune 96, 111, 113, 124-5, 141
New York World 117, 118-9, 121-2, 126, 127
Newman, Noah 14-20
News 94-6; event-oriented 95, 96; values 94; values established by the penny press 94
News as commodity 105-6; composite of 102; selection 67; sources 71
News interval 68, 69, 71
News publications, 17th century, 29-30
Newsgathering 182-3, 185-6,
Newspaper industry 180, 183, 185
Newspaper readers 180, 184-5
Newspaper reading 92-3
Newspaper Reporting Today 188
Newswriting, techniques of 180, 182-3, 186
Niles' Weekly Register, general content 78-88
Nipmuk Indians 15
Nonpartisanship 107
North America, British (colonial era) 25

Northwestern University 184, 187

Oath of a Free-man 26-7, 29
O'Brien, Frank M. 98
Objectivity 10, 20, 50, 149, 180-9; American
Revolutionary press and 51-61; and
emphasis on official sources 222; and
professional standards 64; and science
66, 74, 132; and the marketplace of ideas
96; and the penny press 93; and realism
90; and reporters 94-5; and values 223; as
brake on reporting 221; as writing style
149, 152, 162; boundaries of, modern and
17th century (Puritan era) 33; concept
of, pre- and post-Revolution 61; defined
67, 90, 160-1; forms of 150, 152; goal of in
pre-Revolutionary period 53; goals of
164; Hezekiah Niles's definition 76-7;
ideals of 149-58, 163; in government and
political reporting 24, 33; in journalism
textbooks 223; in modern times 24; in
religious publications 17th century
(Puritans) 24; model of 152; myth of 163;
press as "open to all parties but
influenced by none" 52-3; of religious
discussion (Puritans) 33; synonyms 131;
traditional view for newspapers in
colonial times 51-3; under Puritans 24
Ochs, Adolph 120
Office of War Information (1942) 162
Official reality 193, 195, 198
Ohio State University 186
Olin, Charles 182
Oral communication 10-2, 14

Paley, William S. 197
Palmer, John [pseudonym] 31
Pamphlets 26, 28, 31-2
Park, Robert 181
Parker, James 46, 53
Parliament (of Great Britain) 51
Partiality, consequences of (Revolutionary
era) 52-7
Parton, James 92, 95-8; on balance in
reporting 97; on initial reactions to
penny press 92, 95; on news as a novelty
in the 1830s 95; on the party press 92; on
truth 96
Party press, the 70, 77-8; 90-4, 97;
contrasted with the penny press 92-4;
editors' mutual insults in 93; function of
93; inherent problems 94; purpose 91;
reflects class differences 92;
"Patriots" (Revolutionary era), definition of
52; denial of objectivity 52, 57; partisan
press seen as a conquering hero 61
Payne, George Henry 98
Pearson's 139
Pennsylvania, early press, 34n8
Pennsylvania Gazette 42, 43

Pennsylvania Ledger 60
Pennsylvania Packet 61
Penny press 69-70, 73-4, 90-5, 97, 108-11,
153, 159, 164, 181; and news values 94;
and reporters' role 94-5; initial reactions
to 92; relationship to society 92-3;
watchdog role of 92
Pentagon Papers 229
Pew Research Center for the People and
the Press 222
Pfeiffer, Pauline 186
Phantom Public, The 132
Philadelphia, Pa. 38, 41-3, 56, 58, 60; British
enter 59; early press in 32
Philadelphia Daily News 200
Philadelphia Public Ledger 93
Photography 111
Political model 91, 92, 97
Politics 39, 41, 43-4, 47
Polk, James K. 103, 105
Pollard, James 97
Porter, Philip W. 186
Postmodernism 232
Powers, Francis Gary, U2 pilot 228
Preamble to American Association of
Newspaper Editors canons 161
Printers 36-8, 41-8
Printing 181
Printing press 37, 47, 48
Profession, qualities of 188
Professional associations 154
Professional guidelines 157
Professional standards 1, 73-4, 131, 181
Professional status 149
Professional values 71
Professionalization 156
Progressive Era 150
Propaganda 150
Propositions Concerning the Subjects of
Baptism and Consociation of Churches 27
Protective Tariff 84-5
Protestants, Protestantism 31
Proto-objectivity 73, 134
Pseudo-events 159
Public journalism 224, 232
Public Ledger 172-3
Public opinion 162
Public Opinion 132, 185-6
Public opinion research 184
Publick Occurrences, both Forreign and
Domestick 10, 26, 29, 32, 38
Publishers 36, 48
Pulitzer, Joseph 72, 118, 121, 126, 134, 156
Pulitzer Prizes 181
Pullman, George 156
Puritan press; boundaries of 27-8;
monopoly 25-6, 32; news publications 29;
output of (types of publications) 26
Puritan religion and objectivity 23-33
Puritans 38, 40, 43, 47; and bias in political

publications 30-2; and boundaries of the open press 27-8; as champions of a free press 24; and education for all 25; as intellectuals 24-5; as liberals 25; and minority opinions 23, 27-9; and multiple viewpoints 27; and objectivity 23-33; and objectivity in news 29-30; and open or objective religious argument 23, 27-9, 33; printing monopoly of 25-6, 32; religious writings 26-9

Quakers 32
Queen Anne's War 13
Queen Mary II 13

Radio Networks 192, 193-4, 203
Radio's Golden Age 192, 203
Rather, Dan 20
Rationalization, work 155
Raymond, Henry J. 97
Readers 167-70, 172, 174-8; as citizens 168, 173, 176-7; as consumers 168, 170, 173-4, 176-8; expectations of 36, 38-9, 41, 43-8
Readership studies 167, 171-7
Realism 111-3
Realism Movement 90, 94
Reformers 156
Rehoboth, Mass 15-6
Reid, Robert 187
Relationship to society 91, 92, 93; Samuel Bowles III on dishonesty of 93
Reliability 38
Reliable source 10-20
Reporter and the News 186
Reporters 94-6, 181-2, 184-6; attitudes and objectivity of 94-5; roles 94, 95, 96; rules for conduct of 95-6; women as 185-6; work routines 95-6
Reporting 181, 185-6, 188
Reputation 10-1, 13, 20
Responsibility in journalism 91, 93, 94, 96; James G. Bennett and emerging notions of 93-4; old and new concepts merged 94
Reston, James 207
Reuters 112
Right to know 92
"Right to lie" 228
Riis, Jacob 141-2
Rind, William 53
Rivington, James 57-9, 60, 73
Rivington's New-York Gazetteer (also called *Rivington's Gazette and Loyal Gazette*) 57-8, 60
Rockefeller, John D. 131
Roosevelt, Franklin Delano 162, 195, 197
Roosevelt, Theodore 118, 139, 142
Rosenberg, Charles 107-9, 113
Ross, Charles G. 90, 97, 186
Rothman, David J. 158

Royal Gazette, The 55-6
Runyon, Damon 224
Russell, Charles Edward 142-4
Rutenbech, Jeffrey B. 99

Sacco-Vanzetti 153
Saerchinger, Cesar 194, 196
Saltonstall, Nathaniel 13
Saltonstall, Richard 12
San Francisco Examiner 121
Saratoga, New York (battle and British surrender), coverage of 59-60
Sassamon, John 15
Saturday Evening Post 167, 169, 171, 173
Schechter, A. A. 195, 196, 200
Schiller, Dan 3, 4
Schools of journalism 153, 156
Schudson, Michael 3, 4, 224
Schurtz, Carl 139-40
Scientific method 94, 97, 107-14, 134, 150, 227
Scientific rationalism 153
Scientific Revolution 150
Scopes Monkey trial 153
Scotland, Scots 51, 54
Scott, John Morin 45-7
Scribner's 142
Scripps, E.W. 120-1
Scripps, McRae 119
Sensationalism 150, 160, 164
Sewall, Samuel 13-4, 24, 32
Shanks, W.F.G. 97
Shepard, Thomas 27
Shilen, Ronald 97, 98
Shirer, William 202, 225
Shuman, Edward 181
Shute, Gov. Samuel 39
Siegal, Allan M. 233
Sigma Delta Chi (Society of Professional Journalists) 132, 183-4
Silverblatt, Art 205
Sinclair, Upton 142-3
Sloan, Wm. David 77-8
Smallpox inoculation 40
Smith, Elbert B. 97
Smith, William E. 97-8
Smith, William Jr. 45-7
Snow, John 110
Social Darwinists 156
Social Gospel 156
Social science, research in 180, 184, 189
"Son of Liberty, A" [author] 53
Sons of Liberty (Patriot organization, Revolution) 57
South Carolina 54-5; colonial assembly of 56
South-Carolina and American General Gazette 51, 54-5
South Carolina Congress 54
South-Carolina Gazette 51
South-Carolina Gazette; and Country Journal

51

Space broker 159
Spanish American War 66, 119, 127
Specialization 153
Spencer, Herbert 107, 111-2
Springfield Republican 99
St. Louis Globe-Democrat 188
St. Louis Post-Dispatch 186
St. Louis Republic 186
Stahl, Leslie 230-1
Stamp Act (1765) 51, 53
Standardization 150, 153
Standardized rates 159
Standards 153
Standards for empirical research 154
Standards for journalists 156
Stanford University 184, 187
Starr Faithful murder 153
Steam press 95
Steffens, Lincoln 131, 136-8
Stensaas, Harlan S. 97
Stevenson, Adlai 72
Stewart, Donald 98
Strout, Richard L. 210
Subjectivity 10, 14, 20
Success 139
Sulzberger, Arthur Hays 211
Survey research 184
Sustaining radio 195
Swing, Raymond Gram 196, 200

Tarbell, Ida 131, 136-8
Tea Act 54
Telegraph 66, 68-71, 73-4, 95, 100-6, 112-3
Television 201-3
"Think pieces" 188
Thomas, Isaiah 61
Thomas, Lowell 194, 203
Thompson, Hunter 231
Thompson, Susan 98
Thornton, Brian 91, 99
Time-and-motion study 155
Timeliness 11-3, 105
Timothy, Peter 51-4, 56, 60; press closed to
    Loyalists 54
Tonkin Gulf 228
Townshend Acts 51
Truman, Harry S. 186
Truth 90, 91, 94, 96; Harry Croswell on 90;
    importance of, cited in 1830s letters to
    editors 96; James Parton on 96
Truth held forth and maintained 32

Union of Soviet Socialist Republics 189
University of Chicago 181
University of Illinois 184
University of Minnesota 184
University of Missouri 180, 182, 184, 186,
    188
University of Wisconsin 180, 184, 188

Vandercook, John W. 199
Veracity 10, 12-4
Vietnam war 135, 185
Villard, Oswald Garrison 119, 120, 127
Virginia, early press, 34n8
Virginia Gazette 53

Walley, Thomas 13, 19
Wampanoag Indians 15
War of 1812, 86-7
War coverage 100-2
Waring, Thomas R. 214
Washington and Lee University 181
Washington, Booker T. 139
Washington, George 58
Washington Globe 91
Wasp 90
Watchdog role of the press 92
Watergate 135
Watertown, Mass., 61
WCAU radio 200
Webb, James Watson 108
Weekly Register 73
Weekly Rehearsal 44
Wells family, printers, 53, 56, 60 (see also
    individual names)
Wells, John 54-6
Wells, Robert 51, 54
Wells, William Charles 55-6
Wesley, John 44
White, Paul 197-200
Whitefield, George 44
Wichita (Kan.) *Eagle* 224
Wicker, Tom 193, 221-2
Wile, Frederic William 194
William and Mary, King and Queen of
    England, 31
Williams, Walter 180, 186-8
Williamsburg, Va. 53
Wilson, John 17, 19
Winthrop, John 30
Winthrop, Waitstill 13
Wise, David 228
Witchcraft 10, 11, 20
Wolfe, Tom 231
Wolff news service 112
"Woodstein" 229
Woodward, Bob 229
Work ethic 157
Work routines of journalists 91, 94-6
World Telegram 152
World War I, 149, 150, 164, 180-1, 186
World War II, 162, 180

Yellow journalism 74, 131, 150, 153
Yeoman myth 156
Yorktown, Va. (defeat of Cornwallis) 56
Yost, Casper 186
Zynda, Thomas H. 184

Editors

Steven R. Knowlton is a professor of journalism at Hofstra University. Prior to going into academics, he spent 18 years in newspaper journalism. He holds a Ph.D. in history from Washington University in St. Louis. This is his sixth book.

Karen L. Freeman is a staff editor at the *New York Times*, where she has worked on the National, Metro, Business, Science and Circuits sections and on the Editorial and Op-Ed pages. Before joining the *Times*, she was a professor of journalism at Pennsylvania State University.

Authors

Maurine H. Beasley is a professor in the College of Journalism at the University of Maryland. She earned her Ph.D. in American civilization at George Washington University. She is the author, co-author or editor of eight books dealing mainly with the history of women journalists and journalism education. A former reporter for the *Washington Post*, she is also a former national president of both the American Journalism Historians Association and the Association for Education in Journalism and Mass Communication.

David R. Davies is an associate professor of mass communication and journalism at the University of Southern Mississippi. A former reporter for the *Arkansas Gazette*, he earned his Ph.D. in media history at the University of Alabama. He is the author of *The Press in Transition, 1945-1965*, and editor of *The Press and Race: Mississippi Journalists Confront the Movement*.

Hazel Dicken-Garcia, a professor of mass communication, is the author of *Journalistic Standards in Nineteenth-Century America*, which received the Kappa Tau Alpha award for the best book in the field in 1989. A member of the Academy of Distinguished Teachers at the University of Minnesota, where she has taught for more than 25 years, she earned her Ph.D. at the University of Wisconsin.

Bruce J. Evensen is a professor in the Department of Communication at DePaul University, where he teaches journalism and journalism history. He earned his Ph.D. from the University of Wisconsin. For 10 years before that, he was a broadcast journalist and network news chief, based in Washington, D.C., and Jerusalem. He is the editor of *The Responsible Reporter* and author of *When Dempsey Fought Tunney, Palestine and the*

Editors and Authors • *245*

Press and *God's Man for the Gilded Age: D.L. Moody and the Rise of Modern Mass Evangelism.*

Lynn Boyd Hines is Professor Emeritus at Drury University. He earned a Ph.D. at the University of Pittsburgh and worked as a broadcast journalist in both radio and television. He is the author of *Broadcasting the Local News: The Early Years of Pittsburgh's KDKA-TV.*

Carol Sue Humphrey is a professor of history at Oklahoma Baptist University. She is the author of *Debating Historical Issues in the Media of the Time: The Revolutionary Era, The Press of the Young Republic* and *"This Popular Engine": The Role of New England Newspapers During the American Revolution.* She serves as Secretary of the American Journalism Historians Association.

Barbara M. Kelly is a cultural historian whose research focuses on nonverbal communication, with particular emphasis on the "built environment." She is the author of *Expanding the American Dream; Building and Rebuilding Levittown,* a study of architecture and middle-class values. She is chair of the Department of Journalism and Media Studies at Hofstra University.

Sheila McIntyre specializes in early American communications and teaches early American history at SUNY-Potsdam. She earned a Ph.D. at Boston University and has been a visiting professor at Boston University, Harvard University, Carleton University (Ottawa), and the University of Ottawa. She is working on a complete volume of the *Collected Letters of John Cotton of Plymouth* for the Colonial Society of Massachusetts Press.

David T. Z. Mindich, a former assignment editor for CNN, is chair of the Journalism and Mass Communication Department at Saint Michael's College. He is the author of *Just the Facts: How "Objectivity" Came To Define American Journalism* and *Tuned Out: Why Americans Under 40 Don't Follow the News.* He is the founder of Jhistory, an Internet group for journalism historians, and in 2002 received the Krieghbaum Under-40 Award for Outstanding Achievement in Research, Teaching and Public Service from the Association for Education in Journalism and Mass Communication.

Joseph A. Mirando is a professor of journalism and coordinator of graduate studies in communication at Southeastern Louisiana University. He earned his Ph.D. from the University of Southern Mississippi and has authored more than 50 journal articles and scholarly papers, mainly on the history of journalism education. Prior to becoming an educator, he worked as a reporter or copy editor for newspapers in five states.

Randall Patnode is an assistant professor in the Department of Communication Arts at Xavier University in Cincinnati. He earned his Ph.D. in mass communication from the University of North Carolina. His research focuses on the history of communication technology and new media.

Donald Shaw is Kenan Professor in the School of Journalism and Mass Communication at the University of North Carolina, where he specializes in journalism history, reporting and the agenda-setting function of the press. He earned his Ph.D. in communication at the University of Wisconsin. He has served as a visiting professor at a number of universities and presented numerous papers, talks and lectures abroad.

Wm. David Sloan, a journalism professor at the University of Alabama, has written, co-authored or edited 25 books. Many are on media history, such as *Historical Methods in Mass Communication* and *Perspectives on Mass Communication History*. His edited book *The Media in America: A History*, now in its sixth edition, is the most widely used textbook in the field. He is the founder of the American Journalism Historians Association. He has served as president of both the AJHA and Kappa Tau Alpha, the national honor society in mass communication. In 1998 the AJHA awarded him its Kobre Award for lifetime achievement. On its 90th anniversary, KTA selected him as one of the five most important members in its history. He received his Ph.D. in mass communication and United States history from the University of Texas. Before going into teaching, he worked as an editor on four newspapers.

Douglas B. Ward is an assistant professor at the University of Kansas. He is a former editor at the *New York Times* and is an occasional contributor to the *The New York Times Book Review*. He received his Ph.D. in mass communications from the University of Maryland.

Julie Hedgepeth Williams teaches journalism at Samford University in Birmingham, Ala. She received her Ph.D. in media history from the University of Alabama. She is the author of *The Significance of the Printed Word in Early America* and co-author of *The Early American Press, 1690-1783*, and *The Great Reporters: An Anthology of News Writing at Its Best*.